# Conjugations

**SOUTH ASIA ACROSS THE DISCIPLINES**

A series edited by Dipesh Chakrabarty, Sheldon Pollock, and Sanjay Subrahmanyam

Funded by a grant from the Andrew W. Mellon Foundation and jointly published by the University of California Press, the University of Chicago Press, and Columbia University Press.

*The Powerful Ephemeral: Everyday Healing in an Ambiguously Islamic Place*
by Carla Bellamy (California)

*Extreme Poetry: The South Asian Movement of Simultaneous Narration*
by Yigal Bronner (Columbia)

*Secularizing Islamists? Jama'at-e-Islami and Jama'at-ud Da'wa Pakistan*
by Humeira Iqtidar (Chicago)

*The Social Space of Language: Vernacular Culture in British Colonial Punjab*
by Farina Mir (California)

*Unifying Hinduism: Philosophy and Identity in Indian Intellectual History*
by Andrew J. Nicholson (Columbia)

*Islam Translated: Literature, Conversion, and the Arabic Cosmopolis of South and Southeast Asia*
by Ronit Ricci (Chicago)

South Asia Across the Disciplines is a series devoted to publishing first books across a wide range of South Asian studies, including art, history, philology or textual studies, philosophy, religion, and the interpretive social sciences. Series authors all share the goal of opening up new archives and suggesting new methods and approaches, while demonstrating that South Asian scholarship can be at once deep in expertise and broad in appeal.

# Conjugations

*Marriage and Form in*
*New Bollywood Cinema*

SANGITA GOPAL

*The University of Chicago Press    Chicago and London*

**SANGITA GOPAL** is associate professor of English at the University
of Oregon. She is coeditor of *Global Bollywood: Transnational Travels of
Hindi Film Music.*

The University of Chicago Press, Chicago 60637
The University of Chicago Press, Ltd., London
© 2011 by The University of Chicago
All rights reserved. Published 2011.
Printed in the United States of America
20 19 18 17 16 15 14 13 12 11      1 2 3 4 5

ISBN-13: 978-0-226-30425-0 (cloth)
ISBN-13: 978-0-226-30426-7 (paper)
ISBN-10: 0-226-30425-6 (cloth)
ISBN-10: 0-226-30426-4 (paper)

Library of Congress Cataloging-in-Publication Data
Gopal, Sangita.
        Conjugations : marriage and form in new Bollywood cinema /
    Sangita Gopal.
            p. cm. — (South Asia across the disciplines)
        ISBN-13: 978-0-226-30425-0 (cloth : alk. paper)
        ISBN-13: 978-0-226-30426-7 (pbk. : alk. paper)
        ISBN-10: 0-226-30425-6 (cloth : alk. paper)
        ISBN-10: 0-226-30426-4 (pbk. : alk. paper)   1. Married
        people in motion pictures.  2. Couples in motion pictures.
        3. Motion pictures—Social aspects—India.  4. Motion picture
        industry—India—Bombay.   I. Title.   II. Series: South Asia
        across the disciplines.
    PN1993.5.I8G568 2011
    791.430954—dc22                                2011013546

*To my parents,*
*Ganesh Gopal Iyer and Shyamosri Iyer*

# Contents

# Figures

# Acknowledgments

This book owes its greatest debt to my mother, Shyamosri Iyer, and her sister, Manjushri Chowdhury. They were avid cinephiles, and I spent my girlhood constantly accompanying both to the movies. While my mother favored regional and foreign films, my aunt was partial to Hindi popular cinema. I was omnivorous, consuming everything that came my way with gusto—from schlocky horror movies by the Ramsay brothers that played in rundown theaters to film-society fare like Godard's *Masculin/Feminin* thronging with bearded Marxists. My academic pursuit of cinema in subsequent years, I believe, is an attempt to bring order to and endow with context this early and indiscriminate film-viewing. I have had the great fortune of receiving guidance from several remarkable teachers and colleagues. My professors at Presidency College and the University of Kolkata, among them Sukanta Chaudhuri, Amlan Dasgupta, Subhadra Sen, and Kajal Sengupta, introduced me to the pleasures of critical thought and historical research and taught me how cultural artifacts impinge upon the conduct of our daily lives. Samik Bandhopadhyay's film appreciation course at Chitrabani showed me how interpretation intensifies the enjoyment of cinema, and his analysis of the Odessa steps sequence from the *Battleship Potemkin* remains to this day my pedagogic model.

At the University of Rochester, where I did my graduate work, my teachers Kamran Ali, Thomas di Piero, Morris Eaves, Thomas Hahn, Anita Levy, David Rodowick, and Sharon Willis unfolded for me new and exciting worlds of thought. From professors James Longenbach and David

Bleich I learned the value of asking difficult and uncomfortable questions, and Nigel Maister's wry wit ensured that I stayed grounded. I am especially grateful to my dissertation advisor Bette London, who guided me through the research and writing process and continues to be a generous mentor. Her attentive reading, sharp critical insights, detailed feedback, and unfailing support have proved invaluable to me over the years. I would also like to thank my graduate school cohort—Shera Ahmad, Mark Anderson, Mark Berretini, Mark Betz, Edward Chan, Jennifer Church, John Consigli, Kelly Hankin, Narin Hassan, Amy Herzog, Tammany Kramer, Nick Newman, and Jill Stuart—for the many lively discussions that proved crucial to my intellectual formation.

My current place of work, the University of Oregon, has served as a very hospitable environment. This project has been supported by research leave from the English department and by fellowships and travel grants from the College of Arts and Sciences, the Humanities Center, the Center for the Study of Women and Society, the Center for Asian and Pacific Studies, and the Center for Race and Sexuality Studies. In addition, I have profited immensely from scholarly exchanges with colleagues across a range of disciplines. I thank Michael Aronson, Elizabeth Bohls, Ken Calhoon, Mai-lin Cheng, Maram Epstein, Karen Ford, Lynn Fujiwara, Michael Hames-Garcia, Warren Ginsberg, Ellen Herman, Shari Huhndorf, Lamia Karim, Kathleen Karlyn, Jon Lewis, Leah Middlebrook, Dayo Mitchell, Daisuke Miyao, Sandy Morgan, Priscilla Ovalle, Irmary Reyes-Santos, Dan Rosenberg, Paul Peppis, Tres Pyle, Carol Stabile, Lynn Stephen, Deborah Song, Cynthia Tolentino, Janet Wasko, and Harry Wonham for their thoughtful feedback and generous research inputs. I owe a particular debt to David Leiwei Li, whose extraordinary work on contemporary Chinese cinema has inspired me to think more rigorously about the relationship of intimacy, globalization, and film form. Our long conversations opened up new avenues of inquiry and helped me to redefine the scope of this book. Jenifer Presto's impeccable taste ensured that I ironed out several clunky formulations and awkward turns of thought. I thank Chuck Kleinhans and Julia Lesage for the gift of an intellectually invigorating and emotionally sustaining friendship. I am most grateful to my students, who endured many hours of substandard, poorly subtitled film prints of 1970s and 1980s Hindi cinema to produce insightful readings, often drawing surprising connections that were most useful to me.

This is a propitious time to be a student of Indian cinema, particularly of the popular variety. The last two decades have witnessed a surge of interest in this field, and there are now several excellent studies, both academic and otherwise, from which I have benefited. Sumita Chakrabarty's pioneering study of Hindi popular cinema first suggested to me the rich dividends of approaching Indian postcoloniality through its popular cinema. Madhava Prasad's elaborations on privacy and film form in his seminal work, *Ideology of the Hindi Film*, have been central to my thoughts on conjugal states in New Bollywood cinema, and I am grateful for his support and encouragement over the years. My use of the term *New Bollywood* expands upon and modifies Ashish Rajyadaksha's influential observations on this subject, and I have learned a lot from his interventions on the listserv cinemasouthasia. In methodological terms, Lalitha Gopalan's innovative conception of Indian popular film as a "cinema of interruptions" has been very generative for my understanding of film aesthetics, and I thank her for inspiring me to work on the horror genre. Amit Rai's attempt to locate "Bollywood" in India's evolving new media ecology enabled me to think anew the relation between film form and the field of social and industrial forces that it inhabits. I have profited immensely from our discussions. Ranjani Mazumdar's work on cinema in relation to the city has shaped my views on the contemporary "urban film," while Ravi Vasudevan's call that we continue to attend to the "cinematic instance" through a study of "micro-narrational" units has served as a guiding principle in several sections of this project.

My conversations with Moinak Biswas about Bengali cinema allowed me to refine and nuance my conception of the popular. I thank Sharmistha Gooptu, Madhuja Mukherjee, and Abhijit Roy for sharing with me their ongoing research so I could complete my work in a timely fashion. Bhaskar Sarkar's sharp insights on post-Partition Bengali melodrama enabled me to rethink my notion of conjugality in new Bengali cinema, and I am ever grateful to him for asking penetrating questions that always open up new lines of reflection. Priya Joshi's advice at an early stage in this project that I "follow the money" was very timely, and I thank her for motivating me to study the industry. Film historians Priya Jaikumar and Neepa Majumdar not only led by example, but immediately responded to many queries as I was feeling my way through the archive. Neepa's theoretical insights on film music and sound fundamentally informed my arguments in chapter 1. I thank William Mazzarella for sharing with me his research in progress and for his incisive observations on desire, consumption, and popular culture in contemporary India. Richard Allen, Ulka Anjaria, Anustup Basu, Corey Creekmur, Manishita Dass, Jigna Desai, Rajinder Dudrah, Rachel Dwyer, Tejaswini Ganti, Nitin Govil, Philip Lutgendorf, Sudhir Mahadevan, Purnima Mankekar, Monika Mehta, Sujata Moorti, Manjunath Pendakur, Rosie Thomas, and Daya

Thussu have provided generous feedback at various stages of this project, and it has been much enriched by their suggestions.

My focus on conjugality has been crucially informed by the excellent corpus of scholarship on gender by South Asian feminists. Historian Rochona Majumdar's rethinking of the marriage form and its relation to modernity has been particularly important to my work. I also thank her for being such a careful reader and stimulating interlocutor. Her profound love of popular film made for numerous enlightening discussions. I am grateful to Anjali Arondekar, Srimati Basu, Bishnupriya Ghosh, Gayatri Gopinath, Geeta Patel, Jyoti Puri, Sangeeta Ray, and Sudipta Sen for sharing with me their keen insights on the law, sexuality, and visual culture in contemporary India. Conversations with Chad Allen, Lisa Duggan, Imke Meyer, Robert Reid-Pharr, David Shumway, Patricia White, and Linda Williams have helped me locate my work in a wider field. Toral Gajarawala—despite her protestations that she is not cinematically oriented—has gifted me with many a critical gem. Heidi Schlipphacke and I were writing our books at the same time, and our frequent intellectual exchanges have left their mark everywhere in this work. I owe a particular debt to Manisha Mirchandani—cinephile extraordinaire—whose friendship has nourished my life and scholarship.

My research could not have been completed without the support of the entire staff at the National Film Archive of India in Pune. I thank the director, Mr. Shashidharan, who ensured that my limited research time was used optimally. I am truly grateful to the librarian Ms. Joshi for her many helpful suggestions. Ms. Iyer and Ms. Kshirsagar in the documentation section made resources available, while Mr. Dhiwar organized screenings on short notice. I also thank the librarians at the Film and Television Institute in Pune and the National Library in Kolkata for their research assistance. In Pune, Gayatri Chatterji and K. S. Pillai shared with me their fathomless knowledge of cinema, while Bisakha Ghosh and Jasomati Mukherji's warm hospitality made these visits especially delightful.

I am most grateful to the three anonymous reviewers of this book in manuscript form for their meticulous readings and thoughtful suggestions, which made the revision process a real pleasure. Alan Thomas at the University of Chicago Press has been a wonderful editor, generous with his advice and feedback and patient in guiding me through the publication process. Randy Petilos instructed me in the nitty-gritties of preparing and submitting a manuscript, responding to my many queries with alacrity and humor. I thank him and Jeong Chang for their help with the images. My gratitude is due to Nick Murray, whose thoughtful and meticulous copyediting greatly improved the manuscript. I also thank Mary Gehl for her assistance and guidance with page proofs, and Laura Avey for her help with publicity, as well as Jan Williams for preparing the index.

It is difficult to adequately convey the debt I owe my family. While my interest in cinema originates with my mother, my father, Ganesh Gopal Iyer, encouraged me to pursue an academic career and supported me through all its ups and downs. My brother Shankar Iyer has always taken a great interest in my work, and his critical acuity helped me sharpen several of the arguments in this book. My work has been much improved by my sister-in-law Tammany Kramer's eye for detail. I thank Binky, my two-year-old niece, for showing a precocious interest in Bollywood dance numbers. I drew frequently upon the wide-ranging knowledge of Bengali culture of my mother-in-law, Jayanti Sen, and her facility with the language. I also thank my extended family, among them Lyn Bigelow, Anirudh Chari, Sujoy Chowdhury, Anindita Kumar, Ayesha Mallik, Sanjoy Mukherjee, Debdatta Sen, Debal Sen, Sharmila Sen, Devika Sen, Malika Sen, Panchali Sen, and Sujaya Sen, for always being up for going to the movies with me! I can hardly count the many ways in which my husband, Biswarup Sen, has contributed to this work. Without him, the book would not be. My daughter Mohini Shyama arrived as I was finishing this project, and I thank her for filling each day since with sweetness and light.

A portion of chapter 1 was first published as *"Singin' in the Rain*: Conjugality and Hindi Film Form" in *Feminist Studies* 37, no. 1 (Spring 2011) © Feminist Studies, Inc. A portion of chapter 2 was first published as "Sentimental Symptoms: The Films of Karan Johar and Bombay Cinema" in *Bollywood and Globalization: Indian Popular Cinema, Nation, Diaspora*, edited by Rini Bhattacharya Mehta and Rajeshwari Pandharipande (London: Anthem Press, 2011), © Anthem Press, Inc.

# Conjugating New Bollywood

Director Anurag Kashyap's *Dev D* (2009) is an utterly faithless remake of the most frequently adapted work in Indian film history, Saratchandra Chatterji's 1917 novel, *Devdas*. This tale of a man who transgresses traditional norms but fails to become a modern, self-actualizing individual, captures the disorienting effects of the sudden arrival of modernity in colonial Bengal. Saratchandra's eponymous hero falls in love across class lines but cannot defy social sanctions and be with his beloved Paro. When she is forced to marry another man, Devdas proceeds to self-destruct. Though drawn to the courtesan Chandramukhi, he cannot stop mourning Paro, and so he drinks himself to death. First adapted to film in 1928 by Naresh Mitra and then more famously by P. C. Barua in 1935, *Devdas* has been remade many times in multiple languages. At least nine films bear the title *Devdas*, and countless others are inspired by it. As recently as 2002, Sanjay Leela Bhansali's opulent recreation of *Devdas* featuring Hindi cinema's biggest stars—Shahrukh Khan and Aishwarya Rai—opened at Cannes and put the singing-dancing Bollywood spectacular on the global radar. Made on an "indie" budget with no recognizable stars, *Dev D* is an odd sort of remake. While serial adaptations usually testify to the enduring relevance of a work, this film does the opposite. Kashyap demonstrates how this tragic tale of a man destroyed by desires that he can neither embrace nor abjure is no longer resonant in contemporary India. In all previous renderings of this novel, Devdas is unable to conjugate with either of the women who love him because he fears the modernity they represent. At the same time, having been transfigured by love, he cannot find refuge in traditional patriarchy. So his only recourse is dissolution and death at Paro's door. Dev D, however, pulls back from the brink, gets over Paro, and moves on with Chandramukhi. While Kashyap's turn to a classic establishes this film's cultural genealogy, Dev D's survival signals the coming into being of a new Hindi cinema.

My point of departure for this inquiry is the observation that classic Hindi cinema—an entire system of filmmaking analogous to classic Hollywood[1]—gives way at the turn of the millennium to a new cinematic order, one that I designate as New Bollywood. I am specifically interested in how aesthetic forms and industrial practices in post-1991 Bollywood films are aligned with the social and cultural forces that constitute Indian modernity. I study this phenomenon by analyzing the remarkable appearance of a postnuptial "couple-form" that takes the place of Hindi film's standard romantic duo. If classic cinema was concerned with recounting a love story that ended in marriage (or death), contemporary film begins its narratives with the couple already conjugated. The couple's "right to be"—once the source of narrative conflict—is no longer in question. The central problem that animates this book is this: How can we read *through* the couple-form in New Bollywood cinema in order to arrive at the connections between the celluloid figuration of conjugality, film form, the institutions of cinema, and the social life of the movies? In the following pages, I look at works that feature the postnuptial couple to show how their portrayals of the vicissitudes of marriage and domesticity capture key cinematic developments of the postmillennial era. By analyzing the crucial changes in the couple-form as well as graphing the network of forces and institutions within which it is reformatted, this project demonstrates how classic Hindi cinema has morphed into the New Bollywood.

As I show in greater detail below, by the early 1970s, the unitary structure of Mumbai film[2] began to be dismantled by a series of developments that can be collectively described as "Bollywoodization."[3] For example, the "social" film—the super-genre that had dominated the classic period—gave way to the *masala* (lit., "mixture of spices") film, its campy equivalent, as well as a whole new category known as "B-circuit films." The emergence of a state-supported parallel cinema movement that sought to produce "good cinema" had the effect of pushing the industry toward greater commercialization as film budgets expanded and star casts multiplied. Further, Hindi film became far more integrated with other forms of media—as exemplified by the proliferation of film magazines like *Filmfare, Stardust,* and *Cine Blaze,* as well as the phenomenal popularity of television shows like *Chitrahaar* and *Phool Khile Hain Gulshan Gulshan.*[4] The process of Bollywoodization would come to fruition in the socioeconomic regime put in place by the liberalization of the Indian economy in the early 1990s. The integration of the Indian economy into the global marketplace and the rise of an urban, consumerist middle class provided a suitable context for a wholesale restructuring of the movie industry and the emergence of radically novel styles of filmmaking. Thus, even though New Bollywood cinema's[5] genealogy goes back to a set of processes that had been at play for a while, it only begins to emerge as a distinctive product in the post-liberalization era.

This new cinema differs from its predecessor in many significant ways. Vast changes have occurred at the industrial end. The film industry is now much more capitalized and regulated, the division of labor and the process of movie production are being professionalized and rationalized as never before, the modes of movie distribution and exhibition have been drastically altered, the film business is more closely integrated with other sectors of the entertainment industry, filmmaking is now incorporating a lot of high-end technology, and the nature of the film audience has changed dramatically. In short, the emerging system has all the trappings of a culture industry. At the same time, the films of the new cinema are markedly different from those of the previous era. If classic Hindi cinema was characterized by a self-imposed homogeneity enforced by the all-embracing format of the social film and the *masala,* New Bollywood embodies a multiplicity of genres and is stunningly diverse in its output: the lavish spectacles of Karan Johar or Sanjay Leela Bhansali; the so-called NRI blockbusters featuring Shah Rukh Khan;[6] romantic comedies with Akshay Kumar and Imran Khan in lead roles; genres like science fiction and horror; socially conscious films like *Lagaan* (Land tax, Ashutosh Gowariker, 2001) or *Rang De Basanti* (Paint it yellow, Rakyesh Omprakash Mehra, 2006); gritty productions from Ram Gopal Varma's "Factory"; and low-budget, offbeat "indies" like *Ghosla Ka Khosla* (Ghosla's nest, Dibakar Banerjee, 2006) and *Hyderabad Blues* (Nagesh Kukunoor, 1998).

New Bollywood is not the only cinema whose emergence is congruent with the processes of economic globalization. Many other Asian cinemas have witnessed a similar restructuring of film form as a response to the demands of the global marketplace. Writing on new fifth- and sixth-Generation Chinese cinema, David Li has suggested that we must read "the exemplary Chinese film texts of the past two decades . . . as symptomatic of globalization at large."[7] Writing in a similar vein, a commentator for the *New Bangkok Post* sums up the current state of Thai cinema by observing, "The past decade of 'New Thai Cinema' was carpeted with thorny red roses and characterized by unfulfilled expectations. Two or three directors have matured into brand names of their own, but otherwise the industry has largely been driven by a sad mix of cheap, capitalistic impulses and a general lack of confidence."[8] And the editors of a book entitled *New Korean Cinema* point out that "the cultural phenomenon which critics now routinely refer to as 'New Korean Cinema' is qualitatively different from the pre-nineties cultural cinema," and go on to ask, "What has happened to South Korean cinema since the early 1990s? And in what sense can it be said to be new?"[9] Such inquiries point to the emerging relationship between cinematic form and global market logic. My analysis of New Bollywood cinema can thus be seen as one among many possible interventions that seeks to shed light on this general problematic.

In what follows, I first offer a very brief history of Hindi cinema and its relationship to social and political developments in India. This section situates classic Hindi film within the framework of the Nehruvian state, discusses how a historical crisis in the Indian state coincided with the rise of *masala* and parallel cinema, and offers an account of the post-liberalization landscape of the 1990s. Whereas the first section analyzes the social and economic factors that accompany new cinema, the next section offers an "internal" history of Hindi film in the period 1970–1990 to show how Bollywoodization begins to change the contours of popular film and culture and paves the way for New Bollywood. The third section deals with the category of conjugality and its centrality to popular film. Here I look at the couple-form in both classic and contemporary Hindi cinema in order to demonstrate its critical value as an analytic category. The concluding section lays out my methodological commitments and provides a brief overview of the book.

## Cinema and Society in Post-Independence India

Cinema as a mass medium occupied a unique position in the first few decades after India's independence. Nehruvian policy prohibited private use of the airwaves, so all broadcasting was state-controlled and strictly monitored.[10] With no incentive to be popular, the governing aesthetic for both radio and television amounted to a sort of "socialist realism" whose guiding vision was framed by bureaucratic overseers. Cinema, on the other hand, continued to remain in private hands after independence, and was undoubtedly the prime purveyor of popular entertainment in the country. Though it carried the taint of a guilty pleasure, the social film nonetheless aspired to be a nationalist-bourgeois form. The industry itself was a curious amalgam of makeshift elements. In the colonial period, the industry had been organized around a studio system similar in many respects to that of Hollywood.[11] By the early fifties however, a variety of factors—a rise in the entertainment tax, the influx of indigenous capital, the prohibition on the construction of movie theaters, and the increasing clout of distributors—led to the sudden demise of this system.[12] What emerged in its place was a patchwork arrangement characterized by hundreds of small producers, dubious modes of financing that often involved "black money" coming from the Mumbai underworld, and a vast army of actors, music directors, and film technicians who operated as unfettered agents. The system was very loosely structured, with the three sectors of production, distribution, and exhibition remaining largely autonomous, held together by informal social networks and verbal agreements. The films themselves were also cut-and-paste—dialogue, songs, dance numbers, and fight sequences were manufactured piecemeal and then assembled to create the final product. Production schedules were erratic—a single film could be completed in a matter of few months, or might take years as producers shot a few reels and then used these rushes to procure financing, while star actors and actresses (on whose drawing power the system was heavily dependent) would often commit to four or more productions simultaneously. Consequently, total output was high and kept increasing with each decade, a paradoxical outcome for a system structured by these inefficiencies.[13]

Though a fully commercial medium, Hindi cinema had to reconcile its profit-making impulses with a nationalist orientation it had inherited from the colonial era.[14] During what I term its classic period (1947–70),[15] Hindi film was shaped by three imperatives: it aspired to be a national cinema that was socially responsive; it sought to remain commercially viable by drawing as large an audience as possible; and it desired to articulate with the various currents of modernity. This triple calling led to the development of a textual form that characterized almost all the films of this period. The social film drew on multiple genres—musicals, romantic comedy, action-adventure, and drama—in order satisfy the demands placed upon the medium.[16] Thus the typical film focused on one or more "relevant" issues; included add-ons like rural vignettes, comedy routines, and thrills that helped to draw in the masses; and utilized devices like song and dance in order to promote contemporary fashions and lifestyles. So perfect was this formula that the social film survived almost intact for two decades and produced such masterpieces of Hindi cinema as *Awara* (Vagabond, Raj Kapoor, 1951), *Mother India* (Mehboob Khan, 1957), *Sangam* (Union, Raj Kapoor, 1964), and *Ram Aur Shyam* (Ram and Shyam, Tapi Chanakya, 1967).[17]

The state of the nation began to change in the early seventies. The country faced a series of crises that threatened its stability: the Bangladesh war in 1971, the failed monsoons of 1972 and 1973, a drastic rise in world oil prices that led to a recession, a severe depletion of foreign reserves, and growing unemployment. Prices rose steeply, by 22 per cent in 1972–73 alone. The grim economic scenario led to widespread political unrest, with numerous strikes breaking out in crucial sectors—education, transportation, and even among the police force. These protests culminated in the so-called JP (Jayaprakash Narayan) Movement, a hostile coalition of left- and right-wing forces opposed to the ruling Congress Party, which began a campaign of mass mobilization and civil disobedience that threatened to destabilize the entire system. The government responded by proclaiming a state of internal emergency on June 25, 1975, allowing it to suspend fundamental rights and civil liberties. This unprecedented state of affairs lasted for almost two years. When Indira Gandhi finally revoked the emergency in 1977, she paid a heavy price for her quasi-fascist adventure by being defeated in the polls. However, the coalition government that came into being did not last long, and the Congress Party and Mrs. Gandhi regained power in 1980.[18]

In spite of this return to the status quo, the events of the decade revealed deep fractures in the national body politic. The paternalistic conception of the state—ensconced in the colonial formula that the government equaled *ma-bap* (mother-father)—came to be seriously questioned as sections of the population began to feel that their interests and concerns could never be met by those in power. This alienation came to be refracted in cinema through the figure of "the angry young man," best captured by Amitabh Bachchan's classics of angst and violent discontent: *Zanjeer* (Chain, Prakash Mehra, 1973), *Deewar* (Wall, Yash Chopra, 1975), and *Trishul* (Trident, Yash Chopra, 1978). Bachchan's heroes challenged the notion that the state and its politicians embodied the common good and offered in its stead a populist and violent individualism. This feeling of disenchantment became a central thematic of seventies Hindi film and amounted to a rejection of the contract implicit in the social film. Henceforth Mumbai cinema would begin to retreat from its goal of addressing "the people" as a totality. The biggest hits of the era—the "angry" Bachchan films, action-oriented dramas like *Sholay* (Flames, Ramesh

Sippy, 1975), or youthful romances like *Bobby* (Raj Kapoor, 1973) and *Jawani Diwani* (Youthful Craziness, Narendra Bedi, 1972)—contained little or no "public service announcements."[19] This change in address signaled the end of the social film and the rise of *masala*. As one recent commentator remembers,

The popular films of that era are often referred to as *masala* films, associating the blend of spices used in Indian cooking with the distinctive blend of film ingredients: broad comedy, improbable action (sometimes referred to as "dishoom-dishoom" after the sound used to represent the punches), uncomplicated romance, and copious amounts of melodrama. After the heroes traverse the plots full of coincidence, sit through at least one item number performed by special guest star Helen, and have some dishoom-dishoom with a henchman or five, traditional family values would be upheld, greed and dishonor would be punished by legitimate authority figures, and the world would be set right.[20]

Having disavowed the task of creating products for the "putative" good of the people, *masala* ended up as a much more entertainment-driven version of the social film. With its flashy aesthetics, tongue-in-cheek humor, and multiple star casting, *masala* was a formal reflex of the Bollywoodization of Hindi film. Epitomized by the work of directors like Manmohan Desai—*Amar Akbar Anthony* (1977) and *Naseeb* (Destiny, 1981)—*masala's* universal currency as a categorical term and its memorializing in recent Bollywood films like *Don* (Farhan Akhtar, 2006), *Om Shanti Om* (Hail to Peace, Farah Khan, 2007), and *Once Upon a Time in Mumbai* (Milan Luthra, 2010) is a testament to its seminal role in redefining Hindi film.

The waning of the social film meant that the burden of creating a cinema that explored facets of everyday life fell to other hands. Around this time, the commercial sector witnessed the rise of small-budget films in a realistic register that were concerned with detailing middle-class life. These films thematized urbanization, alienation, and a nascent consumer culture.[21] The state, in turn, began to promote a cinema with a "social conscience." The film industry had been clamoring for funding assistance and other concessions from the state for decades to no avail. The government finally got into the act in 1960 and set up the Film Finance Corporation, a body whose primary goal was to "to plan, promote and organize an integrated and efficient development of the Indian film industry and foster excellence in cinema."[22] As Madhava Prasad has pointed out, by the end of the sixties the government was finally concerned that Hindi cinema was failing in its appointed role of educating and improving the masses and thus launched, "a state-sponsored movement that sought to give substance to the idea of a national cinema." By offering tax relief to films that had the right sort of content, the government "launched a financial policy aimed at the development of 'good cinema,' which for most people associated with the project meant a cinema that was realist, narrative-centered, developmental, and culturally distinctly Indian."[23] This initiative was responsible for launching what would be known as "parallel" cinema. Mrinal Sen's *Bhuvan Shome* (1969) was the movement's first notable success, and it was followed by films like *Sara Akash* (The big sky, Basu Chatterji, 1969), *Uski Roti* (Our daily bread, Mani Kaul, 1969), *27 Down* (Avtar Krishna Kaul, 1974), *Maya Darpan* (Mirror of illusion, Kumar Shahani, 1972), *Garam Hawa* (Hot winds, M. S. Sathyu, 1973), *Manthan* (The churning, Shyam Benegal, 1976), *Albert Pinto Ko Gussa Kyo Ata Hai* (What makes Albert Pinto angry? Saeed Akhtar Mirza, 1980), and *Aakrosh* (Cry of the wounded, Govind Nihalini, 1980). These Hindi-language films were complemented by a number of releases from regional centers that featured directors like G. Aravindan, Adoor Gopal-akrishnan, Girish Karnad, Ketan Mehta, and others. The parallel cinema movement was quite diverse, spanning the gamut from socially realistic films about peasant oppression and the urban lower classes to more experimental fare in conversation with international trends like the French New Wave, Third Cinema, and the Latin American new cinema.

Dependent on government financing and the patronage of the educated middle classes, parallel cinema flourished until the mid-eighties, when it disappeared somewhat abruptly from the Indian film scene. It is possible that television, which came into its own during this decade, siphoned off some of its reformist energies. As the government realized television's entertainment potential—especially after color broadcasting of the 1982 Asian Games proved to be a major draw—it was keen to cash in on the medium's growing and captive audience. Thus, as Nalin Mehta has pointed out, the hugely successful soap *Hum Log* first aired in 1984 after a US-based NGO convinced the state-owned Doordarshan to start a television series with family-planning messages couched as entertainment. The series, sponsored by Maggi Noodles, proved to be a sensational hit, with more than 80 percent of India's 3.6 million television sets tuned in to *Hum Log* (Us folk) every week.[24] The show's success spawned a wave of socially aware serials—*Buniyaad* (Foundation, 1986), *Rajni* (1985), *Nukkad* (Street corner, 1986)—that aired during the last half of the eighties.[25] The medium's stature was even more firmly established by the phenomenal success of the televised versions of the two greatest epics of Indian culture—the *Ramayana* and the *Mahabharata*.

Hindi cinema thus entered a transitional phase in the period 1980–1991. The migration of socially relevant content to television spelled the death of parallel cinema,[26] and *masala* too was in its last days, in spite of Amitabh Bachchan's continuing star appeal. The ensuing vacuum was, to some extent, filled by the rise of the B circuit. Targeted exclusively at economically disadvantaged audiences in both rural and urban areas, B movies—produced on shoestring budgets, featuring second-tier actors and technicians, and exhibited at decrepit movie theaters—could be considered as a down-market form of *masala*. Interestingly, B-circuit products show stronger genre ingredients. The period also witnessed the return of the action film, in a somewhat more "lumpen" incarnation, and the rise of women-centered revenge sagas like those directed by N. Chandra and Rajkumar Santoshi.[27] Even more significantly, entirely new genres like the horror movie and the teen flick began to affect the marketplace. These, as well as other genres like romantic comedy and science fiction, would later become New Bollywood staples.

The advent of New Bollywood was strongly conditioned by the socioeconomic changes of the 1990s. At the beginning of the decade, the Indian economy had reached a so-called "point of no return." The notorious "Hindu rate of growth" that had plagued Indian development ever since independence had dwindled from 2.5 percent per annum to a miniscule 0.8 percent by 1991. More alarmingly, the country had a severe balance-of-payments problem and was teetering at the edge of bankruptcy. Thus, the central bank had refused all new credit, and foreign-exchange reserves had been depleted to the point that India could barely finance three weeks' worth of imports. The government, under the guidance of Finance Minister Manmohan Singh,[28] enacted a set of revolutionary measures that constituted a major turning point in the nation's history. According to one analyst, "In return for an IMF bailout, gold was transferred to London as collateral, the Rupee devalued and economic reforms were forced upon India. That low point was the catalyst required to transform the economy through badly needed reforms to unshackle the economy [*sic*]. Controls started to be dismantled, tariffs, duties and taxes progressively lowered; state monopolies broken, the economy was opened to trade and investment, private-sector enterprise and competition were encouraged, and globalization was slowly embraced."[29]

This "liberalization" completely transformed India's economic and cultural landscape. The loosening of licensing laws, the lifting of restrictions on imports, and the relaxation of barriers against the entry of foreign capital had a combined effect of jump-starting the entire Indian economy.

Within a year of the reforms the growth rate had gone up to 5.3 percent. The upward trend in the growth rate proved to be stable; between 2002 and 2005, for example, it equaled 8 percent, the second highest rate in the world. The country's GDP had topped $800 billion by 2005 (and was projected to be the third highest in the world by mid-century), and more than a hundred Indian companies had achieved a capitalization of more than $1 billion, including such global brand names as Tata Motors, Jet Airways, Wipro Technologies, Reliance Infocomm, and Infosys.[30] This boom had multiple consequences in other areas of social and cultural life: a renewed push toward urbanization; a massive increase in conspicuous consumption; a doubling of the middle classes, which, by 1999, comprised 50 percent of all urban households; the introduction of new industries like information technology and telecommunications; and an unprecedented explosion in media with the introduction and rapid spread of cable and satellite television, privatized FM radio, and the Internet.

Two of these factors—urbanization and the rise of the middle classes—have been crucially important in facilitating the creation of New Bollywood. The first is a nationwide phenomenon—while established megacities like Delhi and Mumbai continue to grow and prosper, smaller towns like Bhopal, Chandigarh, or Meerut have begun to emerge as major urban centers in their own right. The rapid growth in urbanization has been accompanied by a significant change in the population's class composition. The economy's strong performance saw a total of 103 million people move out of poverty between 1985 and 2005, thus massively boosting the size of the middle class, current estimates for which range between one hundred and four hundred million. According to one global consulting firm, by 2025 the middle class in India will comprise more than 40 percent of the population.[31] As a result, India's consumer market, currently ranked twelfth, is projected to be the fifth largest in the world by then. This exponential increase in the size of the market has been accompanied by a rapid change in the nature of consumption, with a move away from basic necessities to discretionary spending. Thus while food, beverages, and tobacco accounted for 56 percent of all consumption in 1995, that percentage is currently down to 42 percent and is expected to be only 25 percent in 2025, allowing for much higher expenditure on lifestyle products, leisure activities, communication, and entertainment.[32] All these projections assume that the consumerist lifestyle, which is currently limited to only 15 percent of the population, will grow to embrace the rest of the country. But this aspiration for an "all-India market" may never be achieved unless, as Partha Chatterjee has said, "the full historical process of a bourgeois democratic revolution can be completed."[33] It is in this "possible India," characterized by the essential parameters of modernity—urbanization, middle-class formation, consumerism, and globalization—that New Bollywood is located.

## From Bollywood to New Bollywood

The term *Bollywood* was allegedly coined as an afterthought by a film journalist commissioned to write a news column about the Hindi film industry. As Bevinda Collaco recalls,

I was given a studio beat to do. I was not happy with the name of the column Studio Roundup and thought of "Flipping around Follywood," but it sounded too harsh. I settled for "On the Bollywood Beat" instead. From a studio roundup column I began commenting on what was happening off the sets too and it turned into a gossip column. In no time at all the stars were calling up to find out why they were mentioned in Bollywood and others to find out why they were not mentioned in Bollywood. I guess they were responsible for giving my word longevity.

While I worked at *Cine Blitz* in 1978, 79 and 80, I used the word prolifically, but I never thought it would get official international usage. Actually I don't know whether to laugh or to cry when I see my word become common usage.[34]

Collaco's playful coinage was probably inspired by the then current mode of Mumbai filmmaking.[35] As we saw above, by the early seventies the *masala* had become Hindi film's signature form. By then, a rampant commercialization of Hindi cinema was a fait accompli. As the radical filmmaker K. A. Abbas wrote in 1977, "With a limited number of cinemas and those too being monopolized by the producers of commercial glossies, there is an exhibition bottle-neck which makes it virtually impossible for any off-beat, no-star, low-budget picture to get playtime. This is called free trade, according to the law of supply and demand that governs that market in cement, steel—or cinema entertainment."[36] In other words many of the features that we now associate with New Bollywood were already present in the *masala* film of the 1970s. Thus a trade publication, *Film Blaze*, draws attention to changing mores in the industry in the 1970s, rhetorically aligning it to transnational corporations. The notion that the Hindi cinema industry resembled the modern, profit-driven corporation, and that it had unfortunately abandoned its native roots in search of a Westernized look, had become widely entrenched, as the following quotations from anonymous correspondents in film magazines from the 1970s demonstrate:

Giant-size, multi-star cast extravaganzas are becoming fashionable and profitable, just like multi-nationals minting money. So all the BIG banners fancy for giant-size outfit, starring giant-size talents and giant-size make-believe technicians [sic]. Since they believe the best technicians are only born overseas, there is a spree for hiring super technicians from abroad. The foren-touch and foren-feel make the difference . . . [and] . . . many are joining the giant-size foren-brain bandwagon [sic].³⁷

To provide something for everybody and everything for somebody, the producers of Hindi cinema have cooked movies about people from a never-never land. This has resulted in the prosperity of regional movies that have definite people, of a definite region, with realistic habits, hearths and homes. Hindi film producers have surely to own the blame for creating a *faceless* cinema.³⁸

Today, most Hindi filmwallahs seem least interested in holding up the mirror either to nature or authentic environmental problems. With a sudden and convenient love for amnesia, they hold this mirror up to other mirrors. Mostly phoren-made [sic].³⁹

The common concern here is that the industry had lost touch with the "real," exhausted its creativity, and was merely reproducing tested formulas to hedge the risks of rising production and exhibition costs. Many also felt that the malaise in Hindi cinema could be attributed to its predilection for copying Hollywood. Indeed, the word *Bollywood* begins to connote this mimic-mode. As another anonymous correspondent put it humorously, "And what do you know folks? Bollywood's fast catching up with Hollywood. Some of our biggest names have leanings towards the gay side of life, but as I have said before, we haven't yet caught up with Hollywood. There gay is great, here homos are no-nos!"⁴⁰

The misgivings and anxieties displayed by these writers—condensed around the increasing use of *Bollywood* as the name for Hindi cinema— points to a very real process that I have alluded to. In this decade, Hindi cinema becomes far more susceptible to the logic of capital, renounces its nation-building role, aspires to become mere "entertainment," and promiscuously embraces a range of foreign styles as it moves from a "nativist" to a globalized art form. The sardonic and superior tone typical of film journalism of this era, as well as the reporting in trade journals and fanzines, bear testament to the fact that the process of Bollywoodization—understood as a "provincializing" of the norms of Hollywood—is firmly under way.⁴¹

The transformation of Hindi cinema is strikingly illustrated by a "linguistic revolution" that occurs in the pages of film magazines. Throughout the 1970s, fanzines like *Stardust, Super, Star and Style,* and *Cine Blitz* are witness to the emergence of "Hinglish"—a vibrant hybrid of Hindi and English. Hinglish words like *foren/phoren* and *fillum/phillumi* repeatedly indigenize the English language, while hybrid sentence constructions incorporate vernacular slang, such as *bilkul,* (just like), *bakwas,* (nonsense), *bindaas* (laid-back), to stretch the semantic reach of English. Further, the structural bilingualism that postcolonial theory has since identified as the basis of urban, middle-class Indian identity is repeatedly enacted in profiles and feature of stars like Jaya Bhaduri, Shabana Azmi, Amitabh Bachchan, Shatrughan Sinha, and Sanjeev Kumar, who, it is felt, are able to successfully negotiate a persona that is simultaneously Indian and cosmopolitan.[42] This melding of Hindi and English (and of Western and Indian identities) was less apparent in the actual films from the 1970s and was actively resisted in some quarters.[43] Today, however, this strand of Bollywoodization has emerged triumphant, and Hinglish is the near-ubiquitous idiom through which New Bollywood, television, and all other media speak to their urban and globalized audience.

Another aspect of Bollywoodization that takes off in the 1970s is the diffusion of cinematic signification into brands, lifestyles, and celebrity culture. First, we note a concerted effort in the fanzines and film press to link cinema to adjacent consumer economies like fashion, cosmetics, fitness, and body-building through promotions, contests, and the visual and verbal overlap between story and advertising content. Film magazines begin to detail the day-to-day lives of stars, including what they buy and wear, as well as "makeover" stories that teach readers how to look and live like a star. At the same time we witness the creation of "instant" celebrities like Protima Bedi or Katy Mirza as well as a greater attempt to involve readers and fans in publicizing films and the consumer lifestyles embedded in them. This tendency too has come of age: we witness today a complete integration of advertising, marketing, retailing, mobile communications, and many related sectors of the entertainment industry. Finally, we find an increasing focus on the overseas market: stories that recommend a more proactive, state-based export policy, features on the sojourns abroad of various stars and film crews; analysis of the international reach of commercial Indian cinema; and repeated references to Hindi cinema's diasporic fan base in the United Kingdom, the United States, Australia, and Fiji. Here again we see a foreshadowing of the contemporary scene—for today's New Bollywood cinema is simply unthinkable without its global dimensions.[44]

As this brief overview suggests, many of the features and movements that are associated with what I am calling New Bollywood began taking hold in the 1970s. The gradual dissolution of classic Hindi cinema gave rise to a set of processes that can collectively be referred to as Bollywood-ization. The eventual result of these processes was the institution of a new paradigm of Mumbai film that came into being in the early 1990s.[45] Certain key features—the growth of the diasporic market as a major source of revenue for the Hindi film industry; the emergence of the NRI films featuring characters located in London or New York; the tie-ins between film and other entertainment industries; the dissemination of Bollywood as a global brand;[46] genre formation; the rise of multiplex exhibition; and the blurring of lines between popular and parallel cinema—argue for the distinctiveness of New Bollywood. *New* is necessary in order to emphasize that post-liberalization Mumbai film, while owing much to changes in the previous two decades, is nonetheless a radically new art form that must be analyzed on its own terms. Thus, while 1970s *masala* was putatively made for the masses, New Bollywood cinema's address is deliberately narrow and aimed at a transnational, urban, middle-class audience. Again, the movement away from the song-and-dance sequence and the development of distinct Hollywood-style genres like horror and comedy challenge the notion that New Bollywood is merely a contemporary reiteration of older forms. Indeed, post-liberalization cinema's obsession with remakes—*Om Shanti Om* is a perfect case in point—shows a pervasive tendency to cite, exaggerate, and historicize *masala* aesthetics, thus announcing its break from this lineage.

To conclude, let me clarify my use of some crucial terms. I use *Hindi cinema/film*, *classic Hindi cinema/film*, and *Mumbai cinema/film* interchangeably to refer to Hindi films produced in Mumbai in the period 1947–1970. *Social* film refers to the master genre (that subsumed romance, comedy, action, and social drama) that was characteristic of the classic era. By *Bollywoodization*, I denote the set of processes (described in this section) that came into play in the early seventies and had the effect of unsettling the classic paradigm. By *masala*, I mean the genre that replaced the social film at the beginning of the 1970s, and also (somewhat more loosely) the entire period between 1970 and 1991. *New Bollywood*—the subject of this book—refers to the entire world of cinema—industrial practices, financing, exhibition, audience, tie-ins, and of course the films themselves—of the post-liberalization period (1991–present). The term *Bollywood* is a catch-all moniker, variously used to signify contemporary cinema, *masala*, classic Hindi film, and even products from the colonial period.[47] When I do use it at all, I mean it to signify Hindi film in general.

## Conjugations

Heterosexual couple-formation has always been at the heart of all film narrative. Virginia Wright Wexman begins her classic study on the celluloid couple with the statistic that "85 percent of all Hollywood films made before 1960 have romance as their main plot, and 95 percent have romance as either the main plot or a secondary plot."[48] While no such data is available for Indian cinema, even the most cursory examination of its corpus would suggest that love and romance are as central to it as they are to Hollywood films. Why is it love that makes the movies go around? For Wexman, this "emphasis on courtship and romance is a function of the movies' place within American—indeed world—culture as a commercial enterprise based on the concept of mass production."[49] I would parse Wexman as saying the following: If modern capitalism is driven by consumption (i.e., the urge to possess objects), then romantic love is the ideal type of this general desire. This explanation holds for Indian cinema as well. Cinema was, as we saw, the only audiovisual medium not placed under state control in the aftermath of independence. In order to be commercially viable, its logic was tied to that of a libidinal economy where a circuit of commodities is the setting for a staging of desire. As a result, it, too, was driven to structure its narratives partly around the all-too-familiar trajectories of boy meets girl, love encounters obstacles, boy gets girl.[50]

While this formulaic journey from romance to nucleated conjugality was easily accomplished in the case of Hollywood, such a clean resolution was rarely possible within the framework of Hindi cinema. Here the couple has to bring its desire for autonomy into equilibrium with familial mores, community norms, and the imperatives of the state. Such accommodations are typically not required of the Hollywood couple since it is believed that the affairs of the state or of the community have little bearing on affairs of the heart. It has always been otherwise in Hindi film: the right of the couple to constitute itself as an autonomous unit of social reproduction was never a fait accompli but had to be achieved through struggle. The couple's "right to be" was thus a source of dramatic conflict and complications. In addition to predictable sources of authority—like a father or landlord—the couple was also asked to directly advance the nation-state's interests. For example, in Raj Kapoor's *Sangam* (1964), the wealthy Radha loves her social equal Gopal, but at Gopal's urging, she marries the impoverished Sundar because he is a soldier and has sacrificed for the nation. In return, she reaps the reward of a consumerist middle-class domesticity. *Sangam* illustrates how Hindi cinema's couple-form is a function of the conjugation of several forces: the industry's desire to placate a state hostile to its commercialism (Radha gives up her desire for the good of the nation); the ambivalent relation to capitalist modernity on the part of both the industry and the state (she gets a household but not with the person she loves); and the alliance between traditional patriarchy and the modern state (it is Gopal who speaks for the state). The union of two individuals in Hindi films of the classic period is always inflected by larger concerns, and the couple's "right to be" is a contingent and contested issue. To unpack this version of conjugation, we must briefly examine the complicated dynamics between family, marriage, state, and capitalism in colonial and postcolonial India.

Prior to the nineteenth century, the Indian family functioned as an economic as well as a reproductive unit that was part of a highly extended kinship network. The family, and thus the domestic sphere, was continuous and interdependent with *samaj*, that is, society. As Indrani Chatterjee has shown, the conjugal bond was only one of several strains that comprised the family network in pre-nineteenth-century India. Other relationships including friendships, patronage, service, and dependencies equally constituted the precolonial family and continued to "refashion the social and political processes of a later period."[51] By the mid–nineteenth century, however, the effort to separate family and society began in earnest. Successive colonial administrations strove hard by means of legislation, social work, and reformist propaganda to recreate the Indian family as a private domain.[52] The attempt here was to draw a firm boundary between the interior familial space—governed by traditional "native" norms—and the external colonial order. This project would be upstaged by a nationalist reform movement that focused on issues like intercaste unions, widow remarriage, companionate conjugality, and women's re-education in order to rethink the family as an instrument of a specifically *Indian* modernity. As scholars like Partha Chatterjee, Tanika Sarkar, and Mytheli Sreenivas have shown, the familial sphere, by the turn of the twentieth century, became a highly politicized domain that was thought of *both* as a reservoir of a resistant Indian tradition (embodied especially in the figure of the woman) *and* as the crucible within which a progressive nation could be forged.[53] This "new" family resembled neither the old feudal clan nor the privatized nuclear entity typical in capitalist cultures.[54] It must therefore be analyzed as a thoroughly modern formation that arises at a very specific conjuncture—the intersection of colonialism and capitalism. This hybrid formation, as Rochona Majumdar points out, leads to the consolidation of the "arranged marriage." As she observes, it is not as though arranged marriages are archaic, while "love marriages" are modern; rather, this opposition itself is a marker of Indian modernity.[55]

Classic Hindi cinema captured the entire dynamic surrounding love, marriage, and family in modern India. On the one hand, as a commercial medium subject to the laws of capital, it represented desire as the reciprocal longing of two freely choosing individuals. Hence every story line coming out of Mumbai had a romantic plot that featured a pair of lovers finding fulfillment against all odds. At the same time, as an industry that saw itself as participating in the nation-building project, it felt obligated to acknowledge and work with the extended family as the locus for political and cultural change. This double imperative necessitated the creation of a distinctive version of the couple-form. Writing about the legal aspect of conjugation, the historian Nancy Cott has argued, "No modern nation-state can ignore marriage forms, because of their direct impact on reproducing and composing the population. The laws of marriage must play a large part in forming 'the public.' They sculpt the body politic."[56] The couple-form in Hindi cinema is of similar importance because its contours and alignments map out the ways in which the diegetic space of a romantic saga reconciles competing notions of nationhood, community, and individual freedom. That is why psyche or psychology plays such an insignificant role in classic film—the crux of its love stories was always a matter of resolving conflict among a set of social and political vectors. In *Sangam*, Radha's emotions do not determine her choice of Sundar over Gopal; the nation's needs serve as the final arbiter. In short, then, the form of the couple in classic Hindi cinema served as a mechanism that enabled the conjoining of private desires and public concerns. The variations in couple-form were consequently a function of how these twin demands were equilibrated. In most cases, the romantic duo achieved union only on the condition that it be reintegrated within the folds of the extended family and its community. Hence the famous "last shot" of classic Hindi cinema that shows newlyweds flanked on both sides by the entire clan. In other cases, the transgressions on the part of the lovers could only result in death. The couple—constituted by free romantic love and yet simultaneously submitting to the authority of kinship groups and the community—functions as a node that connects to several features and aspirations of classic Hindi film: its mass address and commercial appeal, its aesthetic form comprised of "attractions" like song and dance, the family mode of production that organized the film industry in this era, commercial cinema's conflicted relationship to the state, Hindi film's attempt to communicate the operations of modernity, and its bid for a national market. In short, the couple-form encapsulated the entire set of values and forces that constituted the field of Hindi film and can serve, therefore, as a powerful analytic category with which to study this cinema.

The post-liberalization era in Hindi cinema installs a qualitatively different conjugal form. The typical plot shows the couple as already united: new cinema *begins* at the moment at which classic cinema ended. The change in topos implies a shift in discursive function. In his survey of modern love, David Shumway acutely observes that the most important characteristic of romance is that "whatever its attitude towards marriage, it does not depict it; . . . it may give an account of an extended courtship ending in a marriage made in heaven, but it cannot tell the story of a marriage."[57] New Bollywood cinema disavows traditional romance and replaces the problematic of romance with one concerned with intimacy.[58] It attempts to record the vicissitudes of marital life, thus locating narrative and dramatic conflict within the couple's private space. Whereas in classic cinema the obstacles to romance—intolerant fathers, jealous rivals, conniving villains, dominant ideologies—were always external to the two lovers, the impediments to dyadic bliss in new cinema—miscommunication, distrust, extramarital attractions and affairs, nervous disorders, psychic possession—are internal events that mark the couple as a distinct and separate entity. This metaphysical shift is vividly represented on screen—most couples are depicted as living alone in sleek, modern apartment buildings or homes, in stark contrast to characters in classic Hindi film, who were part of large households packed into old-fashioned ancestral *mahals*.[59]

The cinematic focus on the nucleated, postnuptial pair suggests that the couple-form is being put to a use very different from that of the romantic duo in classic cinema. One of my central suggestions in this book is that the postnuptial couple produced by new Bollywood serves as a ground for elaborating on the citizen-subject of the emerging post-liberalization state. Two conditions need to be met if this project is to succeed. First, the couple must be extracted from the domain (and dominion) of the social—the extended family, the clan, and the community—in order to be properly individuated. In other words, the couple-form must project the citizen as an independent agent who exercises free choice within the framework of middle-class consumerist society. Second, the couple must be "technologized," that is, be inserted into a network of material objects, lifestyle attitudes, sociological trends, and financial and economic metrics, in order to demonstrate its "applicability" to the new set of social and cultural parameters that define the contemporary.

My analysis of new Bollywood film charts this double movement of isolation and insertion that leads to the formation of the couple-form in its contemporary mode. As I show in the first chapter of this book, the marginalization of the song-and-dance sequence in current cinema is a marker of the couple's newly found independence. The universality of song and dance, I have shown elsewhere, arose from the crucial function it served in providing a space—a kind of safe house—where the couple could be privatized without challenging its ties to the kinship network.[60] In New Bollywood film, the couple is "unhoused" from song and dance. The latter recedes from center stage to the soundtrack to become an object of nostalgia, while the couple is now able to posit itself as private and sovereign. It need no longer have recourse to the artifice of the romantic duet. We see a similar conversion of the stylistic and narrational elements of classic Hindi cinema into "film effects" in the so-called NRI film that caters to diasporic audiences. In these films the family is displaced from a site of power to one of affect, thus radically altering its meaning and implications for the couple. Rather than acting as an impediment to the couple's desire, the recoded family now functions as an enabler of its greater mobility. In fact, part of my argument here is that the "Hindu extended family" in recent Bollywood cinema is enclosed in quotation marks so that Bollywood can develop a new grammar of emotions that express emerging modes of subjectivity. Finally, the couple's radical isolation from previous attachments is most strikingly demonstrated in two New Bollywood genres—horror and the multiplot film. In what I term *new horror*, the point of departure for every plot is the couple's decision to move into a new home that locates them far away from kith and kin, and the ensuing encounters with the supernatural isolate them even further from all social connections. In the multiplot film the couple is placed alongside other random couples with whom they share only a contingent relation, thus emphasizing the point that every married pair must go it alone.

The processes of isolation release the couple-form from previous dependencies and grant it the sovereignty required of its new role as an independent actor in a marketized order. At the same time, the new properties of the couple-form allow New Bollywood to be conjugated with a set of externalities that constitutes emergent Indian modernity. Thus, the decline of song and dance and the consequent distancing of the soundtrack has led to a greater integration of movie music with the record industry, DJ sampling, mobile downloading, and other ancillary domains. The new grammar of the NRI film has found resonance with diasporic practices: Bollywood extravaganzas, the revival of folk music and dances, Hindu summer camps. Horror's intrinsic focus on materiality has allowed its contemporary version to become a precise cataloguer of India's consumerist culture, while the new modes of exhibition surrounding the multiplot film align it with current trends in the entertainment industry. These correlations demonstrate the importance of the couple-form for an understanding of New Bollywood. Tracing the changes in the couple's makeup and analyzing its modes of interconnectivity with the outside enable us to access the meaning of the "new" in today's cinema.

## Methodology and Plan of the Book

It is my guiding premise that New Bollywood can be properly understood only when placed alongside the ensemble of forces that constitute Indian modernity. Though primarily a study of film form, this book nonetheless examines contemporary practices in industry, technology, urban development, marketing, and other areas that tie in with new cinema. Such a strategy does not imply that I am committed to the notion of art as "reflection" or "derivation." The specific form of New Bollywood cinema—or any art form for that matter—cannot, I believe, be deduced by means of economic or sociological analysis; it is an original creation that must be analyzed on its own terms. However, aesthetic form is efficacious only when it functions as a node in a network of associated elements that constitutes a field of activity. Only when we factor in all the other nodes in the network as well as the lines of force connecting them can we ascertain the full import of aesthetic form.[61]

An example will clarify the point I am making. The Steadicam—a stabilizing mount for a motion picture camera that allows a very smooth shot even when the operator is moving quickly over an uneven surface—was, until recently, not a part of Bollywood's cinematographic repertoire. In my discussion of Ram Gopal Varma's *Raat* (Night, 1991) and *Bhoot* (Ghost, 2003), I suggest that the Steadicam's growing popularity in the post-liberalization era signals three distinct but interrelated processes: the rapid technologizing of Bollywood cinema and its industrial reorganization, the emergence of horror as an up-market genre aimed at middle-class audiences, and the drive toward stabilizing a first-person perspective of narration that psychologizes the couple. The disembodied mobility of the Steadicam captures the modern in its velocity and angularity, enables a detailed probing of objects that expresses the phenomenology of middle-class life, and uses extended point-of-view shots, a generic norm of all horror, in order to adumbrate and isolate the subjectivity of the couple. The Steadicam thus functions as an analytical node that connects technology, sociology, and aesthetics in New Bollywood.

My analysis of New Bollywood is based on close readings of a wide range of titles that exemplify crucial ways in which the couple-form has changed in structure and function. At the same time, I employ complementary modes of research in order to establish the connections between this new aesthetic form and its social and material context. Thus, I carry out extensive archival research of film magazines in the 1930s to demonstrate the importance of song and dance in classic Hindi cinema and thus establish the significance of its decline in New Bollywood. In my chapter on the NRI film I examine Mumbai industry practices to establish linkages between the redefinition of the feudal family and the decline in the "family mode of production." I also draw upon an extensive interview I conducted with the director Rituparna Ghosh to show how New Bollywood functions as a "technology" that can be appropriated by regional cinema. To reiterate what I have already stated, I treat aesthetic form (of which the couple-form is an instance) as neither a reflection of material reality nor an autonomous site of cultural signification, but as one among the many "things" that make up the entire field of cinematic presentation. Hence, while my main focus is on the couple-form, the book examines a wide assortment of "actors" integral to the staging of New Bollywood: fan letters, camera technology, interiors, concession stands, Ram Gopal Varma, urbanization, jewelry, exhibition chains, middle-class demographics, Dolby sound, the Bollywood B circuit, nonresident Indians, third-rate monsters.

Each chapter investigates how a formal property of classic Hindi film is reformatted into a contemporary configuration: thus the song-and-dance sequence recedes into the soundtrack, the feudal saga transforms into family romance by recalibrating the role of affect, B-circuit horror is upgraded into a yuppie brand, the social film is fractured into multiplot narratives, and vernacular cinema gets a makeover by means of global chic. In each of these cases there is a corresponding modulation in couple-form that points to a new arrangement of aesthetic and material elements: the "backgrounding" of the soundtrack allows the couple's intensities to be released from song and dance into entire narrative while also facilitating a synergy between cinema and the sound industries; the reworking of the family saga empowers the couple-form and signals the transition from a family to a corporate mode of filmic production; the detailed description of the nucleated, middle-class couple in new horror films dovetails with the formation of a distinctly middle-class lifestyle in urban areas as well the rise of the Hollywood-style genre film; the multiple couples represented in "multiplex film" correlate exhibition space and narrative structure; the adoption of New Bollywood technologies of representation by a regional cinema—in this case Bengali film—prepares a vernacular tradition for the global marketplace by reorienting the normative structures of the *bhadralok* (middle-class) couple. In brief, the book as a whole demonstrates how the cinematic couple functions as an index of the new directions that Bollywood has taken in the last two decades.

# When the Music's Over: A History of the Romantic Duet

In the final sequence of *Slumdog Millionaire* (Danny Boyle, 2008), Jamal and Latika's lips freeze in a brief screen kiss. Almost immediately, Boyle goes to credits intercut with a Bollywood-style song-and-dance number—"Jai Ho"—that enacts how this kiss feels to the long-suffering, long-separated sweethearts. This couple is twice constituted—first through a kiss and then in the performance register of the romantic duet. By formally separating the kiss from the song, Boyle evokes the uneasy relationship between these modes of affection in popular Hindi cinema. By locating the kiss in the diegesis but consigning the song to the credits, this Bollywood-inspired global blockbuster revises the aesthetic codes of Hindi cinema where the song sequence rather than the kiss has historically functioned as an engine of couple-formation. I start with Boyle's film because it captures fundamental shifts ongoing in New Bollywood cinema whereby the kiss, banished from the screen since the 1930s, is making a reappearance, while the song sequence, which has long served as the primary expressive device for constituting the romantic couple, is being sidelined. If "Jai Ho's" extra-diegetic location references this gradual disappearance of the romantic duet as an engine of couple-formation, Jamal and Latika resemble a New Bollywood couple in other regards. Though he is Muslim and she is Hindu, their relationship is not thwarted by parental interdiction (they have none); nor do societal norms (they are waifs and command no social capital) inhibit their union. What temporarily comes in their way is chance and Salim's (Jamal's brother) illicit desire for Latika. Once a global game-show and Jamal's "street cred" turn the slumdog into a millionaire, he can have the girl and kiss her too. *Slumdog Millionaire* thus cites the couple's emergence in New Bollywood cinema as private, nuclear, and typically located in urban space with weak links to family and community. This couple-form, I argue here, conjugates with an unfolding project of aesthetic reform whereby the song-and-dance sequence is no longer as ubiquitous as it once was. I explore two important periods in the conjunction of song and dance and couple-formation in the history of popular film. I track the emergence of the romantic duet in the first decade of sound and explore how it illuminates Hindi commercial cinema's relation to modernity, nationalism, and public culture. I then turn to a number of recent films to see how they, in turn, modify the song-and-dance sequences' relation to couple-formation. In brief, this chapter examines why the couple-form once conjugated with song and how this tie is now dissolving.

## Sealed with a Song

From its very beginnings, the song-and-dance sequence has been a feature of Indian popular cinema. Rationales for the persistence of the performance sequence range from the culturalist (song and dance in Indian tradition) to the sociological and techno-industrial, though no single approach may be fully capable of explaining this enduring phenomenon.[1] Song sequences come in a wide variety—devotional songs, songs celebrating festivals and rituals, "cabaret" numbers staged in nightclubs, and so on. While such song situations can be naturalized (people after all do sing at parties, temples, or weddings) and thus folded into the narrative, the romantic duet–which is our focus here—tends to break entirely free of the narrative milieu. It operates as an adjunct module within whose space sovereignty is accorded to the couple by means of the formal characteristics of the song sequence itself, its mode of production, and the extent of its circulation. These include the containment of the song sequence (it has a beginning and an end); its disregard for realist codes (it is not subject to the laws of continuity); its mode of production (highly diffuse with composer, lyricist, singers, musicians, actors, choreographer, director, and producer contributing to the end product); the convention of playback singing (the stars on-screen lip-synch to songs recorded by playback singers); and finally, its extra-cinematic life (on radio, TV, cassettes, CDs, as ringtones, in nightclubs, weddings, on the web).[2]

So while the song sequence might appear paratactical, excessive in relation to the narrative, I would suggest that what the song adds is so much more than a kiss. I make my case by tracking the emergence of the romantic duet in certain key films of the 1930s alongside critical and fan discourse around the celluloid fashioning of conjugality. In these discussions, the couple and their figuration become the grounds for debating broader issues such as cinema's implication in nationalism, its commercial imperatives, its "publicness" as technology and art form, and its social effects as an agent of the modernity. In this decade, Indian cinema sought to legitimate itself by participating in the mainstream nationalist project; thus cinematic discourse was recast from "the cosmopolitan mode of the 1920s to an increasingly bourgeois nationalist mode in the 1930s."[3] As a "native enterprise" trying to compete—in the face of a colonial state hostile to it—with imports from Hollywood and Britain, the film industry had impeccable *swadeshi* (lit., "of the nation") credentials. Yet, the nationalist elite were wary of the industry's output on two counts: first, films were viewed as frivolous, sensation-based instances of a debased modernity; second, the increasing popularity of cinema as a mass medium made the colonial state and its nationalist adversaries alike anxious about its mobilizing power. One way to fix this public-relations problem was to improve the product and make it a worthy bearer of national culture, so that cinema could redirect its technological prowess to not only entertain but also enlighten the masses. One must view the debates around the aesthetics of coupling (i.e., song-versus-kiss), in the context of this quest by the film industry for greater legitimacy, while keeping in mind that the shape and extent of reform was also set by cinema's status as a profit-making enterprise.

The song's emergence as an instrument of couple-formation, I suggest, helped resolve this push and pull. I illustrate this by examining in some detail song sequences from three early sound films, Nitin Bose's *Chandidas* (1934), Franz Osten's *Achhyut Kanya* (The untouchable girl, 1936), and V. Shantaram's *Admi* (Life is for living, 1939) to demonstrate that even though the song sequence has always been critiqued for its mimetic deficit—people do not sing and dance in real life—it enabled Hindi popular cinema to capture the particular stakes of couple-formation in India. In all three films social problems like casteism are approached through the framework of cross-caste romances, and although such transgressive conjugality might not always find a happy narrative resolution, the song sequences allow us to sensually experience the stakes of such coupling. Made by the three leading studios of the 1930s—New Theatres in Kolkata,[4] Bombay Talkies in Mumbai, and Prabhat in Pune—these films tackle the most urgent social issue of decade, caste discrimination, and thus reveal the reformist leanings of the social film. Though, as shall see below, each film embraces a different ideology (from the uncompromising romanticism of *Chandidas* through the sentimental idealism of *Achhyut Kanya* to the radical realism of *Admi*), their use of the song sequence to enact modes of conjugality whose time has not yet come coexists with a tragic narrative conclusion in which such couples do not find social sanction. Interestingly, the later films enter into intertextual relations with song sequences in the former—thus illustrating the progressive consolidation of the romantic duet as well as the song sequences' tendency to break free of and circulate apart from the film. Indeed, the very fact that these couples find fulfillment *only* in song and dance points to the failure of the reformist film to enact a truly democratic union, thus reinforcing the conformism of a commercial cinema structured by elite nationalist ideologies. At the same time, the pleasure offered by the romantic duet, its extra-cinematic reach, and the citational relation of these sequences to each other ensure that the vision of conjugality offered by the song survives the narrative conclusion. By assembling the couple through the two representational modes of narrative and performance, popular film form provided a nationalist resolution to the "couple question" even as it continued to draw upon cinema's technological capacity to figure modernity and conjure for the public the pleasure and promise of romantic love.

As a quintessential sign of the modern, romantic love is a favored subject of cinema globally, since film, a technology of modernity par excellence, is especially suited to embody couple-formation in a sensuous mode. The centrality of romance in Indian cinema must therefore be viewed in this light: as the technology was introduced to India, so was the celluloid couple. Cinematic explorations of love would serve as excursions into the ideas, concepts, habits, and techniques, as well as the sights and sounds of modernity. From the early days of sound (the first sound film was *Alam Ara* [Ardeshir Irani, 1931])—and even in the silent period—couple-formation emerged in Indian cinema as a key site for negotiating the still unconstituted national body.[5] For instance, in the 1921 Bengali film *Bilet Pherat* (Foreign returned, N. C. Laharry), the Westernized hero's unique views on love and matrimony make for some trenchant satire, while the Gujarati production *Telephone Ni Taruni* (The telephone girl, Homi Master, 1926) explores an interethnic marriage between a working girl and a leading lawyer. Films like *Bhaneli Bhamini* (Educated wife, Homi Master, 1927) and *Gunsundari* (Why husbands go astray, Chandulal Shah, 1927) connected women's education to more egalitarian conjugal relations, while *Andhare Alo* (The influence of love, Sisir Bhaduri and Naresh Mitra, 1922) and the silent *Devdas* (Naresh Mitra, 1928) put forth in the figures of the childhood lover and courtesan competing models of romantic desire.[6] The reformist social film—set in the present and dealing with contemporary problems like caste discrimination, modernization, female emancipation, urban life, alcoholism, gambling, and divorce—was the emerging bourgeois genre of the 1930s and 1940s, and conjugality occupied its thematic core. Couple-formation across the lines of caste and ethnicity—though doomed in the end—was a way to imagine a more democratic social body, while romantic choice modeled not only subjective freedom but also forms of political sovereignty.[7] Though the cinematic couple-form expressed what Madhava Prasad has called the "desire for modernity," it also had to figure in issues of cultural difference, that is, it had the charge of being simultaneously modern *and* Indian.[8] What pressures did this double charge exert on Indian cinema's representation of conjugality? One might approach this question by looking at the face-off between the kiss and the song that occurred in the first two decades of the sound film.

Kisses were not unknown in Indian films—in fact the Bombay Talkies production *Karma* (1929) was infamous for a four-minute kissing scene between Devika Rani and Himanshu Rai (the film allegedly flopped despite this attraction)—but clearly by 1940, they had fallen into disfavor, supplanted by the romantic duet.[9] In March of 1940, a fan letter to the preeminent English-language film magazine *Film India* queried this development:[10] "Why is it that kissing is taking place in Western films but not in Indian films?" only to be told that "the technique of love-making in the East is different. It does not need kisses to express love. Westerners believe love has to be seen to be believed. With the Indian, love does not need so obvious an advertisement."[11] Aside from demonstrating the proactive role taken by film journals in using cinema to consolidate a nationalist pedagogy of romance, this exchange is one of many that reads the kiss or its absence in civilizational terms. Thus a nationalist cinema requires an aesthetic that favors, in matters of love at least, the oblique over the direct mode of representation. One should, no doubt, read this preference for the oblique mode as registering elite anxieties about on-screen carnality, enhanced through techniques like the close-up that transform the visual field and redistribute social power in disconcerting ways.[12] Whatever the reasons for the disappearance of the kiss, the discursive production of this absence as a distinguishing feature of *Indian* cinema is significant. Another reader from Natal in South Africa protests that censoring the kiss interrupts narrative flow, "Just when they are so near, the artists are separated and the audience is required to imagine the rest."[13] Such obtrusive editing, he suggests, undermines cinema as a technology of the real, for it forces the viewer to conjure up rather than gaze upon the future course of screen intimacy.[14] Since the kiss, in order to be visible and pleasurable, would require that the image be magnified through a close-up, realism is construed here not in terms of verisimilitude but of narrative relay. This reader clearly grasps that such editing is strategic rather than a function of underdeveloped filmmaking. A third reader poses the relation between the kiss and song as one of deliberate substitution, motivated by nationalist drives. He remarks, "*Indian* films use a duet to express love. Don't you think they would do well to use a kiss instead?"[15] Threaded together, these three remarks suggest that the disappearance of the kiss and its replacement by song are somehow linked to the emergence of a national cinematic idiom that deliberately forecloses the kiss while siphoning off into song the visceral pleasures of cinema. This formal move, as indicated above, is linked to cinema's desire to recast itself as a nationalist-bourgeois enterprise.

The response of *Film India*'s editor, Baburao Patil, to such fan queries clarifies that this national style deviates significantly from international norms as defined (mainly) by Hollywood cinema. He writes, "Yes, a kiss would be the shortest cut, which perhaps the audience would also like it if it is passionately given. But what about the dialogue writer who wants to spit out love through the painted lips in the shape of senseless words? Then there are the censor boards with their unromantic inspectors—won't they fall to pieces if they see a good longwinded kiss on the screen? They haven't even kissed their wives."[16] Indeed, a kiss as an expression of love would not only render more sensory pleasure but would also be more real, rational, and economical—after all, song sequences do add considerably to the extraordinary length of the typical Hindi film and make them mimetically deficient. Patil, however, reads the replacement of kiss by song in productive terms—invoking a mode of manufacture in which the film product is assembled through multiple attractions ("senseless words" add value to the film). Other commentators, such as Baburao Pendharkar, producer-director of Navyug Chitrapat Limited, also note how songs compromise narrative economy: "More than often superfluous songs add to the footage. . . . Songs must be the outburst of intense feelings, at its [*sic*] white heat point. . . . How many intense spots (which have to be sung out) can there be in a picture?"

Though Pendharkar concedes that love, "the ruling subject of many of our social pictures," needs songs to express white-hot intensity, he begs for some moderation in the interests of rational storytelling.[17] Further, while there is no direct reference to the absent kiss here, Pendharkar's figures—"intense feelings," "white heat point"—evoke a metonymic relation between sex and song to suggest that the latter can provide the affective intensities of the on-screen kiss. Further, both Patil and Pendharkar alert us to the productive aspect of the song sequence, at both an industrial (providing employment to composers, lyricists, musicians) and discursive level. It is important to remember that the industry, already subject to punishing levies, had to keep its eye on the bottom line. Patil's views on the kiss/song dialectic are noteworthy in other regards. In playfully alluding to the fusty inspector who has not even kissed his wife, he aligns representational interdictions with social habits and a regulatory regime acutely sensitive to the mobilizing power of cinema and thus wary of the "dangerous" effects of on-screen intimacy on a mass audience. Censorship—in this case the *informal* prohibition of the kiss—as Ashish Rajyadaksha reminds us, is not only about excising a particular view but also about producing a pedagogy of spectatorship and putting in place a reformist agenda, "creating a better cinema—worthy of incarnating the *citizen* as the filmgoing subject."[18] The preference for the song sequence is intimately tied to elite anxieties concerning the feelings that this visceral technology might activate among the "uneducated classes."

At the same time, reformers in the industry were keenly aware that cinema's potential—its social effectivity—could be harnessed for the project of national modernity. To cite a random example from 1933, Mr. Jitendranath Mojumdar bewails that "loose love, easy hugging and cheap kissing with unnatural framing of the plot to lure the gross sense, and pander more or less to the vulgar appetite have decidedly lowered the standards of our films." Tracing these bad uses of the medium to Mumbai cinema's impulse to imitate Hollywood, he says that Indian cinema needs to find its own style and subject. Thus he stresses cinema's capacity to conjure a nationalist mise-en-scène—"homes, furniture, utensils, dress, customs, manners, and all the environs that would come within the lens must be Indian in type and fashion—in conception and execution." How curious, then, that Mojumdar, despite endorsing realism, eschews the kiss that, as fan discourse above points out, is but the natural outcome of an embrace. His parallel desire to put cinema to pedagogic use, evident when he writes that it is "high time for producers" to turn out "inspiring and instructive amusements,"[19] brushes up against cinema's power to reproduce pleasurable, if morally precarious, images. Because song and dance offer audiovisual pleasure without the threat of voyeuristic identification, it might indeed provide a way out of this bind and the couple produced through song could serve as an ideal type of the national-modern.

From the mid-1930s, social films preoccupied with the vicissitudes of conjugality proliferated in the Indian screen. So omnipresent is romance that one reader wearily asks, "How is it that in every social picture love is introduced? Is there nothing greater to be achieved in this world?"[20] Other fans are emboldened by the movies to carve out their own romantic destinies. Thus letters inquiring into the love lives of the stars are interspersed with those asking for advice on matters of the heart: should they marry the person they love or fall in love with the person they marry? How should they persuade their parents to accept the one they love? Is love an essential feature of marriage? How should an inter-ethnic/cross-caste couple go about finding societal sanction? Is a platonic relationship between a man and woman possible? How much premarital intimacy is too much? While it would be a mistake to read these letters as expressing any sociological reality, they do testify to how conjugality on screen excites an emerging discourse about love, marriage, and modernity. Noted film critic K. A. Abbas commends the films of Kolkata-based studio New Theatres in these terms, "Practically all the romantic situations in most Indian films, the lover's hide and seek in duets, the humorous interludes and clever banter owe their origin to Nitin Bose [New Theatres director]. . . . Indeed, Nitin may be given the credit for having taught modern Indians how to make love."[21] Since Bose's films did not include kisses but did consolidate the romantic duet, Abbas's insights, when read together with the fan letters, illuminate the social effects of celluloid romance. Further this new medium could authorize itself by modeling appropriate modes of courtship and romantic deportment. Thus in May 1942, an article debating the influence of films notes, "If the film industry teaches the young Indian maiden that she has a right to marry that fine young man she in love with rather than the elderly, grumpy, oh-so-rich man that her parents have chosen for her, then the film industry teaches a very good lesson." But the same writer also stresses that "love is depicted in a very innocent and elementary [sic] way on the Indian screen. Heroes or heroines never kiss each other or even rub noses. They just touch hands and look at each other with emotion shining out of their eyes."[22] This last comment alerts us that cinema's social legitimacy is intrinsically linked to its aesthetics of embodiment.

This sampling of fan and critical discourse demonstrates that while this replacement of kiss by song was viewed as detrimental to narrative rationality, it was nonetheless a nationalist (and elite) resolution to the couple question. As the romantic duet takes the place of the kiss, couple-formation abandons the realistic register to dwell in the expressive realm of song and dance. But this substitution is a site of ideological struggle. The cinematic couple is a placeholder for the modern, but, as such exchanges around the kiss show, this is a modernity structured by nationalist *difference*. The couple may defy tradition and fall in love across lines of class, caste, and ethnicity and even marry, but they may not kiss. While this prohibition—and the song sequence that takes the place of the kiss—inhibit the mimetic competence of cinema, it nonetheless confers upon this new commercial form a social legitimacy. In order for cinema to circulate as a public good, it must also promote the good of the public.

Scholars of Indian cinema have puzzled over this *informal* prohibition of the kiss—informal because there is no line item forbidding the kiss in censorship norms deriving from the Cinematograph Act of 1928–29 or its subsequent iteration in 1952. One theoretical account for the absence of the kiss comes from Madhava Prasad, who argues that the absent kiss is a code for a more generalized prohibition on representing the private.[23] Since cinema circulates in public places, it must only represent that which is public.[24] Prasad's insights seem to be anticipated in the pages of the film journals, particularly *Film India*, that I have been surveying. Thus Sushila Rani protests the absent kiss in these terms: "It is agreed by all of us and critics shout from housetops that the screen should represent life in its realism. Why then this false sense of decency and modesty in representing romance in its true colors practiced on our screens?"[25] Like Prasad, Rani reads the prohibition of the kiss as the operation of ideology ("false sense of decency and modesty") that limits cinema's capacity to function as a technology of realism ("representing romance in its true colors"). The author goes on to inveigh against the "strange misconception" that kissing is a Western practice and therefore "we should abstain from showing it in our Indian pictures."[26] Invoking the Sanskrit playwright Kalidas and quoting Urdu poetry, she asserts that "our ancient legends, our romantic stories, all abound in numerous and vivid descriptions of love—sometimes becoming so sensuous as to make even me, a moderner, blush."[27] The injunction is the result of a more recent national trait—an invention of tradition, if you will—that weds "personal morals" to "religious instincts" and ends up forcing films to resort to forms of artifice that undercut cinema as a modern and democratic medium.

Lalitha Gopalan, however, sees this relation between cinema and the state as structured by a "productive tension." On the one hand is the statist drive toward regulating national subjects and their tastes, and on the other is the film industry's interest in giving pleasure to the audience. She identifies this tension as enacted through a cinematic technique (a kind of *coitus interruptus*) where the camera cuts away on the brink of an intimate scene, filling this gap with "pastoral evocations of passion—waterfalls, rains, gardens and so on," or inserting extra-diegetic images suggestive of a kiss.[28] Such cutaways occur frequently in song-and-dance sequences that seem to replace and audaciously absorb the missing kiss as a trace. Sushila Rani's ruminations make a similar point as she protests this mode of interruption: "The hero stands exactly three feet away, and bursts out into a pathetic wail which we are asked to believe is a love song. At best this is amateurish and unreal love. The audience which is keyed up to a keen point of expectancy is disappointed"; and again, "Leela Chitnis and Ashok Kumar were a fine romantic team, but whenever it came to a love scene, the most the director could do was bring them tantalizingly close to each other, and cause undue tension in the minds of the audience and leave it at that."[29] Gopalan, however, sees such interruptions not as obstructing but rather as activating (and intensifying) spectatorial pleasure. This Foucauldian reading of the missing kiss not as lack but as incitement allows us to see the song-and-dance sequence as not less but more than just a kiss. While a kiss or even a sex scene would have been economical, the song-sequence is profligate—multiplying streams of pleasure and profit.

Even Sushila Rani makes the same point when she refers to the Pandit Indra, who, in his "capacity as a writer for the screen, has written hundreds of sex-tickling songs and numerous passion-laden romantic situations suggesting advanced stages of human relation beyond the *ordinary stage of mere kissing*."[30] The interdiction against the kiss, as Rani acknowledges, does not imply a de-eroticization of cinematic representations of romance. Quite the opposite. She goes on to quote song lyrics far more explicit than any kiss might have been. But the substitution of song for kiss does undermine a film's claim to realism. Denied a kiss, a "natural" expression of love, the couple must resort to artifice. While such flights into song might enhance viewer pleasure, the couple are not legitimated through narrative realism. But neither are they circumscribed by this narrative. Rather, the song-sequence fully exploits cinema's technological capacity to produce through sound, image, movement, and montage a wholly modern couple. While the missing kiss testifies to the couple's subjection to nationalist censorship norms, the aural component of song and dance is not similarly policed. Scholars on censorship in Indian cinema have pointed to "film music's unique ability to escape the direct purview of the state" since it is not governed by the same rules as the film product. This has "enabled its considerable facility to circumvent state scrutiny and, in turn, to circulate and reproduce via various technologies."[31] The couple formed via the song sequence enjoy new modes of autonomy that are hard to sacrifice at the altar of realism. But these modes are also virtual—not unreal but untimely. I now turn to V. Shantaram's film *Admi* (Life is for living, 1939) and its intertextual references to Nitin Bose's *Chandidas* (1934) and Franz Osten's *Achhyut Kanya* (The untouchable girl, 1936) to investigate how film form in the first decade of sound struggles with and reconciles the cinematic couple's relation to the song sequence.

*Chandidas* is a Hindi remake of Debaki Bose's 1932 film with the same title. This feature, billed as New Theatres' first Hindi super hit, officially belongs to the genre of the saint's life. The film's account of the romance between the eponymous fourteenth-century Vaishnavite poet and a lower caste washerwoman, Rami, becomes the occasion for figuring a more democratic future for India, but the most memorable aspects of this film are its romantic duets, including the famous "Prem Nagar Mein Banaongi Ghar Main" (I shall build our abode in the city of love), featuring the legendary singer-actor K. L. Saigal and Umasashi. The song is set in an empty garden—which was to become the locus classicus of the romantic duet—and the lyrical content is suitably utopic. In the opening shot, Rami is seen singing to herself as she does some laundry, wanting to forsake this world and build her home in the city of love, a house whose threshold, roof, and door are all made of love. The scene cuts to Chandidas, who declares that love will be their friend, neighbor, and companion in joy and sorrow. As it cuts back to Rami, the viewer realizes that she is both surprised and delighted that Chandidas has intruded upon her solitude, and she continues in the same vein, singing that she shall bathe and anoint herself in love. The two principles go back and forth, cuts alternating between them. As the song builds to its climax, Chandidas walks across the frame and in the next shot is seen together with Rami. The two singer-actors, Saigal and Umasashi, now occupy the center of the frame, thus visually consolidating the lyrical claim that love is the only truth. Two other features of this song picturization are worth noting. First, the camera captures the effect of the song on the listener. As Rami sings, as yet unaware of Chandidas, he looks on with rapt attention. As he joins in, the rapture is hers. A series of point-of-view shots convey the effect of the song and thus heighten desire. Second, the actors look at each other, but they are also frontally placed in relation to the camera, so that we can directly apprehend them as conjugal unit. That a romantic duet should announce the sovereignty of love is quite unsurprising,

33

but the longing for a domesticity built on romantic love is indeed quite striking, especially if we put these lyrics in the generic context of the film—a saint's life. Rami desires a household made entirely of love, while Chandidas imagines love as taking the place of friends and neighbors. We encounter here a couple using the romantic duet to imagine a form of nuclear conjugality that is as yet only a potentiality. *Chandidas* concludes with Rami and Chandidas forsaking the social because it is not yet ready for the transformation symbolized by their union, but the song-space has already allowed us to enjoy this couple-form as a possibility.

The critically acclaimed Bombay Talkies hit *Achhyut Kanya* (The untouchable girl, 1936) returns to this terrain but is generically allied to the social film, which, as we saw above, explores contemporary life. This film recounts the tragic love affair between the Dalit Kasturi (Devika Rani) and the Brahmin Pratap (Ashok Kumar). Film historians Rajyadaksha and Willemen credit this production with stylistically defining the Mumbai film product as a song-and-dance entertainment that borrowed from Hollywood the star-system and many elements of film grammar, including continuity editing.[32] But as Vijay Mishra notes, the film's attachment to commercial aesthetics also underwrites a political ideology that makes romance the only form of social action, thus sidestepping a materialist critique of untouchability.[33] Contemporary responses to the film are keenly aware of its glamorization of the caste issue: "The rich dresses of the starving Harijans—[are] a concession to 'pictorial beauty'"—especially with regard to the casting of the uber-Westernized Devika Rani as Kasturi.[34] Critics attribute the sanitization of untouchability to the commercial imperative of a well-managed studio like Bombay Talkies and to the lack of local knowledge on the part of its German director, Franz Osten. Abbas claims that Bombay Talkies is run like a Hollywood studio, and while this creates fiscal efficiencies, streamlining detracts from the creativity and social responsiveness evident in the films emerging from New Theatres and Prabhat studios.[35]

This film's structure—a frame narrative that embeds the doomed romance of Kasturi and Pratap as a flashback—serves to neutralize the transgressive potential of the love story. A middle-class couple whose marriage is in trouble are the audience for this love story. When the film begins, the Dalit woman Kasturi is already dead and deified—described by the narrator as "janma se achhyut, punya se devi" (untouchable by birth, divine by deeds). By the end of the film, Kasturi has served her pedagogical function: the husband, who had planned to kill his wife for her infidelity, is reformed. Mishra's critique thus iterates John Alexander's analysis of the social picture in *Film India*. Drawing a distinction between the idealist versus realist orientation in social films, Alexander says that the former reduces the social problem to the level of the individual, and its solutions are paternalistic. Thus, "they point out that the wealthy have a duty towards the less fortunate. But precisely what that duty is . . . or precisely what the existence of the poor is like, *they fail to convey*."[36] This romanticizing tendency is everywhere in evidence in *Achhyut Kanya*, which is set in the nonspecific setting of "village India" that would become the generic mise-en-scène of the rural in Hindi cinema in the coming decades. While Kasturi and her father are untouchables, there is little attempt to delineate the structural violence to which they are subject. Rather, the misery visited upon them is attributed to villainy, cultural mores, and a mob mentality. Further, the ease with which Kasturi and Pratap meet and conduct their courtship seems implausible given the subsequent evocation of a rigid caste society that would never permit them to marry. In *Chandidas*, Rami expresses her frustration and rage, but in this film, Kasturi accepts interdictions with a quiescence that allows us to sentimentalize her. Yet this conformity—on her part and Pratap's—does not really save her. Moreover the film's "realism" inheres in its assured deployment of the codes of classical continuity editing and psychologically grounded characters rather than in any indexical commitment to its social setting. At the same time, it succeeds in smoothly incorporating into the narrative several song sequences—two duets and several solos in which the lovers experience the pain of separation.

One in particular, "Main Ban Ke Chidiya" (I am a bird of the forest), shows all the features of the romantic duet identified above, including the spatial centering of the romantic couple in a pastoral setting; the back-and-forth between Kasturi and Pratap that establishes mutuality alternating with a frontal address that endows the couple with iconic value; and lyrics that dream of metamorphoses—the lovers wish to turn into birds of the wild and take flight from a world that proscribes their love (fig. 1). When Pratap is forced into marriage with a woman of his own caste, Kasturi reprises these lyrics in a heartrending solo, "Udi Hawa Mein Jati Hai Gaati Chidiya Yeh Raat" (The bird song is carried by a rising breeze tonight, / Come my love, come meet me), while the lovelorn Pratap sings "Pyar tera kaun hai" (Who is your love?). Though ostensibly about caste, the film is as much a primer on romantic love as a necessary basis for conjugality. Denied each other, Pratap and Kasturi are not able to find any happiness in the socially mandated relationships they enter into, and tragedy ensues. Despite its rural setting, the film's vantage is utterly urban and middle-class. Village India epitomizes stasis—it breeds conformity and thwarts individual desire, whose force once again we

1  Song sequence "Main Ban Ke Chidiya" (I am a bird of the forest), depicting the sovereign couple. (From Franz Osten's *Achhyut Kanya* [The untouchable girl], 1936.)

apprehend in the lyrical and visual intensities of the film's celebrated song sequences.

Made a few years after *Achhyut Kanya*, V. Shantaram's *Admi*, supposedly an adaptation of MGM's *Waterloo Bridge*, has a much more ambivalent take on the individual's relation to the social. Its protagonist, Moti (Shahu Modak), is a policeman who falls in love with Kesar (Shanta Hublikar), a prostitute, but Moti's love is hardly uncomplicated. He is quite judgmental about Kesar's profession and repeatedly abandons her for fear he will be discovered and socially ostracized. Kesar, while aware of Moti's irresolution, is rather helpless once she gives up her profession for his sake. Her dependence is as much financial as it is emotional. Though self-aware and spirited, Kesar remains bound to social norms that will never allow a whore to become a wife; thus, even when Moti is prepared to marry her, she runs away from him. In a dramatic climax, she kills her pimp, and as she is taken into custody, Kesar urges Moti not to abandon the world for love—"prem ke liye duniya na chodna"—a fitting response to the romantic self-absorption of a film like *Devdas* (P. C. Barua, 1935). This more dialectical relation between the individual and society accounts for the greater realism of Shantaram's film,[37] though it stylistically references German expressionism and the *kammerspiel* film.[38]

It is this realist imperative that activates *Admi*'s much-discussed reference to and critique of the more commercially oriented Bombay Talkies products, particularly *Achhyut Kanya*.[39] In the sequence in question, Moti is humming a tune en route to his village when he accidentally walks into an outdoor film set and interrupts the shooting of a song sequence. The scene—where the leading lady is perched on the branch of a tree and is being serenaded by the hero (fig. 2)—skillfully cites in framing and composition the "Main Ban Ke Chidiya" sequence from *Achhyut Kanya* discussed above. The dialogue that comprises the prelude to the song is recited in a highly artificial manner and is thick with romantic clichés. The shooting is interrupted once again as Kesar, who has been following Moti, now pops into the frame. These comic intrusions highlight the contrast between real and "reel" romance, but they also provide a glimpse into cinema's mode of production during this era, including the difficulty of shooting outdoors, where not only people but also sounds and voices constantly obstruct filmmaking. Thus Moti and Kesar are told that they must remain silent because each wasted take costs a princely sum to produce. When the shooting commences, we realize that the lyrics of the romantic duet that speak of going to a "city of love" reference *Chandidas*'s "Prem Nagar Mein Banaongi Ghar Main" but the real-life lovers, Kesar and Moti, burst out laughing at the ersatz rendition of romance, interrupting the shooting yet again. As the lyricist—Panditji—attempts to impress upon them the sublimity of love through filmic stock phrases, Moti and Kesar proceed to parody the on-screen duet with a song of their own that pushes to absurd limits the romantic idealism proffered by love songs (fig. 3). Thus they sing of "prem ki chulha, prem ki roti, prem ki chutney"—stove, bread, and chutney made of love—both citing and parodying the vision of love's sufficiency created in the song from *Chandidas*. Their performance, however, captivates the film director, who immediately offers to fire his leading lady and hire Kesar instead. The satire in this sequence is multilayered. First, Shantaram pokes fun at the Bombay Talkies brand of filmmaking, helmed by the hyper-Westernized Himanshu Rai, his wife Devika Rani, and the many Europeans in their technical team, including the director Franz Osten. Thus the heroine in this sequence speaks Hindi with a strong English accent, smokes cigarettes between takes, and wears a dress underneath her sari. By aligning the artifice of the product with the inauthenticity of the producers, Shantaram makes a case for an indigenous—and therefore more nationalist—aesthetics. Second, this nationalist agenda not only engages questions of cultural authenticity but also invests in realism as the aesthetic mode most suited to showing life as it really is. This sequence satirizes not only the content of the duet but also its form—the very fact that films need songs to show love. Thus Kesar and Moti reflect on the pernicious sociological effects of such *filmi* (lit., "as in films") love on contemporary Indian youth in urban places.

2 The song sequence "Premi Prem Nagar Mein Jaaye" (The lover goes to the city of love) foregrounds the artifice of the romantic duet. (From V. Shantaram's *Admi* [Life is for living], 1939.)

3 Kesar and Moti satirize the conventions of the romantic duet. (From V. Shantaram's *Admi* [Life is for living], 1939.)

Shantaram struggles with staging song sequences, whatever their content, realistically. Thus, in an earlier social film that explores a January–December marriage—*Kunku/Duniya Na Mane* (The world demurs, 1937), Shantaram attempts to find the most natural way of including song sequences in the diegesis by including source sounds.[40] A similar instinct is also evident in *Admi*. As Kesar and Moti sing their parodic duet, the orchestra on set supplies the score, while in the following sequence, Kesar's romantic ballad layers a folk song that is being performed by some villagers offscreen. Yet, despite *Admi*'s critique of the romantic duet and its idealization by other studios, and a concomitant attempt to keep the performance real, the film cannot abjure the expressive possibilities of the song sequence to realize versions and visions of romantic sovereignty foreclosed by the narrative. In the sequence above, we notice that, even in parody, Kesar and Moti manage to find a private mode for communicating desire for each other. Though the lyrics might deride silly love songs from *Chandidas* and *Achhyut Kanya*, Moti's wit and Kesar's erotic playfulness in the course of this performance realize the subjective possibilities of the romantic duet. We must recall that prior to this scene, Moti has been afraid to venture into public space with Kesar—a fact that pains her greatly. But here for a moment, in full public view, those social interdictions are suspended. The policeman and the prostitute sing together, exchange joyful looks, and perform little intimate gestures to give us a glimpse of a couple-form whose time has not yet come.

Thus cinema finds in the song sequence a formal device to accommodate the competing demands placed on it. While the narrative seeks social legitimacy by reproducing the paternalistic ideology of elite nationalism (thus prohibiting certain kinds of desire, curtailing certain modes of enjoyment), the song sequence retains the prerogative of a commercial enterprise to capitalize on the mobilizing potential of cinema. It performs proscribed forms of desire and incites surplus pleasures, thus alerting us to the limits of narrative. This productive function of the song sequence is particularly stark in the reformist films where conjugality does not find social sanction, but even in the more routine productions of the industry, where the stakes of coupling are not so fraught, the song sequence grants the couple an autonomous mobility while simultaneously reminding us that the couple's sovereignty in the narrative is thwarted by the demands of tradition. The dual enunciation of the couple—in narrative and song—points to the complex relation of Hindi film form to the social domain. The narrative relocation of the couple within the extended family/community is a sign of ideological closure. Here the missing kiss is the most direct evidence of cinema's accommodation of conservative social forces, which decree that the celluloid couple may kiss neither in public (where Indians do not typically kiss) nor in private (where Indians presumably do). But the successful nucleation of the couple in the romantic duet and the intrusion of song and dance into the larger culture indicate Hindi film's social effectivity. This double take on the couple might therefore be viewed as an aesthetic solution that fully exploits cinema's ability to disseminate dominant interests and embody emergent formations, while mining its capacity for producing both pleasure and pedagogy.

## From Romantic Duet to Item Number

If the consolidation of the romantic duet was a formal achievement of Hindi popular cinema in the first decade of sound, the "item number" is New Bollywood cinema's contribution to the song-and-dance repertoire. First witnessed in the late 1980s, this sexually charged, upbeat song-and-dance sequence with ribald lyrics and titillating imagery is usually set in a bar, nightclub, or the villain's den. Supposedly derived from "item bomb" (which might be linked to "atom bomb"), the item number, performed by "item girls" (e.g., Yana Gupta or Rakhi Sawant), or a big star in a guest appearance (e.g., Urmila Matondkar performing "Chamma, Chamma,"[41] from *China Gate* [Rajkumar Santoshi, 1998], or, more famously, Aishwarya Rai performing "Kajra Re" in *Bunty Aur Babli* [Shaad Ali, 2005]) begins to show up regularly by the 1990s.[42] This song-and-dance number often has no relation whatsoever to the film, and the "item girl" plays no role elsewhere in the diegesis; thus it might even be played, *Slumdog* style, along with the opening and closing credits. In the words of one commentator, an item number is "pretty much a raunchy music video embedded in a motion picture and is used as a tactic to attract the viewing public."[43] The rise of the item number is linked, as the quotation above suggests, to phenomena like the diffusion of the music video in India as well as the film song's emergence in New Bollywood cinema as "content" to be distributed and commercially exploited across various media. In short, the item number is a telling instance of the song-and-dance sequence's growing irrelevance to the form of Hindi cinema. As such, it is a significant reconstitution of the sizzling nightclub dance number—the "cabaret" number—a standard of Hindi cinema since the 1960s.

A short history of the evolution of the "cabaret" sequence captures certain key shifts in the status of song and dance within Hindi film form as well as in Indian popular culture. The cabaret sequence typically featured a "vamp" rather than the heroine and visually conveyed the dangerous enticements of Western modernity—sex, alcohol, and half-naked women—or rather, conveyed these enticements as dangerous. Rendered typically by the seductive, husky-voiced Asha Bhonsle (sister to Lata Mangeshkar, who lent her higher-pitched timbre to the virginal heroine), cabaret songs were often composed by R. D. Burman (debut film, 1960). Burman greatly expanded the acoustic universe of the Hindi film song, including in it a repertoire of world-music sounds derived from rock-and-roll, salsa, African drums, and atonal music. Further, he made the film song more corporeal (and carnal) by introducing into it what Ashok Ranade has called "the not-so-musical products" of the human voice, including sighs, yodels, roars, whispers.[44] Burman stretched the sensory spectrum of songs, not only through new instruments like bongos and xylophones, but through complex, internally layered songs that expressed the polyphony of modernity, not unlike A. R. Rahman's global hit, "Jai-Ho." This made Burman a master of the cabaret number, whose function was to deliver a sensuous visual and acoustic experience. If the romantic duet was formally *necessary* to the project of Hindi cinema as public culture, the cabaret sequence was motivated more by the market logic of a cinema seeking to deliver sensation. Its narrative function— quite nominal—was thus to code a decadent, Western-inflected femininity that could then be contrasted to the ideal national subject, that is, the heroine housed in the romantic duet.

As Helen, the screen dancer of the 1960s, developed her own stardom and fan following, the narrative rationale for the cabaret number weakened. The celebrated dance number from *Sholay* (Flames, Ramesh Sippy, 1975), "Mehbooba, Mehbooba," (Beloved, beloved) might be viewed as an instance of this. In a related development, the heroine in 1970s cinema became more Westernized, incorporating the youthful sexuality and bodily deportment of a global consumer culture. The heroine's migration out of the romantic duet and into the cabaret was completed in the 1980s, the iconic instance of this being, "Ek, Do, Teen" (One, two, three) featured in *Tezaab* (Acid, N. Chandra, 1988)—a bold and raunchy dance number performed by the heroine, Madhuri Dixit! Dixit's *jhatkas* and *matkas* (convulsive heaves and swings of the body) in this and subsequent dance numbers, definitively completed the blurring of the distinction between heroine (Indian) and vamp (Western) that had been in progress since the 1970s. The sexualized presentation of the *heroine* in this mutation of the cabaret number suggests not only changing social mores but also a considerable shift in Hindi cinema's status as a purveyor of entertainment. It signified, in essence, that cinema could now provide sensuous pleasure without discursively framing it as Western or debased. Further, the heroine, one-half of the romantic dyad meant to embody the ideal unit of social reproduction in Hindi cinema, could now become a locus of visual pleasure outside the confines of the romantic duet. The romantic duet's function as an engine of desire was being attenuated as other modes of sensation became available to the couple.

Thus, even as the heroine migrated out of the romantic duet, kisses (invisible for many decades) made a reappearance on the Hindi screen, famously in *Qayamat Se Qayamat Tak* (From disaster to catastrophe, Mansoor Khan, 1988; hereafter *QSQT*), a film released the same year as *Tezaab*. *QSQT* (often listed among the top Hindi films of all time) is remembered for its melodious romantic duets, a captivating lead pair (it was the first hit film for Aamir Khan and Juhi Chawla), *and* kisses. The revival of the kiss in *QSQT* brings the relation between conjugal sovereignty and the social order into sharp focus. Though it follows, in many regards, the conventions of a feudal family melodrama, *QSQT* was made at a juncture when the full force of free-market reforms and concomitant social and industrial transformations were just around the corner. The protagonists—Raj and Rashmi—are the scions of warring families, but despite this lineage, they clearly subscribe to an utterly different value system. Thus the feudal family is expressed in this film not as continuous with Indian tradition but as sheer despotism. Raj and Rashmi's rebellion—visualized through an on-screen liplock—is not transgressive but the only rational course of action and therefore unexceptional. The authoritarian agency in this film–which would forbid the kiss—is effectively powerless, so that the kiss, while remarkable, seems hardly momentous. Though Raj and Rashmi die, the usual fate of the transgressive couple in Hindi cinema, their deaths are anticlimactic.

Since the release of this film, kisses have been seen more frequently on the Indian screen, and the discursive noise they continue to make suggests a period of transition.[45] Actors—especially those on the A-list—are regularly asked if they will consent to kissing scenes. India's biggest male star, Shahrukh Khan, will not,[46] while the globally renowned female star Aishwarya Rai's smooch in *Dhoom 2* (Sanjay Gadhvi, 2006) made news and provoked an obscenity lawsuit.[47] Even Freida Pinto, who plays Latika in *Slumdog Millionaire*, only conceded to locking her lips with Jamal after Boyle assured her that this kiss was necessary to the plot and would be tastefully screened. The logic of diegetic necessity that is used to justify the kiss points to an underlying anxiety that screen kisses are not motivated by the narrative but function rather to titillate. This is clearly borne out by the excess surrounding discussions of the kiss on Indian screens. Thus actor Emraan Hashmi has branded himself as "the kissing bandit," while actress Malika Sherawat made the headlines with seventeen kisses in *Khwahish* (Wish, Govind Menon, 2003)![48] The amount of attention that the kiss continues to generate indicates that there is more to its reappearance than meets the eye.

As kisses become less sporadic in Hindi commercial cinema, the song-and-dance sequence's role is now less certain. Increasingly, we witness films where songs are either absent, or, if present, strenuously accounted for by the narrative context. Examples would include films about a dance school, like *Aaja Naachle* (Come, dance! Anil Mehta, 2007), or a rock band, as in *Rock On!* (Abhishek Kapoor, 2008), or about the film industry, like *Om Shanti Om* (Hail to peace, Farah Khan, 2007), *Khoya Khoya Chand* (Lost moon, Sudhir Mishra, 2007), and *Luck by Chance* (Zoya Akhtar, 2009). Indeed, song-and-dance sequences are now so spectacularly staged that they have little bearing on the film, as in *Billu Barber* (Billu the barber, Priyadarshan, 2009), except to ironically reflect on Hindi film form. More commonly, film songs are absorbed by the soundtrack, played over credits, or used only in trailers and promotional material, most famously by Ram Gopal Varma in *Bhoot* (Ghost, 2003). Though Bollywood cinema is globally known for its song-and-dance sequences, this once-stable feature of that popular film form is on its way to becoming history in New Bollywood cinema.

## An Industrial Detour

From the mid-1930s through the late 1970s, film music was effectively the only form of popular music in India. Historians suggest that by the 1940s, Hindi-Urdu film song had come to dominate the recorded music market in India. Folk music, locally varied by performance traditions and dialect, did not lend itself easily to a mass-market technology such as the gramophone record, which relied on economies of scale and sought a homogeneous product. Film song proved such a commodity. Thus music director Kalyanji described the principle of the film song in these terms: "We try to write songs so simple that they can be hummed by everybody." Except for a brief period in the 1950s, when culture czar B. V. Keskar sought to purify state-owned radio by banning film music, film songs dominated the airwaves as well.[49] However, the arrival of cassette technology radically restructured the music industry in India. According to Peter Manuel, it ended the hegemony of the Gramophone Company of India (hereafter GCI), of corporate music in general, of film music, and of the "Lata-Kishore duocracy."[50] It led to the rise of other genres such as the non-*filmi ghazal* (songs based on Urdu poems), *bhajan* (devotional songs), and even "indipop," creating for the first time a diversity of products in the music market. The cassette revolution of the 1980s is significant in another regard: it greatly accelerated the conversion of film song into content for circulation in other channels and formats. Films, as noted above, had a hard time holding onto their songs; thus, their broader distribution was only to be expected.

Entrepreneur Gulshan Kumar was a key figure in the cassette revolution. He used this new, inexpensive technology to fundamentally reorient the economics of film music in India. In short, he showed how to turn film music into a database that could be exploited through multiple iterations. Kumar took advantage of a loophole in the Copyright Act of 1957 and a lax enforcement regime to come up with a business practice that, while legal, was nevertheless ethically questionable. The Act of 1957 protected a "musical work" (i.e., the graphic notation of a melody) and a "recording" rather than the performers (this was amended in 1994 to protect "performer's rights"), so that someone wishing to reissue a recording merely had to publish an intent to do so, pay a small fee, and then issue a "version recording" (in effect, a cover) with lesser-known singers using the same lyrics and tune. This enabled Kumar to flood the market with cassettes that were priced at a fraction of what established music companies charged for compilations of film music. Kumar established a distribution network that matched a low price point by retailing cassettes at neighborhood *paan* shops (equivalent of a tobacconist), newsstands, and small grocers. GCI was slow to adopt this new technology, and thus, in a few brief years, Kumar's labels, T-Series and Super Cassettes, had completely revolutionized the production and distribution of film music, effectively commercializing the social life of film song. While film music had been reissued on records and played on the radio from the early days of sound, as Anna Morcom has shown, the commercial life of a song was closely tied to that of the film in which it was featured.[51] The "version recording" might be viewed as a way of turning into capital the tendencies inherent in the modes of production and circulation of Hindi film music. Let us consider the practice of playback. First instituted as lip-synching in order to overcome the technical difficulties of recording on set (noise, etc.), playback soon dispensed with the singing star and evolved into a dual-star system: the on-screen star mouthed the lyrics, but the song was sung by someone else called a "playback singer." Film songs and the artists who sang them had lives apart from their cinematic incarnations.[52] The "version recording" is but another stage in this constitutive split. It builds on the autonomy of Hindi film music by producing yet another iteration. The appeal of the cover needs to be situated in film music's centrality to social life in India, where film songs are informally performed at family gatherings, community events, talent contests, and game shows like *antakshari* and others.[53]

GCI (now called Saregama, Ltd.) initially responded to the T-Series phenomenon by expanding the market for non-*filmi* music and seeking stronger regulations. By the late 1980s, under the stewardship of Pradeep Chanda, the company returned to film music. From its vast archive, it began to repackage and market old songs in collector's editions, giving rise to a small boom in nostalgia. Another trend that further disarticu-lated the relation between song and film was the rise of the remix.[54] In the 1990s, both corporate houses like GCI and new entrants like T-Series and Venus began to prepurchase music rights and sponsor film production. From the movie industry's point of view, this new and highly lucrative revenue channel proved a gift, accelerating the disaggregation of song from film. Songs are now promoted months in advance of a film's release on FM radio and satellite TV, and the current craze for mobile down-loads and ringtones will further deepen the rift between film and film music. Film music, which once commanded 95 percent of the popular music market now comprises 60–70 percent of the fifteen-billion-dollar industry.[55] This decline in market share is due partly to the emergence of other forms of popular music, but the most significant development in the last two decades has been the film song's increasing separation from the film.

The retreat of the song sequence into the soundtrack and the emer-gence of the item number are perhaps the most important formal symptoms of this new commercial logic. The replacement of dubbing by sync-sound is another equally important development. The greater realism effected by both these shifts is crucially linked to a change in the political status of the couple vis-à-vis the social order and juridical structures like the extended family and community. The romantic duet, I have argued above, conferred a sovereignty on the couple in excess of the narrative. As performance, it enacted a private, nucleated, wholly modern couple-form whose time had not yet come. Moreover, the mode of production and circulation of the song sequence conferred a greater legitimacy and publicity on this vision of conjugality. The romantic duet disappears as the couple's right to privacy is no longer in doubt. As song receded into the soundtrack, Hindi film form moved from constituting the couple as private to exploring that couple's interior.

Madhava Prasad has argued that the perception of sound and the per-ception of sound *as* image—implied in characterizing cinema as com-posed of sound-images—are two different things, for in the latter, "the logic and discipline of the visual has intervened."[56] Reading sound as an image demands an a priori facility in the act of reading words and signs; thus it is inevitably linked to modernity and literacy, and takes place at the level of the individual. Sound, on the other hand, can be received, collectively at that, and a response does not require the mediation of the visual. It is productive to think of the song-and-dance sequence in this framework, where the song and its picturization form a composite event. Music *and* movement are received at once, with no necessary primacy attributed to the visual. Here the audience's awareness of the practice of playback is important,[57] for it further reinforces the autonomy of sound. The sound is not produced by the characters but is channeled through them. Further, in most cases, the musical accompaniment is nondiegetic (or nominally diegetic in those instances when an on-screen sound source, such as a piano, yields to a full-blown orchestra). We are simultaneously aware and unaware of the separation of sound and image. In this sense, the retreat of the song into the soundtrack might be viewed as an emergence of the sound-image, whereby sound is disciplined by reading competence and perceived as an image. Thus, as a song plays over the soundtrack, we are meant to perceive it as an element of signification that adds value to the image, but the latter can exist apart from it. In the romantic duet, the song and its picturization were equally crucial to the couple's becoming. However, song's subordination in a soundtrack suggests that the couple can now exist apart from it. This disarticulation needs to be understood alongside the increasing demand by singers for better contractual terms, including profit-sharing and an independent circuit of recognition. Playback artist Sonu Nigam says, "If you hear the hit song 'Kajra re' from the film *Bunty aur Babli*, it's called the Aishwarya-Amitabh-Abhishek song. No one calls it the Shankar Mahadevan-Alisha Chinai-Jaaved Ali song. It's such a wrong attitude, and that's what we want to change," while Kunal Ganjawala states, "You cannot mix the Grammy with the Oscars."[58] This desire for autonomy needs to be put in the context of the numerous sources of value extraction from film music as content, but it is also motivated by a changing media universe, in which TV shows like *Indian Idol* are creating stars who are then developed by music companies. *Indian Idol* star Abhijeet Sawant's debut album sold nearly nine hundred thousand copies—a fantastic figure when we consider that a film album sells about five hundred thousand copies. The music industry in India, long fattened by a steady stream of film music, is undergoing considerable transition at the moment. Blighted by piracy, a problem for music worldwide in the age of new media, its annual profits have fallen from an average of Rs. 1,150 million in the 1990s to Rs. 450 million in 2005.[59] As a recent industry report suggests, its future depends on its ability to capitalize on ancillary channels of revenue and develop genres beyond film music. With this shifting scenario in view, let us return to the couple-form and its songs in New Bollywood cinema.

## Singin' Again

Mira Nair refers to *Monsoon Wedding* as "a Bollywood musical in my own terms." How does this film without a single proper song-and-dance sequence and with music composed by Mychael Danna, "an Indian brother who happens to be Canadian," qualify as a "Bollywood musical?" Indeed, what can this film, a global arthouse hit, tell us about the fate of film music in New Bollywood cinema. *Monsoon Wedding*'s music, an eclectic brew of Punjabi folk songs set to a *bhangra* beat, Urdu *ghazals* remixed by a Delhi garage band called Medieval Pandits, Bollywood samplings, and *filmi sangeet* (film-song) classics, provides an interesting instance of the mutations in form and function that film song is undergoing in the present. A brief review of the film's plot is in order before I review its various uses of music. The film is centered round Aditi Verma's wedding to a US-based engineer, an arranged match to which she has consented upon realizing that her married lover will not divorce his wife. As various branches of Aditi's globally dispersed family converge in New Delhi for the celebrations, family secrets, interpersonal tensions, and Aditi's own doubts bring matters to crisis; as is typical of the genre, however, the film finds a happy (if uneasy) resolution. *Monsoon Wedding* clearly references the wedding extravaganzas that are a staple of the NRI genre in New Bollywood (see chapter 2), but Nair's aesthetic commitments—an improvised script, handheld camera, ensemble cast—are those of independent cinema. Understandably, *Monsoon Wedding* has no conventional song-and-dance sequences or romantic duets, but its use of song definitely converges with broad trends in New Bollywood cinema.

Let us turn first to the film's only instance of a diegetic song sequence. This occurs during Aditi's *mehendi* ceremony (in which a bride's hands are decorated with henna paste). Noted folksinger Madhorama Pencha lustily belts out traditional wedding songs in Punjabi while the women of the household decorate the bride's hands with henna paste and give her advice on being a good wife. The dress, jewelry, gestures, and performance idioms in this scene are specifically Punjabi and as such reflect a post-1990s New Bollywood tendency to produce "ethnic culture" for domestic and diasporic audiences eager for contact with their vernacular roots.[60] Nair's use of Pencha also speaks to urban upper-class India's rediscovery of "folk music"—fueled no doubt by world music's commodification of the "ethnic" and the "authentic."[61] At the same time, the song's naturalistic staging—Pencha's presence in the scene, a visible source of sound, diegetic rationality, the use of sync-sound—also marks it as a product of New Bollywood, a cinema no longer at ease with the attributes of the song-and-dance sequence and its location within Hindi film form. Indeed, this sequence apart, the film repeatedly evokes Hindi film songs in order to show their centrality to social life in India and the diaspora.

Such performances either take the form of group sing-alongs or elaborate reenactments in full dress of entire song-and-dance sequences. In either instance, Hindi film song functions as an instrument to create belonging. The first occurs immediately after Aditi's rather chaotic engagement party, where we glimpse the sinister secrets and simmering tensions that roil the surface of this family reunion. The Verma family joins in a rendition of a song, "Gore, Gore, O Banke Chore, (O fair one, pass by my neighborhood) from *Samadhi* (Memorial, Ramesh Saigal, 1950; music director, C. Ramachandra; sung by Lata and Amirabai), and, momentarily, the family is brought together by the nostalgia evoked by this 1950s classic. The second involves a reenactment of a romantic duet from a popular Bollywood movie—"Chunari, Chunari" (O veil! O veil), from *Biwi No. 1* (Wife no. 1, David Dhawan, 1999). Community events in the Indian—particularly the Punjabi—diaspora have long included such reenactments. But as Nair notes, their inclusion in wedding ceremonies among the Punjabi community in India is a newer phenomena—"unimaginable even 10 years ago."[62] This shared practice of staging Bollywood song sequences bridges, as it were, the difference and distance between the Punjabi at home and abroad. This is the important lesson that Rahul—the "idiot" cousin from Australia learns. Attracted at first sight to the sizzling Neha, Rahul is nonetheless a bit intimidated by her. Thus, when she begs him to accompany her in this dance, he declines, saying, "This is not a nightclub in Melbourne." Rahul's refusal immediately marks him as a *firangi* (foreigner), and he loses her affection. However, when he spots a rival on the horizon, he changes his mind and joins the dance, leading Neha to say, "We made an Indian out of you after all." Thus the reenactment of a film song becomes the means for performing citizenship in the nation of Bollywood—a nation in which the cousin that lives in Melbourne and the one that lives in New Delhi can both dwell. One of the primary objectives of New Bollywood cinema is precisely to provide a common cultural platform for the global Indian.

It makes sense then that Mira Nair's film about global India is also a Bollywood movie of sorts.

While the *mehendi* sequence references the rise of folk music as an autonomous genre that is diversifying the music scene beyond film song, *Monsoon Wedding*'s evocations of Bollywood song-and-dance sequences capture its diffusion in social life. There is, however, a third mode through which Hindi film songs are incorporated in the film. This mode cites the romantic duet's function as a space of becoming for the couple. The first time the maid Alice meets the event-manager Dubey, the soundtrack plays "Aaj Mausam Bada Baiman Hai," (Today the weather is treacherous) from *Loafer* (Slacker, A. Bhimsingh, 1973; music director, Lakshmikant Pyarelal; sung by Mohammed Rafi), and the scene unfolds in lyrical slow motion. In another sequence, when Alice brings Dubey a drink of water, giving him the first sign of her affection, his mates sing "Aankhon Mein Aankhon Mein Ishara Ho Gaya," (Eyes have spoken a secret language), from *C.I.D.* (Raj Khosla, 1955; music director, O. P. Nayyar). These romantic classics on the soundtrack are accompanied by cinematography reminiscent of classic film—camera on tripod, deep focus, high-contrast lighting, and languorous takes.

The coupling of Alice, the maid, and Dubey, the lower-class "event manager," transcends the barriers of class and religion and is, according to Nair, the only "pure" relationship in a film that documents the conjugal anxieties of the upper-middle classes. Yet, in contrast to the couple in classic cinema, whose road to nuptial bliss was strewn with many a thorn, Alice and Dubey's union is unopposed by family and society. Alice has no recalcitrant parents, and Dubey's mother is entirely absorbed by her stock portfolio. As the only lower-class couple in a film concerned with alliances among affluent global Indians, Alice and Dubey's coming together is a poignant, if low-stakes, affair. Though Nair's film does not permit Alice and Dubey to break into a song that celebrates the social transformation that their conjugation represents, the potential of romantic love is sentimentally referenced by Nair's extra-diegetic use of these "golden-age" songs and by her visual recapitulation of a celebrated scene from *Shree 420* (Mr. 420, Raj Kapoor, 1955), in which the protagonists, Raj and Vidya, sing "Pyar Hua, Ikraar Hua" (We have loved, we have acknowledged love) as they walk down Marine Drive, the thoroughfare that skirts Mumbai's celebrated seafront. Against a skyline dotted with modern, high-rise buildings, Raj and Vidya, barely sheltered by an umbrella, are impervious to their surroundings and have eyes only for each other. The fragile beauty of this image is heightened by lyrics that dream of a conjugal future that may, one day, attain to the middle-class comforts signified by the well-lit apartments in the background. As Raj and Vidya sing to each other in the rain, they access a private realm that is sovereign, modern, nucleated and far removed from the public indignities of their everyday life in the shanty slums of Chowpatty. While in the first instance the couple is constituted in and *only* through song, in the second, song's function is much attenuated. Nair's evocation of this scene from *Shree 420* poignantly underscores the historical distance that Hindi cinema has traversed in its depiction of the conjugal couple. In a film where almost every relationship is contingent and compromised, Raj and Vidya's radiant love can only survive as kitsch. Thus the rain-drenched city streets have made way for an ornamental garden whose arboreal excess bears down upon the human figures. As the soundtrack plays song fragments from old Hindi films, Alice and Dubey remain the mute objects of Nair's nostalgic gaze. It serves as an annotation—reminding us of couples past, including Chandidas and Rami, Kasturi and Pratap, Moti and Kesar, and Raj and Vidya, but it is ultimately an accompaniment to Alice and Dubey's union. If song's role in Hindi cinema was prophetic, giving us a couple-form that was yet to be, in Nair's film song functions elegiacally—recalling for us couples past. As a citation, it reminds us that the relation between conjugality and film form that I have explored in the first section is becoming a thing of the past in New Bollywood cinema. It should come as no surprise then that couples in *Monsoon Wedding*—except for Alice and Dubey—freely kiss.

Let us turn next to Yash Chopra's blockbuster *Veer Zaara* (2004) and the highly unusual manner in which it historicizes the romantic duet and its relation to couple-formation in Hindi cinema. This film, unlike Nair's, has many traditional song-and-dance sequences, including a communal *bhangra*, a *qawali* (a Sufi devotional song), and several romantic duets that mark the highs and lows of love's trajectory. One of Hindi cinema's great auteurs, Chopra returned to directing with *Veer Zaara* after a seven-year hiatus (his last film was *Dil To Pagal Hai* [Crazy for you, 1997]).[63] *Veer Zaara* is a Hindu-Muslim love story (other noteworthy examples would include Mani Ratnam's 1995 film *Bombay*, and Amjad Bin Essa's 2001 *Gadar: A Love Story*).[64] Upon its release, it enjoyed critical and commercial success in both domestic and overseas markets. Romantic love in classic cinema usually has two outcomes: marriage or death. In the first case, the romantic dyad makes its passage to conjugality by receiving the sanctions of the family and the state and is thus interpellated into the task of national reproduction, the "nation" being imagined in territorial or cultural terms. Less frequently, death awaits those couples that either cannot or will not submit to this reproductive teleology.

In *Veer Zaara* we witness both outcomes. The Hindu-Indian Veer (Shahrukh Khan) and the Pakistani-Muslim Zaara (Preity Zinta) fall in love. Zaara is engaged to be married to Raza (Manoj Bajpai), the scion of an important political family in Lahore, and on this match rides the future of progressive politics in Pakistan, for it will consolidate two "liberal" factions of the polity. On the eve of the wedding, the relationship of Veer and Zaara is made public, but in the interests of the greater national/familial good, Veer persuades Zaara that she should proceed with her marriage to Raza. For the same reason, Raza agrees to marry a woman who loves someone else, but he extracts a price for this "injustice" by making Veer an offer—that Veer give up his identity, confess to being a spy, and spend the rest of his life in prison in return for Zaara's happiness. If he refuses to do this, Zaara's future will be in jeopardy. Veer—according to the logic of romantic love—naturally chooses the former and disappears into a prison cell, now known only as Qaidi Number 786—which is the holy number for the Bismillah.[65] Zaara, believing he is dead, breaks off her marriage and returns to India to spend the rest of her life running a school for girls in Veer's native village. In the first movement of the film then, unsanctioned love meets with apparent death. Twenty-two years pass. A lawyer, Saamiya Siddiqui (Rani Mukerjee)—a character supposedly based on Pakistani activist Asma Jahangir—reopens the case and visits Qaidi Number 786 with the hope of restoring to him his *"naam, pehchan,* and *mulk"*—name, identity, and country. Veer agrees to go to court on the condition that Zaara's name will not be invoked in public alongside his. After a protracted courtroom drama, Zaara arrives in person, identifies Veer, and the lovers are reunited.

It is noteworthy in this film how the romantic dyad experiences a kind of death linked to the subtraction of a legal identity—Veer becomes nameless. Veer is brought back from this living death in a court of law, but the entity that returns his name to him is not the state but his beloved, for only she can bear witness to his former identity. The restoration of identity coincides with a romantic reunion, though the couple that we are given in the final frames of the film is too old to reproduce. We have moved from living death to fruitless life. In each instance Veer and Zaara escape the reproductive logic of the state—first by stepping out of time—the twenty-two years that Veer spends in prison and Zaara in exile—and then by arriving too late. In this extraordinary ending we glimpse a romantic couple freed from the heterosexist teleologies to which couple-formation has been subject in Hindi cinema. As this couple traverses hand in hand the no-man's-land between Pakistan and India, we are witness to a couple-formation that is asynchronous—an image from the past that arrives in the present and is instinct with the future.

I would like to explore the emergence of this form of social subjectivity by looking at the way the film treats both the historical and the cinematic past. Why does the new couple emerge through a confrontation between two orders of time? Why does the film need a temporal caesura (twenty-two years) before it can move from the one outcome (death) to the other (reunion)? And most crucially, how does the film use music to embody this asynchronous couple? Chopra says that as he was looking for a music director for *Veer Zaara*, he was unimpressed by the work of contemporary composers. He needed sounds that would convey the passing of time that the film enfolds. Rather than commissioning someone to create a retro sound,[66] Chopra resuscitated unused tunes composed by the late Madan Mohan, an industry veteran from the 1950s and 1960s. These compositions were recreated by Madan Mohan's son, Sanjay Kohli, and sung by Lata Mangeshkar. The duo of Madan Mohan and Lata had once created such enduring hits as "Naina Barse" (My eyes weep) and "Tu Jahan Jahan Chalega" (Wherever you go) from Raj Khosla's classic films *Woh Kaun Thi?* (Who was she? 1964) and *Mera Saaya* (My shadow, 1964). If Chopra's revival of this celebrated collaboration, posthumous in the case of Madan Mohan, is another mutation of the nostalgia boom noted earlier, it is also a nod to the greater sonic realism in New Bollywood cinema.

The success of the film in both "old" and "new" India, among the beneficiaries of globalization and those who trail behind, might be due in some measure to the deft ways in which it maneuvers discursive and cinematic registers through a skilful and effective musical management of temporality. In short, a new couple-form is given to us in the body of the old. Aesthetically, by using music remaindered from a time past, Chopra grafted an old sound onto a young body. All those themes, affects, subjects, and protocols of representation and performance that characterized pre-1990s Hindi cinema are neither nostalgically mourned, transformed, or discarded; rather, they are confronted and negotiated, even as the film participates in the visual and narrative economy of New Bollywood. The film thematizes the transformation that Hindi cinema has undergone in the last decade by exploring form at the level of content. At its core is a love story that is utterly conventional—Veer and Zaara's love is structured by idealism and driven by sacrifice; as such, it is the stock-in-trade of Hindi film melodrama. Yet in being recounted by a decrepit old man in a prison cell to a young woman who belongs to another time as a series of flashbacks, the film takes a cliché and endows it with historical

value. The temporal displacement turns generic conventions into historical content.

The film's title sequence perfectly condenses this strategy. The images of mountains and waterfalls locate the spectator in the cyclical time
of nature, but the Urdu narration in Yash Chopra's own voice that accompanies these images immediately bisects these visuals with history.
In Hindi cinema, Urdu lyric poetry frequently serves as a shorthand for
the trauma of partition—the division of the land in 1947 along communal lines into India and Pakistan. From the red and white outfits of the
principals that mirror the Yash Raj logo to the yellow fields that we have
encountered in earlier Chopra films, including *Silsila* (The affair, 1981)
and *Dilwale Dulhaniya Le Jayenge* (The brave heart will take the bride,
Aditya Chopra, 1995), the title sequence spins a dense, intertextual web
that evokes nostalgic affects that prepare us to mourn for a narrative that
we have yet to encounter. Particularly noteworthy is Chopra's use of the
seventy-year-old Lata Mangeshkar to render the opening song "Yeh
Hawa" (This breeze). Mangeshkar's voice reveals its age, and so a sound
arrives from the past, as it were, to be synched onto the contemporary
body of Shahrukh Khan. In fact, since Veer and Zaara's love unfolds
through a series of songs, the fact that the expressive register of romantic
interiority—songs—are out of time with the visual embodiment is particularly significant. In the last segment of the titles, however—as Zaara
is shot with a gun—we break out of one habit of viewing and must recall
the spectacular final scene of *Dil Se* (From the heart, Mani Ratnam, 1998).
Ratnam's film ends with a shot of the couple exploding into flames, signifying the impossible union of a citizen and a terrorist.[67]

Since Veer and Zaara's love is so firmly located within a discursive and
cinematic past—that is, if it is meant to be merely an object of nostalgia—then why not let Veer languish in a prison house of memories? Why
does Saamiya, a human rights lawyer, enter his cell with the intention
of returning him to the land of the living? What valence, after all, can
Saamiya's truths—freedom and identity—have for a romantic subject for
whom the abdication of the self is the fulfillment of a romantic destiny?
Can she—equipped with the liberal values of individuality and sovereignty—find a way to communicate with the kind of historical and social
subjectivity that he embodies? She comes in to remedy past wrongs, but,
although the typical subject of a human rights violation might be a victim of state violence, such is not the case with Veer. It is not the state of
Pakistan that takes Veer's name away; rather, as Zaara's fiancé reminds
us, the state only comes in to the extent that it can misused by those in
power—a characteristic that the Indian state shares with the Pakistani

one. The state aids Raza by momentarily holding Veer in custody, but Veer chooses his own incarceration. By giving up his name, Veer is only doing what is expected of him according to the codes of romantic love, but can the legal language that Saamiya brings with her ever adequately comprehend these codes?

Saamiya tries to frame Veer and Zaara as historical subjects. What century (the word she uses—*saadiyo*—also conveys the sense of "era") are they from, she wonders, that each would waste all this time in memory of a fleeting love? Their temporal irrationality—the fact that they are so profligate with time—suggests to her that maybe she needs to locate them in a different register altogether. In this remarkable moment the human rights lawyer finds herself face to face with an unfolding of humanness that the secular language of law cannot entirely navigate. And yet it is the task of Saamiya and the film to bring justice to these fugitive subjects. We have to ask, To what end? Are Veer and Zaara the bodies that the state must capture to reform itself? Is this what instituting the rule of law in developing countries means? What does it mean that Saamiya—on behalf of the state—atones for a wrong that the state did not commit?

Nivedita Menon has pointed out that in a historical sense "justice" is constituted by specific moral visions, but the discourse of the law is predicated on the assumption that justice can be "obtained once and for all by the fixing of identity and meaning."[68] The meaning delivered by the law as the just one then gets articulated in complex ways with other discourses constituting identity and tends to affirm dominant and oppressive possibilities rather than emancipatory and marginal ones. Law and justice have long been sundered in the world of Hindi cinema— therefore, as many have observed, the police always arrive too late. By the time the body is handed over to the state, justice has already been meted out. It is Saamiya Siddiqui's charge to articulate law with justice, but to do so she has to enter the moral and affective space that energizes her subjects. Veer and Zaara's reunion happens in a court of law in Pakistan, which acts as a guarantor for the right of a Hindu and Muslim couple to be together if they so choose. Yet their actual coming together occurs in song-space in the course of a romantic duet, "Tere Liye" (For you). The introduction of a four-minute song in the film's final moments is very unconventional for Hindi cinema.[69] This is especially so in the context of a courtroom drama where the climax is reserved for dramatic revelations and reversals. Chopra deliberately suspends the flow of narrative, stretching out Veer and Zaara's longed-for, long-awaited, reunion. The song plays through the soundtrack (in a concession to the greater realism that we are witnessing in Hindi cinema now). So too, the scene begins in a realistic register. A series of shot-reverse shots alternate between Veer and Zaara and record for us their reactions. However, the conventions of continuity editing are rapidly abandoned as editing and camera-movement become much more expressive. Dissolves, frame inserts, and a 180-degree shot whose tempo is matched to that of the song convey the intensity associated with the romantic duet. Though the couple never quite breaks into song, the narrative delay effected by the song's duration at this climactic juncture reminds us that Veer and Zaara waited a long time for the law to bring them justice, so now it must in turn wait for their private reunion. It also gestures toward other modes of conjugality that still await their day in court.

Let us turn in conclusion to the itinerary of song and dance in *Dor* (Rope, Nagesh Kukunoor, 2006). The director, Kukunoor, was an environmental engineer in Atlanta, Georgia, until he returned to his country of origin to make *Hyderabad Blues* (1998). Shot on a shoestring budget of Rs. 17 million and completed in the brief space of seventeen days,[70] this film is a by-the-book "indie" product. In this romantic comedy about an Indian-American negotiating the complexities of an arranged marriage in his hometown, Hyderabad, the actors speak a mixture of Telegu, English, and Hinglish. It was a runaway hit in metropolitan India and pioneered a wave of Hinglish films. Kukunoor's subsequent films all retain this "indie" core. To take two examples, *Bollywood Calling* (2001) takes a satirical look at commercial Hindi cinema through the eyes of a failed Hollywood actor trying to make it in Bollywood, while *Iqbal* (2005) is about a deaf-mute Muslim boy from a village who is trying to find a place on the Indian cricket team.

*Dor*, produced by Sahara One and Percept Film Company, is tellingly dedicated to 1970s director Hrishikesh Mukherjee.[71] It opens with a long, wide, slow pan of the kind of mountainscape that has long served as a locus classicus for the romantic duet. But Kukunoor resets our expectation by cutting to a close-up of the protagonist Zeenat (Gul Panag), perched on a ladder and hammering some nails into the outside walls of a hut. Her lover, Amir, comes up from behind and attempts to steal a kiss. He is thwarted, not by her modesty (as is usually the case in a duet where the heroine turns away from a kiss), but by the nails she is gripping between her teeth. Her task concluded, they kiss. The film then cuts to its second female lead, Meera (Ayesha Takia), who is dancing for her husband, Shankar, to a popular Bollywood hit—"You Are My Soniye" (You are my beloved), from *Kabhi Khushie Kabhi Gham* (Sometimes happiness, sometimes sorrow, Karan Johar, 2002) playing on the radio. Shankar does not get a kiss because the arrival of his father interrupts the couple's idyll. The camera pulls back to frame them through a wire screen, capturing their thwarted sovereignty. This opening intercut establishes our two protagonists—Zeenat and Meera—as contrasting historical subjects, located on either side of the kiss/song divide that I have been exploring here. While Zeenat works for a living and marries Amir against the wishes of his family, Meera is under the authoritarian gaze of the feudal family, her desires expressed through Bollywood songs.

However, globalization brings us all into a common present. Thus Zeenat and Meera's husbands go to Saudi Arabia as migrant workers, and, by accident, Amir ends up killing Shankar. Saudi (sharia) law decrees that Amir's life will be spared if the wife of his victim forgives him, and so Zeenat goes looking for Meera to seek this pardon. Zeenat has no name or address but only a picture of the murderer and his victim. She knows that the family lives far away in Rajasthan, but she is the kind of determined and self-determining woman for whom this quest is inevitable. We enter the fabular domain of a knight on an impossible quest, but the knight in question is a woman—a very modern, self-assured one at that. Zeenat is at once the knight of a romance and the protagonist of a novel. Her quest has the inexorability of the former and the psychological arc of the latter. The film's narrative is ordered by chance—the miraculous appearance of the *bahuroopiya* (professional impersonator, played by Shreyas Talpade); the many coincidences—and thus resembles Hindi film melodrama. Its notion of character is novelistic, while its mise-en-scène is iconic. Film citations—songs, dialogues, posters—are almost the only indices through which the milieu is detailed and historically situated. Snatches of song—from *Kabhi Khushie Kabhi Gham* and then "Kajra Re" from *Bunty or Babli*—serve as temporal markers. Our other access to context, what stops the milieu from being entirely symbolic, are the landscapes, vernacular architecture, and costumes. These settings—the lush mountains and stone huts of Himachal, the crumbling *havelis* (palaces) and rolling sands of Rajasthan—have been invoked and archived in the movies. Though *Dor* has no song-and-dance sequences, it is as though the milieux and visual styles of song and dance spill over and spread to the entire film.

The *bahuroopiya* and Meera are enthralled by the movies. The former entertains his dupes by ceaselessly reprising dialogues from old films and mimicking 1970s stars like Dev Anand and Rajesh Khanna, while Meera expresses herself by dancing to the tune of popular Hindi songs playing on the radio. In one striking sequence, Meera (now the veiled and grieving widow) suddenly bursts into an energetic jig in a deserted street. It would seem as though only Zeenat is afflicted by no such Bollywood addiction. Her subjectivity does not need the movies to express itself but can be unfolded through other means. This is particularly interesting if we consider that she is the most "forward-looking" character in the film. Though dependent for her life and happiness on the less-autonomous Meera, she clearly sees herself as more progressive and proceeds to give Meera a feminist education while concealing from her the real reason for the visit. When Meera learns Zeenat's identity, she feels angry, vengeful, and betrayed. But for the sake of friendship and in gratitude for all the lessons in independence that Zeenat has taught her, Meera in the film's ticking-clock finish (recalling the climax of countless melodramas) runs to the train station to deliver her pardon. Zeenat, in the closing shot of the film, holds out her hand and helps Meera up into the train that is rushing into their uncertain future.

*Dor* is a highly self-conscious form of cinema that marks itself as New Bollywood through this reflective relation to Hindi film form. This is also a temporal plot since, through such citations, it can historicize its own emergence out of Bollywood. From the song sequence "Ding-Dong, O Baby Sing a Song" (from Subhash Ghai's 1983 film, *Hero*) that Meera and Zeenat watch in a decrepit provincial movie theater to the *bahuroopiya*'s charming imitations, *Dor* archives the function of song and dance in Indian social life (of the backward kind) and the immersion of the masses in their seductions. It is as though the song-and-dance film has turned into a cultural shorthand for precisely the kind of world that the film sets out to change. But can the song-and-dance sequence in film be so easily overcome? Or is it still needed to stage unanticipated becomings? The film concludes, as we have seen above, with a queer conjugation—Zeenat, the widow Meera, and a soon-to-be-pardoned Amir are now together. Interestingly, we have had a prior glimpse of such an odd triangle in a scene that comes closest to a song-and-dance sequence. In a desertscape that is both stunning and absolutely empty, Zeenat, Meera and the *bahuroopiya* dance to an item number "Kajra Re" playing on FM radio (fig. 4). Zeenat, first skeptical and then bemused, eventually joins in (fig. 5). As this unlikely threesome strut and shake with increasing abandon, heterosexual conjugality's queer future is vividly foretold.

The three modulations in the formal organization of the song-and-dance sequence that I have sketched above suggest that as film song reinvents itself as a purely industrial product, the stable relation of narrative to song and dance outlined in the first half of the chapter weakens. New Bollywood cinema no longer needs the song-and-dance sequence to deliver the sensations of coupling, and the narrative allows the couple access to sovereignty. This aesthetic shift also draws attention to a rewriting of the contract between popular cinema and its public that is

4  Zeenat, Meera, and the *bahuroopiya* dance to "Kajra Re" playing on the radio. (From Nagesh Kukunoor's *Dor* [Rope], 2006.)

5  Zeenat, Meera, and the *Bahuroopiya* enact new conjugal arrangements through dance. (From Nagesh Kukunoor's *Dor* [Rope], 2006.)

ongoing in post-liberalization India. If the double enunciation of the couple in both narrative and song and dance enabled Hindi film form to reconcile public interests with a commercial agenda, popular cinema's contemporary transformation as corporate entertainment allows the celluloid couple access to privacy without the intervention of song and dance. As a consequence, the song-and-dance sequence is presented as an asynchronous object, whose time has already passed or is yet to come. Here the performance sequence attaches to couples that are out of joint—

the poor, the old, the queer—to produce for us modes and affects that cannot be reconciled with the emerging norm of heterosexual nucleation. The song's affinity for marginal subjects, I have argued, is aligned with the multiplication of entertainment options and film music's struggle to retain its commercial dominance in a rapidly mutating media environment. In the next chapter, I look at another instance of New Bollywood cinema's reconstitution of Hindi film aesthetics in the wake of industrial transformation. We turn there to the NRI genre (films made for nonresident Indian audiences) to examine how its figuration of conjugality and the Hindu extended family is motivated by a desire to convert the narrative protocols of Hindi cinema into "film effects" that memorialize the conventions of 1970s Bollywood cinema.

# Family Matters: Affect, Authority, and the Codification of Hindi Cinema

Pyaar. Pyaar. Pyaar. Throughout South Asia you can't get away from it. Perhaps the rise of Love has something to do with cinema, or independence from the British or globalization. . . . In India (the most disco nation on earth) Love is a glittery madness, and obsession, broadcast like the words of a dictator from every paan stall and rickshaw stand, every transistor radio and billboard and TV tower.[1]

While this observation from Hari Kunzru's novel *Transmission* (2004) might have limited sociological value, it is most certainly true that Hindi cinema has historically been obsessed with love, especially the fortunes of the courting couple. The romantic duet, as we saw in chapter 1, brought the couple into being and publicized love's sovereignty. But the couple, once constituted, was reabsorbed into the family and held no further interest. As a result, the vicissitudes of the postnuptial state were the preserve of minority film movements like the "middle cinema" of the 1970s and 1980s, which was addressed to an urban, bourgeois audience that putatively desired greater "realism" than the commercial Bollywood blockbuster was able to provide. It was represented by directors like Rajinder Bedi (*Dastak*, 1970); Basu Bhattacharya (*Anubhav* [Experience], 1971, and *Aavish-*

*kar* [The discovery, 1972]); Hrishikesh Mukerji (*Abhimaan* [Pride], 1973) in the 1970s; and Mahesh Bhatt (*Arth* [Meaning], 1982); Vinod Pandey (*Ek Baar Phir* [Once more], 1979, and *Yeh Nazdeekiyan* [Intimacy, 1982]); Govind Nihalini (*Dhristi* [Vision, 1990]); and women directors like Kalpana Lajmi (*Ek Pal* [Just for a moment], 1986) in the 1980s. Lauded by critics, some of these films enjoyed modest box-office success, but they were, for the most part, a niche product.

The past decade, however, has witnessed a proliferation of films centered on marriage and its aftermath. This emphasis on the postnuptial state might well connect with India's rapidly shifting social landscape. A familiar litany of reasons, including the breakdown of the extended family, urbanization, gender mobility, and the global dispersal of labor, are cited for the radical restructuring of family life. While India still has one of the lowest incidences of divorce in the world (1.1 percent in 2005),[2] it has nonetheless witnessed a dramatic escalation, in relative terms, of the divorce rate.[3] The launch of a dating website—secondshaadi.com (lit., "second marriage")—attracted four thousand members within the first month of its operation and the attention of the international press with stories in Reuters and Time.[4] This same period has also witnessed an explosion of films across a number of genres preoccupied with conjugality. It commenced with conjugal allegories. Mani Ratnam's *Bombay* (1994) and *Dil Se* (From the heart, 1998); Anil Sharma's *Gadar: A Love Story* (2001); and Yash Chopra's *Veer Zaara* (2004) explored the link between intimacy and nationalism from all sides of the political spectrum. Urban dramas about troubled marriages—*Saathiya* (Beloved, Shaad Ali, 2002), *Chalte Chalte* (Opposites attract, Aziz Mirza, 2003), and, most recently, *Life . . . in a Metro* (Anurag Basu, 2007)—jostled for space with comedies. The latter spanned the gamut from broad (*Shaadi No. 1* [First marriage, David Dhawan, 2005] and *No Entry* [Anees Bazmee, 2005]) to slick (*Mixed Doubles* [Rajat Kapoor, 2006]) and *Main, Meri Patni aur Woh* [Me, my wife and the other, Chandan Arora, 2005]). Marital discontent was also at the heart of emerging genres like sex-noir (*Murder* [Anurag Basu, 2004]; *Jism* [Body, Amit Saxena, 2003]); and horror (*Bhoot* [Ghost, Ram Gopal Varma, 2003]; *Raaz* [Secret, Mukesh Bhatt, 2002]). In other words, the troubled couple was ubiquitous—from A-list epics like *Kabhi Alvida Na Kehna* (Never say goodbye, Karan Johar, 2006) to low-budget "indie" comedies about swinging couples like *Mixed Doubles*. Between films that were preoccupied with marriage across a number of registers and a small handful of films—*Chameli* (Sudhir Mishra, 2003), *Girlfriend* (Karan Razdan, 2004), and *My Brother . . . Nikhil* (Onir, 2005)—that confronted same-sex desire explicitly, if only in a subplot, the heterosexual courtship romance that ends with a closing shot of a married couple surrounded by a loving joint family all but disappeared from New Bollywood cinema.

Yet films affirming the extended Hindu family were precisely the fare that in the mid-1990s revived an ailing film industry, bruised by the spread of television and video piracy. They included the landmark *Hum Aapke Hain Koun!* (Who am I to you? Sooraj Barjatiya, 1994); *Dilwale Dulhaniya Le Jayenge* (The brave heart will take the bride, Aditya Chopra, 1995); and the crossover hit *Monsoon Wedding* (Mira Nair, 2001). These films present the trials and triumphs of family life in India and the diaspora through melodramatic narratives and spectacular song sequences that celebrate the rites and rituals of Hindu marriage. If galloping divorce rates are the context for postnuptial cinema, these domestic dramas must be situated against an equally rapid expansion of a wedding industry now valued at $11 billion,[5] suggesting an intensification of the modes of conspicuous consumption that has always characterized the Indian (especially) Hindu wedding. While the circulation of Hindi cinema in the Indian diaspora and in many parts of the world is not a new phenomenon,[6] such circulation was unorganized, informal, sporadic—fed by a desire for the homeland and its culture or by Hindi films accidently arriving in and connecting with viewers in transitional societies. The industry itself did not pay much attention to these overseas networks. However, starting in the mid-1990s, the industry became alert to the revenue potential of this market. Now it is a common occurrence for big-budget movies to be released simultaneously in more than fifty theaters in the United States, while Hindi movies are often among the top ten in the U.K. box office. This new and extremely lucrative market is also diegetically solicited by films set in the West that feature lead characters who are nonresident Indians (NRIs), and the films thematize through family and romance the relation of the diaspora to the homeland. This trend, as elaborated in the introduction, coincided with the liberalization of the Indian economy, the rise of new forms of cultural nationalism that reimagined the relation between the nation-state and its capital-rich diaspora, and the spread of new media technologies, including satellite television, that radically globalized India's mediascape.[7] Hindi cinema's re-branding as Bollywood coincided with the short but extremely profitable reign of the family film, leading Ashish Rajyadaksha to claim that the typical Bollywood film refers to a fairly specific narrative (love stories with lots of song-and-dance sequences that feel good, end happily, endorse "family values," and showcase Indian "culture") and a slick mode of presentation.[8]

The figure most associated with New Bollywood song-and-dance spectaculars that present the vicissitudes of the global Indian family is Karan Johar (known more commonly by his brand name—KJo). Johar made his name through three films that he directed: *Kuch Kuch Hota Hai* (Something is happening, 1998), *Kabhi Khushi Kabhi Gham* (Sometimes happiness, sometimes sadness, 2001, aka *K3G*), and *Kabhi Alvida Na Kehna* (2006, aka *KANK*), and a fourth, *Kal Ho Na Ho* (If tomorrow comes, 2003, aka *KHNH*), that he wrote and produced. Though *Kal Ho Na Ho* was directed by Karan Johar's former assistant, Nikhil Advani, it is fair to say that his close association with all aspects of this film and the strong aesthetic and thematic links that *Kal Ho Na Ho* bears to the other three films directed by Johar merits its nomination as a KJo product.[9] This slim cinematic output apart, Johar's other claim to media fame is a very popular TV talk show *Koffee with Karan*, that features witty, fast-paced interviews with film personalities. Other than starting with the letter *K* (a superstition the director shares with his friend, TV producer Ekta Kapur, whose studio, Balaji Telefilms, is credited with revolutionizing soap programming in Indian television),[10] Karan Johar films are always fronted by Shahrukh Khan, India's most globally renowned male actor, and some combination of the top stars of the past decade, including Kajol Devgan, Rani Mukherjee, Preity Zinta, Saif Ali Khan, Hrithik Roshan, Kareena Kapoor, legendary actor Amitabh Bachchan, his wife, Jaya Bachchan, and their son, Abhishek. They boast big budgets and gorgeous production values, and carry cheesy subtitles like "It is all about loving your parents." Whether set in a summer camp, the likes of which do not (yet) exist in India (*Kuch Kuch Hota Hai*), or against a stylized Manhattan skyline (*Kal Ho Na Ho* and *Kabhi Alvida Na Kehna*), the KJo film explores the lives and loves of the rich and the beautiful, and is driven by melodramatic plots, extreme emotions, and extravagant song-and-dance sequences. In brief, the KJo film assembles many of the features that we associate with post-1970s popular Hindi cinema, or Bollywood—melodrama, elaborate musical numbers, fairy-tale endings, and a large cast of stars—and then proceeds to exaggerate these features, making big, glittering films that return their weight in gold at the box office, particularly the overseas box office comprised of diasporic Indians in the United Kingdom, the United States, Australia, and, to a lesser extent, Fiji, Trinidad, and the Middle East. How well have these films fared in the diasporic market? The top two spots in an all-time list of overseas blockbusters as of 2008 belong to *Kabhi Alvida Na Kehna* (Rs. 445 million) and *Kabhi Khushi Kabhie Gham* (Rs. 365 million), while *Kal Ho Na Ho* (Rs. 267 million) and *Kuch Kuch Hota Hai* (Rs. 227 million) come in at numbers ten and eleven.[11] But if we look at top earners for the period 2000–2009, domestic and foreign combined, *Kabhi Khushi Kabhi Gham* comes in at number seven, *Kabhi Alvida Na Kehna* at eighteen, and *Kal Ho Na Ho* at twenty-four, while *Kuch Kuch Hota Hai* ranks at number eighteen among all-time earners,[12] suggesting that Johar's films do not fare quite as well nationally. Clearly, the overseas box office belongs to KJo.

There are at least two trends in cinema that characterize New Bollywood. One is film's immersion in a media ecology, including branding and so forth, and the other is an active cultivation of the overseas market. In each case the term *New Bollywood* signals a shift from the object that was Mumbai cinema—whether we understand that shift to be a dispersal of the cinematic object and its assembly with other practices and commodities, or understand it more narrowly to refer to a film product created for overseas consumption, which would also imply a form of branding.[13] On both counts, the category of KJo films seems to epitomize the process of (New) Bollywoodization, a process that intensifies and turns into capital the inherent and informal tendencies of Mumbai cinema. The moniker *KJo* is very revealing. It captures—wittily—the intimate alliance between auteurship and branding that has been a feature of commercial cinema globally in the past few decades.[14] While Mumbai cinema has had a number of directors, such as Raj Kapoor, Guru Dutt, Bimal Roy, Dev Anand, Yash Chopra, Manmohan Desai and Subhash Ghai, who commanded a value analogous to that of the star and exhibited a recognizable style/signature while functioning within the confines of commercial cinema, the emergence of the director as a stable source of a film's value is a more recent phenomenon. The 1990s witnessed the rise of the star-director, a trend signaled in the credits by opening titles like "A film by director X" or "A director X film." Figures like Mani Ratnam, Ram Gopal Varma, Vidhu Vinod Chopra, J. P. Dutta, Raj Kumar Santoshi, and Sanjay Leela Bhansali were widely described in the popular press as "artists" whose distinctive style and unique vision would help Bollywood straddle the gap between creativity and commerce. But this also functioned as a brand identity that helped raise finances and market films, and lent a new legitimacy to popular cinema. We might view such "auteurism" as historical activity, what James Naremore has called (after Raymond Williams) a "cultural formation."[15]

While the moniker *KJo* is a perfect case study of the auteur as brand, publicized through an elaborate network of TV, stage shows, awards ceremonies, fashion, video games, comic books, and even the university lecture tour, the KJo film presents the conventions and industrial modes of Mumbai cinema as a set of "attractions"—melodrama, song-and-dance sequences, stars, dialogues—that add visual and affective value to a product whose underlying narrative protocols adhere quite closely, as I shall show, to the Hollywood model. This disintegration of classic Hindi film form was already inherent in *masala*, but the KJo film in particular and the family film in general turn the form of Hindi cinema into a set of reproducible codes while simultaneously marking a break with it. Thus, while the KJo film—an all-singing, all-dancing, spectacular—might seem far removed from the postnuptial focus and generic inventiveness of the postmillennial films that I listed above, it represents a very important temporal and aesthetic bridge between Hindi cinema's courting duo and New Bollywood's postnuptial dyad. KJo posits a sentimental relation to the feudal family romance and changes it from within. Even more significantly, however, this thematic reformatting is aligned to a formal project that exaggerates the narrative codes and the stylistic toolbox of Hindi film, turning them into "film effects" that commemorate the superseded form.[16] Such a citational relation to film history allows New Bollywood cinema and its conventions to take hold.

## Family Business

The opening up of the diasporic market to Hindi cinema coincided with the release of a number of films thematically focused on the family. As we have seen above, *Hum Aapke Hain Koun!* and *Dilwale Dulhaniya Le Jayenge* (*DDLJ*) were landmark events in this regard, and all KJo productions to date have retained this emphasis on the family. Romantic couple-formation continues to be, as it has always been, at the center of these films, but we notice, as well, a new emphasis on inter-generational cooperation, what Moinak Biswas in a vivid phrase has called a "romance with patriarchy."[17] The social film, or, in Madhava Prasad's words, the "feudal family romance," has traditionally had a conservative conclusion, in which the couple, though romantically constituted, had to be incorporated into the governing ideology of the *khandaan*, or extended feudal family. This usually took the narrative form of reconciliation between the hero and the patriarch. The textual heteronomy of Hindi commercial cinema might be viewed as a formal solution to the problem of accommodating individual desire to social norms, modernity with tradition, and so on. The 1970s marked the exhaustion of the social film as a master genre and a concurrent diversification of the film product. The "big" films of the decade—*Sholay* ("The flames," Ramesh Sippy, 1975); *Deewar* (The wall, Yash Chopra, 1975); *Don* (Chandra Barot, 1978)—show new traits, including an affinity for Hollywood genres like the Western and the gangster movie; greater technological finesse, including a more propulsive camera; the increased use of zoom and telephoto lenses; and a sophisticated use of background sound, parallel editing, and special effects. While stars, especially Amitabh Bachchan in his reprisal of the "angry young man"—a working-class hero who fights injustice through violent and criminal means—continue to grow in influence, this decade is also marked by the rise of name-brand directors with recognizable styles, such as Ramesh Sippy, Prakash Mehra, Manmohan Desai, Yash Chopra, and the scriptwriting duo Salim-Javed.[18] These new developments, however, are not accompanied by a substantial formal shift, though one might argue that during the 1970s and into the 1980s, when cinema's dominance was seriously threatened by television, the heterogeneous form of Hindi commercial cinema ossifies into formula.[19] This decade, as noted above, was also characterized by the rise of a "middle cinema" focused on the vicissitudes of couple-formation in a comedic or dramatic vein. These films, addressed to an emerging urban middle-class, eschewed melodrama, were often women-centered, socially progressive, and director-driven. This and the emergence of a state-sponsored art cinema, as I have indicated above, are important precursors to the contemporary *hat-ke* (offbeat) film (discussed in chapter 4).[20]

The resurgence of the family melodrama in the mid-1990s is therefore particularly remarkable, given that it follows two decades—the 1970s and 1980s—when the representation of family values and romantic conjugality was in a state of flux across a spectrum of films. While couple-formation was a relatively minor note in action-oriented blockbusters, in romantic hits like *Ek Duuje Ke Liye* (Made for each other, K. Balachander, 1981) and *Qayamat se Qayamat Tak* (From disaster to catastrophe, Mansoor Khan, 1988), transgressive lovers chose death over reconciliation with an authoritarian patriarchy.[21] Not only middle cinema but even mainstream films like *Silsila* (The affair," Yash Chopra, 1981) and *Thodisi Bewafai* (A small betrayal," Esmayeel Shroff, 1980), and comedies like *Pati, Patni aur Woh* (Husband, wife and other," B. R. Chopra, 1978) charted the risky territory of incompatibility, infidelity, and divorce. The emergence of the female avenger figure in films like *Pratighaat* (The revenge, N. Chandra, 1987) and *Damini* (Raj Kumar Santoshi, 1993), and the unconventional star turn of KJo's favorite hero, Shahrukh Khan, as a schizophrenic stalker in films like *Darr* (Fear, Yash Chopra, 1993) and *Baazigar* (The gambler, Abbas-Mastan, 1993) all bear witness to a film scene in which the pleasure and promise of romantic love and the power of the family to regulate its members, especially women, were on the wane. Though none of these films mark a radical break with the form, many of them wrestle with it, as "interruptions" or "paranarratives" are attenuated, strenuously rationalized, or nominally present.[22] Even as the courageous Raj in *Dilwale Dulhaniya Le Jayenge* goes from London to Punjab to gain the consent of the bride's father, though the bride herself is willing (at her mother's urging) to elope, other directors like Mani Ratnam and Ram Gopal Varma were giving us distinctly unfamiliar family relations. While Mani Ratnam isolates and fully invests (even overinvests) in the sovereignty of the romantic couple in films like *Roja* (The rose, 1992), *Bombay* (1995), and *Dil Se* (From the heart, 1998), in which the couple, if anything, is hypernucleated,[23] in the films of Ram Gopal Varma the family disappears altogether. As opposed to the gangster of old, who took to a life of crime to avenge his family, the eponymous hero of Varma's film materializes in gangland Mumbai, literally out of nowhere,[24] and films like *Naach* (Dance, Ram Gopal Varma, 2004) and *Ek Hasina Thi* (There was a beautiful girl, Sriram Raghavan, 2004) strain credulity by featuring such radically unmoored protagonists.

Thus the recuperation of the family in the KJo film runs counter to tendencies in Hindi cinema in the previous decades, and even in the present, it is not the only or even the most dominant trend. How do we explain this love affair with the family in Karan Johar's films, even while Hindi cinema has been engaged elsewhere in challenging or entirely circumventing the power of the family? Most critics insightfully link the centrality of the family film to the active solicitation of a diasporic audience, since the ideology of the undivided Indian family links the nation to the diaspora.[25] They argue that "family values" neutralize the threat of globalization while simultaneously reflecting an increasingly sectarian Hindu politics. I would supplement such accounts by suggesting that a focus on the family evokes a sentimental relation to the historical deployment of this theme and trope in Hindi cinema, even as the KJo film thoroughly reinvents what a family means and how it works. Further, this reinvention of the family must be tracked alongside Johar's conversion of Hindi film form into "attractions" embedded in a narrative technique that is strictly Hollywood.

Let us begin by considering Johar's family ties. He belongs to a group of contemporary directors like Aditya Chopra and Farhan Akhtar who come from film families. Johar is the son of veteran Bollywood producer Yash Johar, while Chopra and Akhtar also have famous fathers—the director Yash Chopra and famed scriptwriter-lyricist Javed Akhtar. The film industry in India (and now increasingly in Hollywood) has always functioned like a family business. Dadasaheb Phalke, the putative founder of Indian cinema, made movies under the aegis of a family firm, while the Pune-based Prabhat studios and the producing/exhibiting empire of the Madans, established in the 1920s and centered in Kolkata, were family-owned. Even Bombay Talkies, a Western-style studio with a German director, Franz Osten, and an international film crew, was managed by the husband-wife team of Himanshu Rai and Devika Rani. The decline of the studio system in the 1940s, led to a radical disintegration of the three sectors of the film industry. However, as we shall see below, this family model continued to function until the 1990s and survives into the present. Let us first briefly review the industrial structure from the 1940s through the 1980s, in order to put in context this filial mode of production.

By the post-independence period, films began to be made on an ad hoc basis, largely by independent producers who outsourced and then reassembled the various components of the film, with the star eventually functioning as the one steady source for attracting finance. Unable to access bank loans (since the state did not formally recognize the film industry), these producers were dependent on informal, often illegal, sources of funding (estimates suggest that in the 1970s and 1980s, 25–50 percent of the capital floating around in the industry was "black," or unreported, income), and they raised money by preselling distribution rights. Here again, the star and, to some extent, the track-record of the producer—rather than the script or director—were the deciding factors. The distributors were organized by territory and played a crucial role in bankrolling productions. The exhibition sector comprised, in essence, theater owners who were almost entirely entrusted with marketing films.[26] Moreover, owing to government-imposed restrictions on the construction of new theaters, exhibitors had an inordinate influence, and even when these stringent land-use laws were relaxed, exhibitors continued to resist expanding venues in order to hold on to their bargaining advantage.[27] In essence, from the late 1940s through the early 1990s, the Hindi film industry largely functioned as a "cottage" industry. This fragmented structure was further exacerbated in the 1970s and 1980s by chaotic working conditions that led to escalating costs.[28] There was little horizontal or vertical integration, and the industry could rarely make use of economies of scale. Further, it was not able to sufficiently exploit ancillary revenue streams like music rights, videotapes, or even royalties from exhibitions in other venues like TV, even though films were ideally suited to such remediations. In this regard, as many commentators note, it was quite distinct from Hollywood.[29]

The 1980s were at once the worst decade and a turning point for Hindi cinema. First the state-sponsored spread of television and then the arrival of satellite service greatly depressed the demand for movies. In addition, new technologies like the VCR changed the way people consumed film. As a result, between 1989 and 1993, the number of theaters fell from 13,335 to 13,001, and the number of daily patrons, according to the National Readership Survey, plummeted from 12.2 million in 1986 to 5 million in 1992.[30] Further, widespread video piracy as well as the informal exhibition of films on cable channels by local operators meant that the industry could not capitalize on these new exhibition technologies. Between rising costs and falling revenue, an industry always in crisis found itself in the doldrums. However, by the end of the decade the situation improved somewhat as the industry became alert to the commercial potential of film music. In the early 1990s, owing to music channels on TV, the rise of "indipop" (nonfilmic popular music), and the aggressive promotion of cassettes in the previous decade by entrepreneurs like Gulshan Kumar of T-Series, there was a boom in the music industry.[31] Film producers finally became adept at exploiting film music, selling rights for large sums that helped finance films. The early 1990s also witnessed the rise of the tie-in, corporate sponsorships, and in-film advertising. Greater attention to marketing, especially prereleasing song-and-dance sequences on TV, yielded results at the box office. N. Chandra's *Tezaab* (1988) was one of the first films whose success trade analysts attribute to the aggressive promotion of its title song *Ek Do Teen*. Producers began to spend more than 10 percent of a film's budget on marketing![32] Finally, at the distribution end, films began to open widely so that they could pull in audiences early in order to beat video piracy and illegal exhibition on cable. Films like *Hum* (We, Mukul Anand, 1991) and *Khuda Gawah* (God's witness, Mukul Anand, 1992) were released in 450–500 theaters against the 200-theater average common at the time. A good "initial" was seen as offsetting the higher costs of a huge print run.[33] Further, with the success of *Hum Aapke Hain Koun!* and *Dilwale Dulhaniya Le Jayenge*, from the mid-1990s onward, the overseas market emerged as a big driver of revenues. While the decade of the 1990s put in place structural shifts that are key to understanding the current industrial trends in Bollywood, it is only in the new millennium that the industrial landscape was completely overhauled.

Throughout the period outlined above, the family-enterprise model continued to be operative in the film industry at a functional and ideological level. First, the members of several prominent film families, across generations, were reprising the roles of producer, director, actor, playback singer, music director, and so forth. A few noteworthy instances would include the Kapoors, Anands, Barjatiyas, and, more recently, the Bhatts. Four generations of the Kapoor family have been involved in the industry and their banner—RKFilms—is among the most prestigious in the industry.[34] The brothers Dev, Vijay, and Chetan Anand formed the long-enduring Navketan films, and Vishesh Films was formed by siblings Mahesh and Mukesh Bhatt, and Mahesh's daughter, actress-director Pooja Bhatt. Each family firm acquired a "brand" identity over time—the Kapoors were known for their lavish melodramas in the high Bollywood style; the Anands perfected stylish crime films and cult capers. While the Barjatyas produced treacly love stories thick with family values (their 1989 smash hit *Maine Pyar Kiya* [I have loved] anticipates the discursive elements that would define in the 1990s family film), in the 1980s the Bhatts introduced an edgy, urban product that was aligned with the exploitation film insofar as it dealt with youth culture and topical subject matter. In addition, they kept their budgets low by using newcomers and subscribing to a realist style often shot on location. Great soundtracks and a hefty dose of sex guaranteed a healthy box office. Even in the B-circuit (see chapter 3), the familial mode of production was firmly established, with the five Ramsay brothers dominating the horror boom of the 1980s.

Extended kin networks organized other departments of film-production, including music. The sisters Lata Mangeshkar and Asha Bhonsle dominated playback singing for about four decades, while the father-son duo S. D and R. D Burman and the brothers Kalyanji-Anandji were music composers. Even in collaborations between unrelated partners, like those of the scriptwriters Salim-Javed or music composers Lakshmikant-Pyarelal, the conjoining of names produced the effect of filial affinity. Moreover, the entrepreneurial model centered in the family was not confined to the film industry but characterized the Indian-owned private sector as a whole. Despite the state's stated policy of industrialization and modernization to be implemented through a planned model of economic growth, the family business continued to be the primary unit of private enterprise. As Rochona Majumdar has convincingly argued, the idealization of the joint family in public debates over legislation as well as in quotidian practices suggests that the figure of the propertied subject in modern India was quite different from its liberal counterpart in the West.[35] The family functioned as an alternative power bloc, more local and regional, consolidating its position through marriage alliances and social networks, and inhibiting the forms of mobility required for standard capitalist relations of production to emerge.[36] Though the major industrial houses of this period—the Tatas, Birlas, Goenkas, Modis, and Ambanis—employed a professional managerial class, the top echelons continued to be run by a tight circle of insiders related by blood or marriage. As Ritu Birla has recently shown, these family businesses forged in the colonial period actively contested a governmental demarcation of the economy and culture into the domains of the public and private respectively. Rather, these kinship-based commercial groups asserted their legitimacy by contesting and creatively inhabiting this statist mapping of private and public. Naturally, the fiscal durability of this model relied on an efficient semiotic circulation of the family in culture.[37]

Madhava Prasad has noted that while the mode of production of commercial cinema was profit-oriented, it was not fully industrialized, so that "precapitalist ideologies in which relationships based on loyalty, servitude, the honor of the *khandan* (clan) and institutionalized Hindu religious practices" structured relationships within the industry, the production process, and the cultural content of cinema.[38] Karan Johar's description of how the Mumbai film industry functions in comparison with Hollywood seems to echo Prasad: "In our film fraternity, relationships are stronger than contracts. . . . We've been nurturing these equations for years, and we do it sans agents and managers and assistants. Those of us lucky to be raised within the industry have the word of our fathers, our siblings, and those friends that might as well be family. We're small, and we may bicker, but we've sat in each other's living rooms, and we've built this industry to what it is." Addressed to foreign media giants, with "their big corporate presentations" and their "pie charts," who seek to do business with Bollywood, this blogpost claims, "We might be a little old fashioned in our pitches, but we make films because the nation's heart thumps for it. Appeal to that sentiment, and understand our culture. Employ people who understand this about us, as an industry, and as a country. We're emotional, and we're more connected than you'd think, but we have our patterns. Try to understand who we are as an industry, what works for us and more importantly, for our audiences."[39]

What KJo identifies as unique to the Bollywood mode of production is a network of social relations modeled on the family and business dealings structured by sentiment. He sketches a rhetorical link between the sociology of the industry, audience expectation, and the content of cinema. This familial mode of functioning, Johar stresses, must be reckoned with as Indian cinema globalizes, for it has historical value and renders fiscal advantage. A recent study notes that this model continues to be profitable because it is based on tight social networks; thus "Business relations among different roles in film projects (scriptwriters, actors, producers, directors, and so on) are, ceteris paribus, [more] likely to be influenced by family relations and other types of strong ties in India than in film industries located in countries with other national institutional fields, such as Hollywood. Business relations may hence to a relatively high extent rely upon trust than upon contracts."[40] Ravi Vasudevan has traced the history of this link between a diegetic investment in the creation of a joint family and the industry's own use of this metaphor to enhance its social legitimacy back to the 1940s, when the studio system was being dismantled. Studios were imagined as families, and the same figure—family—is remediated to describe the independent producer-star relation.[41] We must view KJo's invocation of the family in a similar light—as having referential and normative value. It describes an industrial scenario so thoroughly controlled by a few powerful families that they determine the type of all social relations, but this figuration of the industry as family also provides social (and, in the case of Johar, global) legitimacy to a certain mode of production, even as it is undergoing radical transformation.

Let us now briefly detail this mutating industrial landscape, focusing here primarily on the sector of production. As we have seen above, from the early 1990s, the industry fought back against the expansion of media outlets and falling theatrical attendance by capitalizing on ancillary revenue streams, tightening films' links to other media, and by courting the overseas market, particularly the Indian diaspora, with the kind of targeted content that showcased Indian culture and thematized the nation's relationship to its migrants. KJo is closely identified with this product, and he is also very adept at optimizing returns through presold music rights; in-film advertising; product tie-ins, especially with fashion and lifestyle companies; live entertainment shows; and so on. Despite his rhetorical disdain of "graphs," "pie-charts," and other such instruments of professionalization, KJo is skilled at using multiple media channels, including TV, print, and electronic media, to produce himself as a brand. KJo's signature line reads, "Hi, I am Karan Johar and if you do not know who I am, you are not watching TV or reading Page 3 [the celebrity gawker page in English language newspapers]." His 2006 release, *Kabhi Alvida Ne Kehna*, a film about adultery, was promoted by *We, The People*, a talk show on the twenty-four-hour news channel NDTV, which typically features topics like peasant unrest, global warming, and religious fundamentalism. Called the "The Modern Marriage," this episode of the show featured Johar, his male lead, Shahrukh Khan, noted film journalist and pulp novelist Shobha De, a marriage counselor, a psychic, and the founder of an online dating site, shaadi.com. It debated the film in the context of the changing sociology of marriage, with a live audience supplying ethnographic evidence. This emphasis on marketing is notable in an industry that had made few systematic attempts to promote films in the past, relying instead on participatory culture and other forms of fan activity.[42]

Burgeoning advertising budgets and aggressive cross-media promotion are only two aspects of the changes sweeping the Hindi film industry in the present. More remarkable are the ongoing shifts in industrial structure, especially the rise of the corporate conglomerate. According to a major study by The Confederation of Indian Industry and A. T. Kearney, trends indicate that the large entertainment corporation spanning content creation, aggregation, and distribution will emerge as the future model.[43] The report predicts consolidation of various sectors by production houses, organized theater chains, and cable network operators. It indicates that the most significant movement so far has been in film retail and exhibition (see chapter 4). The once notoriously fragmented industry with hundreds of producers and little intersectoral integration has now made way for no more than a dozen major film companies that distribute and retail (and in some cases produce) a bulk of the films. While the creative product still remains under the control of specialized production companies—as of 2005, 90 percent of all films and the top thirty earners between 2003–2005 were thus produced—the study by Mark Lorenzon and Florian Arun Tauebe reveals that there is significant horizontal integration of distribution, marketing, and exhibition.[44] The formal recognition granted to the film industry by the Indian state in 1998 allowed producers to secure bank financing after the Indian Banking Association established norms for film financing. This was followed by a decision to allow 100 percent foreign direct investment in films. In addition, key business associations like The Federation of Indian Chambers of Commerce and Industry (FICCI) and Confederation of Indian Industry (CII) that historically have shied away from the film business, have noted the double-digit growth rates that have characterized the media and entertainment sectors, including film. The industry now enjoys a new level of access and visibility as major Indian corporations like Reliance invest in the movie business. In 2005, Anil Ambani's Reliance Entertainment Group bought 66 percent equity in Adlabs, a film-processing company founded in 1978 by Manmohan Shetty. Since then, Adlabs, now renamed Big Cinemas, has expanded rapidly, building a retail empire of four hundred screens in India, Southeast Asia, and the United States. It has also added production and distribution units.[45] In addition, multinational companies like Sony, Disney, Warner Brothers, and Fox have begun to enter the production and distribution sectors, though recent Bollywood films by Disney (*Roadside Romeo*, Jugal Hansraj, 2008), Warner (*Chandni Chowk to China*, Nikhil Advani, 2009), and Sony (*Saawariya* [Beloved], Sanjay Leela Bhansali, 2007) have all failed at the box office. Interestingly, given the resilience of the domestic market in India, these major companies have opted for a localization strategy, partnering with Indian companies to develop indigenous products.[46]

Corporatization and bank financing have incited operational changes, the most significant being the institution of a new industrial structure and revenue models that are much closer to the Hollywood standard. Distributors are increasingly working on commission, buying films after they are completed rather than purchasing rights in advance. The goal is to distribute profits and risks more evenly along the value chain.[47] Producers secure funds through official channels like banks and private equity firms. This gives them greater control over the product, but it also makes them subject to new kinds of scrutiny as lenders begin to assess film as property.[48] This has introduced practices quite novel to Hindi cinema's mode of functioning. For instance, in the past, projects were pitched to stars via a "narration session" where the director (accompanied often by the producer) would orally present a concept, a storyline, and some crucial highlights. Actors typically received a few pages of script (mainly dialogues and brief directions) on the day of the shoot.[49] Now, increasingly, a bound script serves as the basis for prospecting a project and banks evaluate these "properties" through advisory committees before making a loan. The script is then translated into a screenplay, and shooting schedules and detailed budgets are drawn up in advance. Where pre-production was once "a 20 minute meeting,"[50] 4–6 months is fast becoming the standard among the better-known production houses. While cost overages and time delays are still common, the average turnaround time has shrunk from several years to months in many cases.[51]

Further, financial institutions are reluctant to lend to individuals and prefer to deal with large companies. This has encouraged the formation of conglomerates like Yash Raj Films, UTV Software Communications, Percept Communications, and Pritish Nandy Communications that either hire creative houses like Ram Gopal Varma's K Sera Sera to deliver films or sign on talent with multifilm deals, thus taking advantage of economies of scale. These companies have diversified into other sectors like domestic and international distribution, music, home video, animation, gaming, and television. Some, like Percept Communications, provide ancillary services like talent and event management, media consulting, experiential brand marketing, and even a "Touch and Feel" Bollywood experience for tourists and fans visiting Mumbai. Most recently, these companies have begun to invest in studio infrastructure, technology research, and script development—practices almost unknown in the earlier Hindi film industry.

While an industry model based on *alliances* that can take advantage of scale economies in distribution, retail, and financing while retaining the creative and managerial advantages of small firms in production still remains in place,[52] this situation is rapidly evolving. Ronnie Screwvala's UTV Software Communications is exemplary of the regime change currently underway in the film industry. Dubbed "India's Jack Warner,"[53] Screwvala came to the film industry from the outside. A door-to-door salesman of cable service, and then host of a popular TV game show, Screwvala became a successful television producer before branching out into cinema. Now UTV, involved in movies, television, broadcasting, and interactive (animation and gaming) units, has a market capitalization of $435 million (2007 figures) and is one of India's largest entertainment conglomerates. It has an equity partnership with Disney worth $220 million and has coproduced *The Namesake* (Mira Nair, 2007) and *The Happening* (M. Night Shyamalan, 2008) with Fox; it is therefore the Indian media company with the most prominent global profile. Screwvala has no genealogic link to and little nostalgia for the family mode of production. In his assessment, the film industry was not fully capitalist in the past: "Nobody thought of this as a profit-and-loss [business], . . . they thought of it as a cash-flow [business]. So if a producer-director made a movie and it lost $5 million, he got advances to make his next movie of $5 million, [so in his mind] he'd broken even."[54] Screwvala, however, is wholly committed to creating a media company that is profit-driven like any other modern, publicly traded corporation. For him, this fiscal goal is consistent with his desire to create innovative, nonformulaic films—in short, *hat-ke* movies, for he believes that liberalization has created a sea change in the Indian consumer, who is no longer fixated on brands ("the star" would be one such brand) but hungry for content. The key is to stay high up on the value chain and create scale economies through integration. The CII-Kearney study seems to bear out Screwvala's insights. It suggests that film content will serve as the originary point of an entire economic chain because it has the highest linkages with other mainstream media and entertainment segments, such as TV and music. Generating film content is thus crucial to extracting revenue from the multiple segments with which film connects. Screwvala has little faith in the outsourcing model credited with fueling growth in India, and thus he would like to develop products rather than render services.[55] Thus UTV emphasizes content that breaks with the three-hour, star-driven, singing-dancing family entertainment. UTV films typically run 90–120 minutes. They focus on the script and director, have slick production values, target niche audiences (youth, young professionals—Screwvala repeatedly reminds us that middle-class Indians now spend 11 percent of their disposal income on entertainment), allocate 25 percent of their budget to marketing, open widely, and aggressively exploit revenue channels and fight piracy by shrinking the theater-to-DVD/TV interval of a film to four weeks. Productions are managed in an extremely professional manner. Clearly, UTV sees itself as defining the future of the Indian movie business.

With entrants like Screwvala into the field, established family businesses have had to professionalize, investing in management, process, and planning. Some, such as Yashraj Films, have successfully transitioned to the new order—they were disciplined to begin with. Director Subhash Ghai of Mukta Arts, maker of such blockbusters as *Taal* (Rhythm, 1999) and founder of a state-of-the-art film school, Whispering Woods, notes that "the only organized guy around here is Yash Chopra. There is absolutely no wastage in his productions."[56] Companies like Johar's Dharma Productions and Yashraj Films (production, distribution, music, and home video) have retained a competitive edge by taking the strengths of the family model and reshaping it to meet the new professional standards taking hold in the industry. However, as a sign of the shifting alignments that define New Bollywood, Karan Johar, whose films were typically distributed by Yashraj, has recently signed deals with UTV!

## The Value of Family

The KJo film, I argue, is engaged in a similar project of reform. While the family's ability to evoke sentiment and establish historical continuity is preserved, the KJo film also significantly rethinks the family. This takes the most immediate form of a disappearance of society and the state and a retreat into the family as the only staging ground of action. As such, both KJo's characterization of the industry as family and the content of these domestic dramas seem to reprise the social film, or, in Madhava Prasad's words, the "feudal family romance," which did not need "the kind of integrated production process" that is necessary when narratives are "particularistic, focused on chunks of the real."[57] Prasad links the aesthetic dominance of this heteronomous form to a social totality in which the feudal family is still in power, and the modern, sovereign individual (who is also a citizen) has yet to emerge. Though the law was *formally* vested in the postcolonial Indian state, the feudal family continued as an alternative locus of power. Thus, to give Prasad's vivid example, the police in these films always arrive too late. Justice is meted out according to the laws of the feudal family, but the actual incarceration of the criminal is performed by the state. If the Indian state kept Mumbai cinema at a distance, refused to grant it industry status and thus access to institutional funding, imposed a punitive entertainment tax on film, and functioned as a censoring body, popular cinema remained vested in the ideology of the feudal family and its favored mode—melodrama. The heterogeneous form of Hindi cinema and its weak investment in realism are aesthetic symptoms of this attachment. But the force of the family in the KJo film, as I show below, is quite weak, for there is a shift in emphasis from the family as an absolute power that abrogates to itself a law that is beyond its jurisdiction to the family as a transmitter of values. Its coercion is affective rather than legal or economic.

For example, these films valorize the father's love rather than his authority, and there is an odd reversal of generational priorities. The old do not oppose the desires of the young but facilitate them. Thus mother of the widower-hero Rahul (Shahrukh Khan) in *Kuch Kuch Hota Hai* conspires with his eight-year-old daughter to orchestrate a romantic liaison between Rahul and his best friend from college, Anjali (Kajol). Rahul's father-in-law assists the mother in this task. The grandmothers in *Kabhi Khushi Kabhie Gham* initiate a chain of events that reconciles an autocratic father, Yash (Amitabh Bachchan), to an estranged son, Rahul (Shahrukh Khan again). In *Kabhi Alvida Na Kehna*, the adulterous Maya's (Rani Mukherji) father-in-law, Samarjit (aka "Sexy Sam," played again by Bachchan), upon discovering her affair with Dev (Shahrukh Khan), urges her to leave his son, Rishi (Abhishek Bachchan—Amitabh's son) so that all concerned might move on and make new lives for themselves. Dev's mother, Kamaljit (Kirron Kher) opts to stay on with her daughter-in-law Rhea (Preity Zinta) when the couple separates. In this film, though the parents are the first to learn about Dev and Maya's affair, they do not publicize the news—rather the adulterous couple make a joint decision to break off their impossible relationship and confess all to their respective spouses. The parents, though present, are not the enforcers of morality.

Parents, including fathers, with the possible exception of Yash in *Kabhi Khushi Kabhi Gham*, are hardly the irascible authoritarian figures of the feudal family romance. The child's right to make a romantic choice and the romantic choices of children are mostly encouraged and supported, which signals, if anything, a weakening of the family as a locus of alternative fiscal and ideological power. Affective rather than material ties structure family life, and emotional attachments modify and regulate filial hierarchies. Thus Dev, who is an ill-tempered father in *Kabhi Alvida Na Kehna*, has to be disciplined by the end of the film, while familial dysfunction in *Kal Ho Na Ho* is resolved through effective communication. Moreover, these ties—suddenly contingent in a globalized world order that demands and rewards mobility—must be ritually and gesturally affirmed.[58] Thus the KJo film is littered with hallmark moments—hugs and kisses between parents and children; affections expressed through cards, stuffed toys, privatized handsigns, and nicknames; family-centered song-and-dance sequences; a mise-en-scène cluttered with photographs; and, perhaps most important, frequent exhortations to be more expressive. Thus Rahul's mother in *Kuch Kuch Hota Hai* advises Anjali to speak her heart, while Sexy Sam in *Kabhi Alvida Na Kehna* regrets not showing his love while he still had time. Dev and Maya almost give up on a future together by concealing their true situations from one another, and Yash, the father in *Kabhi Khushi Kabhie Gham*, imperils the unity of his family for ten long years by not showing his affections, while his wife, Nandini (Jaya Bachchan) makes things right by breaking her silence. Not only is interpersonal communication a highly prized value in the world of KJo, but the KJo film is replete with scenes of role-playing through which characters access affects and effects through iterative performance.

This is especially so with regard to heterosexual couple-formation. If romantic love and the arranged marriage had been the two opposing norms of conjugality in Indian cinema, serial monogamy emerges here as a third option.[59] Romantic love in the KJo film is as much about desire as circumstance: relationships can be managed, and love can happen at first or subsequent sight. Thus in *Kuch Kuch Hota Hai*, Rahul and Anjali are best friends, and though Anjali falls in love with Rahul, for him she is just one of the guys. He gives his heart to the alluring outsider, Tina. The broken-hearted Anjali disappears. In the meantime, Rahul and Tina (Rani Mukherji) marry, but Tina dies in childbirth. Eight years pass until Rahul and Anjali meet again, but this time she, long-haired and feminine, is the alluring outsider, and Rahul falls in love with her. So, though Anjali does not get her love at first, she gets him at last. In *Kal Ho Na Ho*, we start out with a triangle: Aman (Shahrukh Khan) and Naina (Preity Zinta) love each other, and Rohit (Saif Ali Khan) loves Naina, but she thinks of him as her best friend. Aman is dying and wants to make sure that Naina finds happiness with someone who loves her, so he teaches Rohit how to make Naina fall in love with him (*"che din, ladki in,"* "six days and the girl is yours"), and she does! Rohit and Naina marry and go on to live a long happy life. The film, told in flashback, concludes with Naina telling her daughter (a la Rose in *Titanic*) that, while Aman was her first love and she will never forget him, she now loves Rohit. In the classic Hindi film triangle, a first love always emerged to threaten the hard-earned contentment of a subsequent relationship. A triangle could only be resolved spatially as one party left the scene, usually as a result of death or sacrifice. Here, Naina might not marry the man she loves, but she falls in love with the man she marries. She is allowed to love twice. In *Kabhi Alvida Na Kehna*, Dev and Maya, both in unhappy marriages, act upon their desire for one another by pretending that each is the other's spouse. This performance frees them up to express their needs and anxieties and better prepares them for their love affair. Thus, while romantic longing might not meet its mark at first, it will do so at last.

This reinvention of the family as a liberatory (and liberal) space and the emergence of serial monogamy are central to the repurposing of the social film that the KJo film engages in. Critics have repeatedly drawn attention to the "look" of the KJo film—the addiction to designer labels; the immaculate interiors; the beautiful people; urban milieus from which all dirt, crime, and poverty have been excised so that even Chandni Chowk, a congested neighborhood in New Delhi, looks as it might in a heritage calendar. If cinema, particularly commercial cinema, has always been adept at inciting desire through a display of bodies and commodities, the KJo film fully harnesses the technological potential of cinema to immerse spectators in a consumerist utopia. This liberation into the world of things in Karan Johar's cinema has been justly read in connection with India's transition to free-market capitalism in the 1990s and the sudden flow of images and commodities into a nation whose economy since independence had been partly socialist, and whose media, including cinema, had been fairly regulated.[60] The focus on the family has been viewed as a countermovement that manages the destabilizing potential of capital by locating it in the closed space of the upper-class, upper-caste Hindu home while appealing to a wealthy Indian diaspora that desires just such a harmonious union between capital and culture. It is true that the KJo film features miniskirted Indian girls back from Oxford who sing pitch-perfect Hindu hymns and other such paragons of flexible citizenship who skillfully navigate the flows and disparate spatio-temporalities of globalization. The mode of subjection in the KJo film is allied to a liberalization discourse that, as Mankekar has pointed out, was viewed as "freeing the creative and productive energies of the people."[61] Equally striking is the new relation between generations and the emergence of the subject through performance. The KJo film is a biopolitical project that brings into being emergent social relations—relations that do not so much reflect reality as construct it. For instance, when Johar was asked why he chose to set *Kabhi Alvida Na Kehna* in New York, despite his claims that his theme—adultery—reflects a growing social reality in India, he responded that he needed to show Dev and Maya conduct their love affair—unhindered and unobserved—in public spaces, and an Indian setting would not allow this.[62] The New York milieu, in other words, was dictated by his pedagogic project of bringing the adulterous couple out into the open so that he could explore the vicissitudes of their relationship—something as yet impossible in India. This spatio-temporal mismatch between the emergent subject and a recessive milieu provides us with another way to think of the disappearance of the social in the KJo film. It is entirely appropriate that the families in KJo films—unmoored in any social reality—seem unreal, because he is imagining modes of being and belonging whose time has not yet come. Here the family does not impose its values but is rather thoroughly revalued.

## Sentimental Symptoms

If the old are not enforcers of the law but facilitators of desire, the young, in effect, have nothing to rebel against. Rather than opposing a tradition that no longer wields any real power, the young invest it with sentiment. Thus they don ethnic gear and dance at festivals, perform rituals, and mimic gestures that memorialize tradition from a vantage that is utterly contemporary. It would appear then that the generations, rather than being at odds, accommodate each other. What, then, in the world of Kjo is the use of melodrama, which in Hindi film traditionally represented the clash between law and authority, good and evil, past and present? Though Johar makes ample use of melodramatic plotting (all his films have "ticking-clock" finales), acting style, and cinematography, this view of the subject as flexible and of the self as managerial substantially diminishes the need for the mode of melodrama, which relies upon the inability of protagonists to act upon their desires or express themselves because of adverse circumstances or social interdictions.[63] In melodrama, conflict usually arises because time is out of joint, and all manner of external misfortune is visited upon the good. The moral order is restored when the tides turn, and time, rather than obstructing virtue, makes it visible. The hero has little to do except be unstintingly heroic, and the villain's change of heart is both necessary and unconvincing. Thus time, what Linda Williams has identified as the temporal dialectic between "just in time" or "too late," is the narrative engine of a melodrama.[64] But in the world of KJo, it is never too late. While chance is an important narrative device (the films thrive on coincidences), failed communication equally drives melodrama in the KJo film. Though this expressive blockage is circumstantial, it is also indicative of a certain cultural logic. Let us look at some examples.

In *Kabhi Khushi Kabhie Gham*, putatively the most reactionary of KJo's films, the patriarch Yash, for all his new-fangled ways, is an unreconstructed autocrat who casts out his son Rahul for marrying someone poor. But Rahul, deprived of his family's wealth, immigrates to the United Kingdom and not only survives but actively thrives. It is very clear that the family wields merely emotional power over its members. The allegiance that Rahul owes his father is underwritten not by necessity but by affect. The once-whole family is remembered through photographs that play a prominent role in the mise-en-scène. The opening sequence, saturated with sentimental iconography, is a montage of photos alternating with fragments of video showing scenes from Rahul's happy childhood, alerting us at once that the film to come will document the disintergration of this family. In the older melodrama, emotional excess speaks to a structure of power (at least this is how melodramatic emotion has been theorized via a repressive hypothesis). Here, emotion represents a particular relation to the past, an excess that cannot entirely be contained by the rationalities of the present. Thus, when Rahul finally returns home after a decade, Yash asks his forgiveness and chides Rahul for having taken such an extreme step in reaction to a parent's words spoken in anger. Yash has to learn that the affective family is also surprisingly contingent. It does not endure but has to be affirmed; while a few angry words can sunder a family, gestures of love can make it whole again. Family is coded with a new form of value.

Melodrama's capacity to monumentalize sacrifice is activated by the KJo film, though the situations do not rationally demand such sacrifices. Thus in *Kuch Kuch Hota Hai*, when Anjali is on the brink of getting together with Rahul, her fiancé Aman arrives and delays this outcome; in *Kabhi Alvida Na Kehna*, Maya, despite her misgivings, does not call off her ill-advised marriage to Rishi because a chance meeting with a stranger convinces her that friendship is as good a reason to marry as love. The members of the younger generation in the KJo film do not *yet* feel entitled to treat romantic love as a sovereign value and act upon their desires; rather, they feel the pressure of older modes of being that valued renunciation over enjoyment and familial (and social) obligations over personal fulfillment. They experience these outmoded affects, and that sustains melodrama, yet these affects are not demanded by the narrative but are in excess of it. Consider the following instance from *Kuch Kuch*

*Hota Hai.* When Rahul and Anjali meet again, he is widowed, but she is engaged. However, the man she is engaged to, Aman (Salman Khan), suspects that her heart belongs elsewhere. He jokes that she will prove a runaway bride. Nor does she experience any pressure from the family. Her mother appears skeptical about Anjali's decision to marry Aman. Why does Anjali refuse to call off this engagement, though it would be so easy for her to do so? She keeps her word to give *Aman* the chance to release her from this obligation, recalling the heroic sacrifice that was the resolution of many a classic Hindi film triangle. Johar's staging of this ticking-clock finale recalls an older economy of desire in Hindi cinema and is, as such, a purely formal homage in a film that otherwise subscribes to a radically altered concept of desire.

In the light of such hesitations, it is significant that the call to free oneself from this superseded economy is issued by the older generation. In each instance, the narrative resolution also entails access to a more expressive mode.[65] Thus Anjali in *Kuch Kuch Hota Hai* has to own up to her feelings for Rahul, Yash in *Kabhi Khushi Kabhi Gham* has to speak his love, and Maya has to overcome repression. In every case the family and an extended kin network—parents, spouses, siblings, in-laws—authorize these transformations. Whereas the family in Mumbai cinema wielded a juridical power that rivaled that of the state, and the protagonist typically shuttled between these poles (that we may also gloss as tradition and modernity), in the KJo film the family is not the arbiter of a (despotic) law that the individual either submits to or needs to escape from to become fully sovereign, but a cultural resource and an affective milieu that enables the self-actualization of its members. At the same time, the older figuration of the family and conjugality in Hindi cinema is aesthetically memorialized—through song and dance, melodrama, and even duration. During an era of shrinking film-length, the KJo film typically clocks in at three hours, sometimes more. Rey Chow has recently described the sentimental *"as an inclination or disposition towards making compromises and towards making do with even—and especially—that which is unbearable. [It] may best be described as a mood of endurance."*[66] She goes on to theorize sentiment "as a vaguely anachronistic affect whose mere survival points to another mode of attachment and identification—and whose noncontemporaneity stands in mute contrast to global visibility."[67] Taking my lead from this compelling reading of sentiment as an accommodation of older modes of filial power and piety, I suggest that we view KJo's "romance with patriarchy" as a sentimental stance in the face of the modes and affects of another time. Paradoxically, this stance is taken not by the older generation but by the younger one. It is an excess of feeling—a form of intensity—toward the old. We must therefore view KJo's exaggeration of the formal features of Hindi cinema as a sentimental symptom that commemorates the superseded aesthetic, even while his films fully assimilate the narrator system of Hollywood.

## Out of Time

Such thematic repurposing of generational relationship and conjugality, I have argued above, is accompanied in the KJo film by an intensification of the aesthetic effects of Hindi cinema. These effects memorialize the form of Hindi cinema—its styles and techniques of narration. They function as set pieces in a narrative schema that cleaves quite closely to the protocols of Hollywood. Let us consider two instances where the stylistic features of Hindi cinema are both referenced and re-coded. The first is from *Kabhi Khushi Kabhie Gham*. This sequence occurs toward the midpoint of the film—a few minutes prior to the intermission. It is part of a long flashback as Rohan learns of the circumstances under which his older brother Rahul left home a decade ago. Here Yash, who has arranged a marriage between Rahul and Naina, the daughter of a business associate, finds out that Rahul loves Anjali, a girl from the wrong side of the tracks. The first part of this 4-minute, 22-second sequence comprises eighteen shots and activates the "high style" of the Mumbai melodrama to represent this face-off between two of Bollywood's biggest stars— Amitabh Bachchan and Shahrukh Khan. Tracking close-ups punctuate 360-degree panning shots, and a thundering background score accompanies this confrontation between father and son—the former channels *parampara* (tradition), while the latter espouses *pyar* (love). The opening two-shot introduces us to the principals, and then we cut to a high angle that constructs a tableau of father and son along a sharp diagonal. The tableau, as Ravi Vasudevan, has argued "displays interruptive, interventionist functions in the flow of scenic construction; . . . the function of this spatial figure is to encode a socially and communally defined address."[68] This opening tableau reminds us that we are in the familiar territory of Hindi film melodrama, where the forces of desire and love oppose each other (fig. 6)—a compositional template most recently reprised in Aditya Chopra's *Mohabattein* (Loves, 1998) and featuring the same actors. The next segment, made up of an alternating series of pans and close-ups, ramps up the melodrama as Yash berates Rahul for being unmindful of his family name, while Rahul claims that love knows no reason. Our sympathies are clearly with Rahul, for his reactions in close-up shape our

6  Rahul and Yash in a tableau representing the face-off between desire and law. (From Karan
Johar's *Kabhi Khushie Kabhi Gham.* [Sometimes happiness, sometimes sadness], 2001.)

response to Yash's class prejudice. But from around shot eighteen, the
sequence shifts gears as Yash begins to express disappointment rather
than rage at his son's "failing." This group of seven shots commences
with one of Yash, in which the camera tilts up ever so slowly, and Yash
appears forlorn and diminished as Bachchan's resonant baritone modu-
lates downward. A series of rapid shot-reverse shots follow that undercut
our former attachment to Rahul's point of view until, by shot twenty-
five, Yash sinks down into an armchair, tired and dejected. We now view
him in profile in the extreme foreground in a deep shot in which Rahul
appears blurred in the background (fig. 7). This composition in depth,
rack-focused, stands in marked contrast to the tableau that opened the
sequence, for it does not "relay" a transcendent meaning (law versus desire) but asks to be read immanently, in the context of the particulars of
the story world. And what are those particulars? Rahul is Yash's adopted
son, and thus Yash's charge that Rahul has failed to act like a "Raichand"
takes on a special resonance. We must read Rahul's submission to the
father's will—he agrees to give up Anjali—not as a capitulation to patriarchal power per se but as the psychic reflex of an adopted child. Shot
twenty-six is a flashback to the eight-year-old Rahul, who learns that he
is adopted and then folds his hands in respect before his "new" father
(fig. 8). It is this promise that Rahul makes good on in the final shot as he
submits to Yash in a gesture that graphically recalls the flashback we have
just seen (fig. 9).[69] Though the scene begins by reprising a classic conflict

7 Rahul and Yash now encounter each other as father and son. (From Karan Johar's *Kabhi Khushie Kabhi Gham* [Sometimes happiness, sometimes sadness], 2001.)

8 A flashback to the child Rahul saluting his adoptive father. (From Karan Johar's *Kabhi Khushie Kabhi Gham* [Sometimes happiness, sometimes sadness], 2001.)

in a melodramatic mode familiar to the audience from countless Hindi films, it shifts to a more realistic register as the framework moves from a sociology to a psychology of the family. Yash and Rahul's confrontation is no longer allegorical but embedded in a particular history. This move from the family as necessary to the family as contingent is underscored by a stylistic shift from Hindi film conventions.

9  Rahul repeats the same gesture of salutation in the present. (From Karan Johar's *Kabhi Khushie Kabhi Gham* [Sometimes happiness, sometimes sadness], 2001.)

In the second example, from *Kabhi Alvida Na Kehna*, there is a similar conversion of the techniques of Mumbai cinema into film effects that add intensity to a narrative structured by the conventions of Hollywood. The lovers Dev and Maya suffer no social or circumstantial constraints—adultery here is driven not by the mistreatment of one spouse by another or even by the return of a past lover but by the nature of the people involved—Dev, who cannot connect with the upwardly mobile Rhea, especially after he is unmanned by an accident, and Maya, who entered into a marriage based on care rather than romantic love. Events are ordered by motivation and psychology—Dev and Maya form a connection because Dev is unhappy in his marriage, and Maya is clearly not in love with the man she is about to marry. These preconditions are quite economically conveyed in the opening sequences. Why Maya speaks so openly and frankly to a stranger, and a male at that, is openly acknowledged and explained away: sometimes it is easier to talk to strangers than to friends—they are free to speak the truth. And what does Dev tell Maya when she expresses concern that if she bases her marriage on friendship there is always the danger that she might fall in love after she is married? He responds that if she does not look for love, she will not find it. But even as he constructs for her this voluntarist version of human action, essentially an ethic of self-control/self-sacrifice, the exchange of looks, body language, and flirtatious wordplay testify that love has arrived unbidden to derail such an ethic.

Consider the scene itself—two people in a garden that is absolutely empty, placed frontally in relation to the camera. Though this framing graphically evokes the convention of frontality in Indian cinema, it is a citation merely. Although frontality has been theorized as instituting spectatorial relations quite at odds with voyeurism, this is indeed a private scene.[70] The "fourth wall" is firmly in place, and the characters are speaking only to each other. Moreover, the camera is very unobtrusive, and the editing is seamless. The camera is placed at eye level, and the sequence comprises relatively long takes alternating with brief interludes of shot-reverse shots. It starts out with a midshot and moves almost imperceptibly closer to the principles, never quite achieving a close-up. In brief, the sequence plays out naturalistically with almost no dramatic emphasis.[71] The conversation comes to a close as Dev urges Maya to hurry up and get married. As they part from each other, they exchange names, and the film makes its first direct allusion to Mumbai cinema as Dev mimics the distinctive speaking style of his celluloid namesake, actor Dev Anand. Almost on cue, the technique shifts gear, and the framing and editing become much more stagey. First the camera pulls back and up to an overhead shot of the two figures parting, and the background score plays the instrumental section of the title song (fig. 10). This overhead shot of two figures walking away from each other (which functions as a visual leitmotif in the film) alternates with a rhythmically edited shot-reverse shot of Dev and Maya looking back at each other even as the overhead camera and the traditional authority that it relays demands that they part. The overhead shot functions as a tableau conveying in a congealed form the social mandate that a married man and a woman on the eve of her wedding have no right to be flirting with each other. This exact composition reappears to remind us of this mandate when, midway through the film, Dev declares his love for Maya (this time in an empty train station in the middle of the night), and Maya is in no position to deny that she loves him too (fig. 11). But unlike that first time, when Dev and Maya walked away from each other, this time Maya ignores the injunction of the tableau and runs towards Dev in an agonizingly long sequence.

It is by now almost a truism that the ordering of events and actions in the Hindi film melodrama is not driven by the motivational logic of a psychological-realist kind but by characters who perform actions that enable the plot to move forward and take its many twists and turns.[72] Since the narrative drive of an externalized form like the melodrama is the initial disturbance and final restoration of the moral order, there is no real suspense in a melodramatic narrative, no unexpected character-driven reversals or projections of action. This is why the tableau performs such an important function in the melodrama—it consolidates the moral

10 Dev and Maya in a tableau formation that enforces the social injunction that they must part. (From Karan Johar's *Kabhi Alvida Na Kehna* [Never say goodbye], 2006.)

11 Dev and Maya repeat the tableau only to transgress it. (From Karan Johar's *Kabhi Alvida Na Kehna* [Never say goodbye], 2006.)

order that the action will fulfill. But Maya disrupts the tableau and takes an action based on her own unique experiences that will run athwart traditional morality. As in the scene from *Kabhi Khushi Kabhie Gham* described above, the transition from an older cultural logic to a newer one occurs via a flashback. Maya recalls key moments with Dev and her husband Rishi, but as these scenes from the first half of the film play back, she reprocesses them and then decides to go with her lover. We witness, in other words, a cognitive remapping that enables Maya to break through one set of habits and emerge into another. What we diegetically experience as Maya's individual agency is also a cultural transformation.[73]

Melodrama was the aesthetic mode best suited to capture the face-off between law and desire, tradition and modernity, but these antinomies are no longer narratively necessary in the world of KJo. His project, as we have seen, puts into place a new kind of family and new modes of subjectivity that are less agonistic, more self-actualizing. We must consequently view his activation of the melodramatic mode and his use of micro-narrational techniques like the tableau and frontality as a memorialization of the older forms of Hindi cinema and the social relations they embody. They are the relics of another time—valuable souvenirs—that evoke sentimental affects and add value at the box office. However, as we saw in the examples above, they must also make way for a mode of narration that is more Hollywood than Mumbai cinema. As such, the KJo film is a transitional object that lingers awhile with a cinematic form whose time is up. Perhaps the most vivid instance of this is the diegetic timeline in *Kabhi Alvida Na Kehna*. The film breaks into three parts. The first segment is sixteen minutes long and occurs on March 21, 2002 (Dev precisely dates it for us). Dev and Maya meet for the first time. They part. She gets married, he has an accident that partially cripples him and ends his career as a football player. The second segment commences four years later, in 2006, and lasts for almost one hundred and fifty minutes. Dev and Maya meet again, have an affair, decide to break it off, and confess their transgressions to their respective spouses, who throw them out. But they do not get together—rather each lies to the other that they have been forgiven, for after all "family is family." So they go their separate ways. The third segment, in which Dev and Maya are reunited, is about twenty minutes long and occurs three years later—in 2009, three years after the release of the film in 2006! This might very well be one of those continuity lapses that Hindi cinema was notorious for. Alternately, the ending lends itself to a different reading. We might view it as another melodramatic set piece—a sentimental gesture to the disappearing moral and aesthetic universe of Hindi cinema. The lovers are reunited in a "nailbiting" climax at a train station, aided by their exes–Rishi and Rhea—who have now moved on and rebuilt their lives. So why does the film need this interval of three years, during which we witness on-screen the lovers pining for each other to the accompaniment of the title song, "Never Say Goodbye"? This flash-forward is motivated by the nostalgia of the KJo film for the cultural logic of Hindi cinema. Infidelity remains a risky subject in Hindi cinema. In *Kabhi Alvida Na Kehna's* most illustrious precursors—*Silsila* (The affair, Yash Chopra, 1981) and *Arth* (Meaning, Mahesh Bhatt, 1982)—marriage vows are broken under extenuating circumstances. Even a recent spate of *hat-ke* films like *Jism* (Body, Amit

Saxena, 2003) *Murder* (Anurag Basu, 2004), and *Life in a . . . Metro* (Anurag Basu, 2007) rationalize infidelity by featuring lonely women trapped in dysfunctional marriages. But Dev and Maya's actions are motivated only by desire—they are each other's "soulmates," and their spouses, Rhea and Rishi, hardly deserve this humiliation! So three years must pass, during which Rishi and Rhea rebuild their lives, and Dev and Maya's emotions are lyrically mediated by song. Both song and the ticking-clock finish in a train station draw on the melodramatic codes of Hindi cinema to transform the adulterous couple into romantic lovers who have paid their dues in time and tears, so that we can now can now root for their union! At the same time, KJo renders such a coda virtual by setting it in the future. It is a happy ending that is out of time.

To conclude then, the KJo film, as a category, takes a distinct stance in relation to the cinematic past and mines certain strains within it. This, as I have shown, is a crucial way in which the KJo film breaks with Mumbai cinema. For not only does this archival relation to Mumbai cinema turn it into a historical object, but the KJo film also evokes the thematic tropes and aesthetic protocols of Hindi cinema, only to transform them. I have traced this through the KJo's multiple iterations of the "family"—as theme, as aesthetic, as a new source of value, and in relation to social and cinematic history. If the *hat-ke* film is marked by its addiction to the new, the KJo film invents a new relation to the old. I examine the emergence of the *hat-ke* genre and its conjugal relations in chapter 4. But let us first elaborate on the intimate alliance between genre formation and the couple-form in New Bollywood cinema by turning to the upgrading of horror from the B to the A category in recent cinema.

# Fearful Habitations: Upward Mobility and the Horror Genre

The centrality of the couple to the emergence of New Bollywood cinema is perhaps most sharply illustrated by the way horror films were reinvented at the beginning of the nineties. Previously, the genre consisted of B-circuit movies aimed primarily at rural and working-class audiences. Immediately after liberalization, Hindi horror suddenly went upscale, recasting itself as a metropolitan product addressed to India's globalizing middle classes. More recently, the success of films like Vikram Bhatt's *Raaz* (The secret, 2002) and Ram Gopal Varma's *Bhoot* (Ghost, 2003) has led to a steady stream of slick horror films that have generated consistent returns at urban venues. This up-market horror wave needs to be analyzed in the context of the many transformations in the Hindi film industry, as well as changes in the economic and cultural milieu of popular entertainment. The rise of this so-called New Horror genre has been accompanied by the creation of several other genres previously absent from the Indian screen. The colonial and post-independence periods were characterized by distinctly indigenous genres—"historicals," "mythologicals," the "social film," and the *masala*. The remaking of horror and the introduction of genres like romantic comedies, action-adventure, and science fiction represent a process of "Hollywoodization" that makes Hindi cinema's taxonomy much more in tune with cinema elsewhere. As in the case of horror, these other genres have also shifted their target audience from the lower end of the film market ("frontbenchers") to affluent, middle-class audiences ("supergentry").[1] Tracking the mechanics of this reversal in market logic allows us to reflect on the rise of the genre movie as a crucial development in New Bollywood cinema.

As genre films solicit new audiences, they need to reformat content in order to appeal to and shape the tastes of this class of spectators. I would like to examine here how the figure of the couple is a locus for such remodulations. The horror genre uses the urban, middle-class couple as the social material through which it reconstitutes its relation to the market, and the genre's formal and phenomenal properties also facilitate a refiguration of conjugality and domesticity that contributes in some measure to its commercial success. If horror's generic identity is intimately aligned with a basic formula, which Robin Wood has expressed as "normality is threatened by the monster,"[2] it stands to reason that the genre's effectivity is significantly premised on the successful evocation/production of the norm understood, as David Russell astutely notes,[3] both as culture and form. Moreover, this norm must be phenomenally experienced by the viewer in order for the eruption of the monster/threat to take effect and for the eventual (though always partial) restoration of order to acquire value. The genre therefore tests both the mimetic and marvelous capacities of cinema—its ability to assemble and shatter "reality." Thus the basic premise of horror is particularly suited to expressing historical shifts, including those pertaining to cinematic form and technology, since it is entrusted with producing the norm and its disruption. Upwardly mobile Hindi horror emerges therefore as an excellent site for examining a changing social and industrial landscape. In this chapter, I first situate new Hindi horror by providing a brief history of the genre, its discursive elements, and its exhibition contexts. I then investigate how the phenomenology of horror is being activated to imagine new social relations, especially in the domain of family and conjugality. Finally, I show how horror's upward mobility is intimately tied to its ability, as a genre, to capture and isolate the life-world of the middle-class nuclear family.

## Hindi Horror and the B-Circuit

Horror films are conspicuous by their relative absence during the classic period of Hindi cinema (1945–1970), an era dominated by the social film—an omnibus form that, as we have noted earlier, included elements of romance, comedy, family drama, action-thrillers, police and detective stories and, of course, song-and-dance sequences. It would not be an exaggeration to say that genre films as such did not exist in Mumbai cinema during this time, except in the B-circuit.[4] Horror was almost completely absent from the screen, and the few films that dealt with the supernatural were old-fashioned ghost stories, in which "the attempt was not to scare as much as to give the love story a new dimension."[5] Films like *Mahal* (Mansion, Kamal Amrohi, 1949), *Madhumati* (Bimal Roy, 1958), *Bees Saal Baad* (Twenty years later, Biren Nag, 1962), and *Bhoot Bangla* (Haunted house, Mehmood, 1965) were less concerned with the horrific than with the extra-empirical dimension of the human—*bhatki hui aatmas*(lost souls), reincarnation, salvation—and with the manipulation of the ghostly by evil human agents.[6] The film historian Pete Toombs confirms this judgment in his comprehensive essay on the history of the Indian horror film, where he observes that "horror was more or less unknown in Indian cinema before the 1970s."[7]

Classic Hindi cinema's disavowal of horror was hardly an exception when one surveys various national cinemas in the global South. Writing on Turkish cinema's golden age, Kaya Ozkaracalar observes that almost all genres flourished in this period, but "besides a few isolated exceptions, it seems that the horror genre was largely missing from the scene."[8] Again, according to Viola Shafik, among the twenty-five hundred full-length feature films produced so far in Egyptian cinema, it seems that only three films deserve to be classified as horror.[9] And in responding to a film critic's article, "Where Has All the Horror Gone?" Mauro Rumbocon points out that a "tentative survey of Philippine film output from 1927 to 1994 reveals a more or less consistent number of horror films produced, namely, one to two percent of the annual output."[10] Even in countries where horror has subsequently flourished, it was absent in the decades under consideration. Thus, one historian of Indonesian film terms the period 1980–86 as the early years of horror,[11] while the reemergence of horror film in Thailand occurred as late as the 1990s with the release of the ghost film *Nang Nak* (1999).[12]

The question of horror's belated arrival in these contexts cannot be properly answered here, but a tentative list of possible explanations would include the following: middle-class censorship of the cinema of sensation, budgeting constraints that limited the scope of special effects, distribution protocols that inveighed against genre-formation, as well as the anthropological fact that many of these cultures exhibit a widespread belief in the existence and efficacy of ghosts and other supernatural entities. Toombs argues that the problem for Indian filmmakers is that it is much harder to exploit images of the otherworldly "precisely because they aren't hidden or lost. They are still very much present in the public's mind as living, contemporary ideas."[13] My intent in the following pages is not to explain the delay in horror's arrival—if that is even possible—but to delineate how the genre has functioned in both its B-circuit and A-circuit incarnations. In doing so, I intend to demonstrate how the process of upgrading enables the genre to produce a radical version of the nucleated couple that is synchronous with developments in social life.

Recall that Bollywood in the 1970s was marked by the gradual dissolution of the classic paradigm, one consequence of which was the replacement of the omnibus form known as the "social film" by the more campy *masala* (lit., a mixture of spices). This same decade also witnessed the rise of horror as a distinct genre of filmmaking.[14] The social film had survived so long as Hindi cinema's sole genre because, as Madhava Prasad has argued, its artisanal mode of production obviated the need for any further genre formation.[15] Since the different elements in the typical film—stars, song and dance, dialogues, comic interludes, choreographed fight sequences—were autonomously valued, all films tried to optimize these multiple streams of profit. There was thus no competitive advantage to specialization and hence no need for the formation of separate genres. The emergence of horror in the early seventies signals the end of one era of Hindi filmmaking and points to the shape of things to come.

Many in the initial wave of horror films were successful in the mainstream circuit. *Nagin* (Female snake, Raj Kumar Kohli, 1976), a revenge saga starring several Bollywood heavyweights like Sunil Dutt, Jeetendra, Rekha, and Reena Roy, was a great success, as was Kohli's subsequent effort *Jaani Dushman* (Life's enemy, 1979). The public were also treated to two notable *Exorcist* remakes—1977's *Jadu Tona* (Black magic, Raveekant Nagaich) and the arty *Geharayee* (Abyss, Vikas Desai and Aruna Raje, 1980). One of the superstars of the previous decade, Rajesh Khanna, took on the role of a horrific serial killer in the 1980 Dario Argento–inspired *Red Rose* (Bharathi Raja), and he followed this a few years later with the campy *Woh Phir Aayegi* (She will return, B. R. Ishaara, 1988). These sporadic hits notwithstanding, horror did not really take hold in mainstream cinema. Indeed, the single most important event in the history of Indian horror film occurred inconspicuously with the release of *Ek Nanhi Munni Ladkhi Thi* (There was a young girl, Vishram Bedekar, 1970). Produced by F. U. Ramsay, the film, based on a father-daughter relationship, was not a big hit, but one particular sequence of the film—featuring a monster—proved to be irresistible to audiences. The Ramsay Brothers (as F. U. and his five sons were collectively known) realized that they had stumbled onto a gold mine and proceeded to release a series of sensationally successful, low-budget horror films that included such hits as *Do Gaz Zameen Ke Neeche* (Two feet under, Tulsi Ramsay, 1972), *Darwazaa* (Door, Shyam and Tulsi Ramsay, 1978), *Hotel* (Shyam and Tulsi Ramsay, 1981), *Veerana* (Loneliness, Shyam and Tulsi Ramsay, 1988), and *Shaitani Illaka* (Devil's domain, Kiran Ramsay, 1990). The first wave of horror was largely driven by the Ramsay brothers. Some noted directors like Mohan Bhakri and Vinod Talwar did enter the fray, but most of the other figures of the early era were undistinguished Ramsay clones and are long forgotten.

What enabled the sudden horror boom of the seventies and eighties?[16] The answer lies in both generic logic and industrial practice. The reigning generic form—the *masala*—lacked the social film's integrative drive and was thus more accommodating of diverse cinematic material. Most Ramsay films were structurally *masala*—they had song-and-dance sequences, action fights, comedy routines, and family melodrama—while featuring curses, monsters, and gory slayings as major themes. In other words horror was hatched as a unique form by being placed inside a more capacious genre. As one perceptive Ramsay fan puts it, "Like most Indian horror movies, Ramsay Brothers films do not closely resemble what most people think of as a horror movie, in that they simply add an additional horror 'track' to the traditional Bollywood formula. Thus, viewers of a Ramsay movie should be prepared for a lot of other elements that may or may not have any connection to the movie's central supernatural plot—singing, dancing, melodrama, and alleged "comedy."[17] Thus, the eighties horror film still remained within the horizon of *masala*, even though—as we shall see below—it stretched this form to its limits.

If the horror film's popularity was parasitic on that of *masala*, a secondary and equally important reason for its enormous success had to do with its commercial status. Because it could not capture the mainstream market, the genre got plugged into what was known in India as the B circuit. This vast sector of the film industry consisted of small distribution companies dealing in low-budget products, reruns, soft porn, downmarket imports, dubbed films from other languages, and other marginal products. B movies typically played in decrepit movie theaters that operated on razor-thin margins in lower-income urban and suburban neighborhoods, small towns, and the semirural hinterlands. As S. V. Srinivas has noted, the severely undercapitalized B circuit is "witness to repeated interventions by both distributors and exhibitors which result in the destandardization of a film's status as an industrial product. Another distinction of the B circuit is its questionable legality: condemned prints, uncensored films, censored films with sexually explicit interpolations, and prints whose rights have lapsed are to be found circulating here."[18] Horror as a genre possessed attributes—sensationalism, action-oriented plot line, simplistic structure, low production cost—that made it ideal for this improvised and ramshackle circuit of exhibition and reception. Further, new technologies that were leading to a decline in the movie-going public also spurred the genre film. The introduction of the VCR meant that Indian directors now had far greater access to foreign (mainly American) material and were able to "rip off" stories from these sources. Mohan Bhakri, for example, would ask his assistants to watch two Hollywood horror films every day to find out what effects and stunts could be "sampled" for the film he was working on. Whether "stolen" or not, plot lines were invariably formulaic, making the product easier for audiences to absorb. A tongue-in-cheek web posting entitled "How to Make a Ramsay Horror Flick" provides a realistic recipe for the generic horror text: "The film should always have a dark flashback beginning. Now the film should time travel roughly by 100–150 years A.D. (after demon). . . . The heroine should be 'ultra modern' which means she should be very 'open.' And by open we don't just mean open-minded" . . . and so on for fourteen easy steps.[19]

Given the genre's positioning in the B circuit, production values were on a low budget. Thus, though horror films replicated the tendency of the *masala* film to hedge its bets by featuring multiple stars, their casts comprised second-tier actors and actresses. The Ramsay films did have a constant pool of fairly well regarded actors, including the veteran Deepak Parashar, the sirens Huma Khan and Aarti Gupta, and the comedians Jagdeep and Rajendranath, but these were the exception rather the rule. The same logic was employed when it came to producers, directors, scriptwriters, and music directors. To take one example, while the 1962 hit *Bees Saal Baad* employed the famed composer Hemant Kumar to write the score—one of the songs from its soundtrack, "Kahin Deep Jale Kahin Dil," won both the Filmfare Best Lyricist and Filmfare Best Female Playback Awards that year—eighties horror films invariably had indifferent music scores composed by undistinguished musicians. Nor was there any motivation to upgrade the product; despite the box-office success they enjoyed, the Ramsays did not increase their budget and production values significantly and continued to target the same audience as before. The entire Ramsay oeuvre (and that of its imitators) is unmistakably B-movie: garish and unconvincing sets, monsters that veered to the side of kitsch (frightening animals, leather-masked demons), imitative stories (clones of *The Exorcist*, Hammer Films–inspired Gothic horror, avatars of Hollywood monsters like Jason and Freddie), and predictable narratives.

This product—based largely on sensation and spectacle—was ideal for its audience. The guiding assumption was, as Pete Toombs puts it, "that they will be most popular with rural audiences and the urban poor and treated as rather a joke by everyone else."[20] I propose to analyze the fundamental features of B-horror by looking at two films that are recognized universally as Ramsay classics. In 1984 the Ramsays released the title most associated with the Indian horror boom—*Purana Mandir* (The ancient temple, Shyam and Tulsi Ramsay). Then in 1990 they released what would be their last hit, *Bandh Darwaza* (The closed door, Shyam and Tulsi Ramsay). Though they had numerous hits in their thirty-year career, these two classics embody the essence of the Ramsay approach.

## Purana Mandir *(The Ancient Temple)*

*Purana Mandir* has a plot line that was standard in the Ramsay oeuvre: following a violent standoff, a rich feudal landlord is cursed by the demonic magician Saamri: every woman in his family is condemned to die at childbirth. We flash forward around one hundred and fifty years to the present (1980s India). The last male descendant of the family's line has one child—a daughter—and he is determined to avoid the curse by not allowing her to marry. This is in keeping with Hindi melodrama's standard formula that has the father strongly opposing his daughter's desires. The girl and her suitor, however, are equally determined that their love should bear fruit and resolve to remove the curse once and for all. They journey back to the ancestral mansion that is adjacent to the old temple after which the movie is named. After a series of encounters that involve a lot of carnage, the demon Saamri is vanquished through the power of the holy *trishul* (a Hindu ornamental weapon) and then exorcised through burning (fig. 12). While the film is full of thrills and wonderfully creative in its depiction of monstrosity and human attempts to come to terms with it, what is equally striking is how it well it functions as a platform for generic multitasking. First, scenes of horror are punctuated by the numerous song-and-dance sequences typical of all Bollywood products. Unlike the standard *masala* film, however, the *Purana Mandir* song-and-dance sequences serve no apparent diegetic purpose: the couple in question are not courting but already betrothed. The film also contains a comedic module involving goofy fights between a local leader and his followers and a group of inept and cartoonish gangsters. This subplot has a very tenuous relation to the main story line—the hero's friend becomes "pals" with the gangster boss in order to make money off the local leader—and thus functions as an almost entirely autonomous component. The

12 Saamri, an old-school Bollywood monster. (From Shyam Ramsay's *Purana Mandir* [The ancient temple], 1984.)

comedic routine is highly motivated in being a parody of the enormously popular Hindi "Western" *Sholay* (Flames, Ramesh Sippy, 1975). In other words it functions hypertextually, as a link to participatory culture that evokes the social life of cinema, and exhibits the self-reflexivity that has characterized Hindi film form since the 1970s.[21]

### *Bandh Darwaza* (The Closed Door)

*Bandh Darwaza* reprises many of *Purana Mandir*'s main features—a primal event from the past with macabre consequences, a young couple in love, song-and-dance routines, many fight sequences, and a fearsome monster (Nevla), played by *Purana Mandir*'s Ajay Agarwal. As one would expect, the difference between the two formulas is negligible: whereas the monster Saamri merely destroys, Nevla sucks blood and thereby acquires a sexual dimension that the former lacked.

What theoretical insights can we glean from these two paradigmatic texts? First, Ramsay horror functions exclusively in the field of the social. The horrific is evident to and impinges on all the characters that populate the text, and its exorcism is also collectively enacted. The realm of the monster is immanent and continuous with the human one. In other words, ghosts or demons not only exist, but they do so in a space approachable by humans. Thus, in both *Purana Mandir* and *Bandh Dar-waza*, the protagonist-couple (whose mission is to lift the curse that hangs over their family) can journey right into interior spaces that houses the malevolent spirit. In *Purana Mandir* these are the ancient (*purana*) temple, where Saamri's beheaded corpse is interred, and the medieval dungeon hidden in the depths of the old family home, where his head lies entombed. In *Bandh Darwaza* these are the labyrinthine rooms of a house hidden atop the notorious Black Mountain. The boundary between monster-space and human-space is completely permeable, allowing unrestricted passage from both sides. Thus, monster-space is entirely within the ambit of the social. No better proof of this is required than the last episodes of both films, in which the burning (and consequent exorcising) of the demon happens in front of a large assembly of villagers. It is the not the body of the protagonist but the entire body politic that is rid of the curse in these final scenes.[22]

This conception of horror is therefore quite different from Hollywood's. Here, ghosts, demons, and other supernatural entities are imagined as inhabiting a space that is adjacent to the natural world, whereas in Hollywood, the horrific is situated at the psychic level. Consequently Hindi horror cinema cannot be analyzed by standard Western theories of the genre. For example, Robin Wood's seminal thesis—that the function of the horror film is to challenge our established notions of normality through the figure of the Monster[23]—would be hard to apply to Ramsay horror films. To take their immanent entities and ask them to stand in for repressed objects (as the Monster does in the Wood thesis) may be placing too great an ontological burden on them.[24] This is not to argue that Indian society is nonrepressive, but to make the much more limited claim that figures like Saamri and Nevla cannot, by dint of their semantic and cultural status, *represent* counterhegemonic forces as Wood and his followers envision them. Precisely because Saamri is posited as actually existing, he cannot, in the language of semiotics, function as a signifier for anything else. Nor is the typical Ramsay text amenable to the sort of psychoanalytically based feminist analysis that sees horror as an instance of the male gaze.[25] The Ramsay monster does not discriminate between genders. Saamri, for example, attacks individual women and men, and even the entire social network where the protagonists are located. It is interesting to note that New Bollywood horror films introduce a "gendering" that is quite absent in Ramsay horror. In New Horror classics like *Raat* (Night, Ram Gopal Varma, 1991) and *Bhoot* (Ghost, Ram Gopal Varma, 2003) it is always the woman who is privy to the ghost world and is possessed by it. The designation of the woman as victim, I argue, is crucial to New Horror's strategic aims—encumbering the woman in this way keeps the couple apart and not fully realized, thus enabling the narrative to stitch the couple back together in a newly fashioned manner.

The Ramsay world posits an epistemology of horror that has a strong bearing on the question of couple-formation. Neither member of the conjugal pair is privileged with respect to monster space; what they know, either individually or as a pair, is common stock, in principle knowable by all humans. In most films of the period, the demon is revealed to and accessed by all and sundry—parents, friends, even strangers. Thus, in both *Purana Mandir* and *Bandh Darwaza*, the protagonist-couple "share" the horror with another couple, the father of the female protagonist, and numerous family retainers. Their relationship with the monster is therefore "objective" in a way that tales of possession are not. This objectivity is further secured by the placement of horror alongside songs, fights, romance, and comedy. This amounts to a sort of "secularization" in the sense that the horror world gets no ontological priority in the diegesis. In sum, though the couple in these movies is thrown into the horror world, the being of the couple is in no way dependent on the devolution of the horrific. Horror is external to the couple, which is fully constituted prior to its emergence and is in no way modified or modulated by its agency. That is why horror never strikes inside the home, for to do so would take it outside of the ambit of the social. In both *Purana Mandir* and *Bandh Darwaza* the couple *travel* to encounter horror. There is a telling moment in *Bandh Darwaza*. When Nevla approaches the hero's friend's wife (illustrating once again its social networking aspect), who is in her bedroom, he looks through a lattice window at her and calls to her. She obeys and becomes his next victim. The woman's fate is inevitable; what is significant here is the monster's inability to cross into her private space. As an utterly objective entity, it is unable to operate at the level of the psychic and is compelled to lure its victim into the space of the social.

To sum up: Horror appeared late in the history of Indian cinema, and when it did so, it was not as a full-blown genre but as a variation on the dominant *masala* format. The fact that horror needed to be housed within *masala* suggests that it had not yet found its true form. For all its popularity, Ramsay horror remained in the B circuit and could never acquire the respectability accorded to mainstream productions. Only with its upgrading in the post-liberalization era does horror begin to emerge as a distinct and legitimate film genre. The "incompleteness" of horror in the Ramsay era is, as I have shown above, signaled by the relative unimportance of the couple-form. In both *Purana Mandir* and *Bandh Darwaza* the lead couples are already conjugated, and the horrific is not at all instrumental in their consolidation. Couple-formation, however, does become central to contemporary Indian horror cinema, and this shift points us toward the genre's evolution into the discursive form that I call New Bollywood.

## The Beginning of New Horror

Ram Gopal Varma's *Raat*, was released in 1991, the same year in which the Indian economy underwent a sea change by being "liberalized."[26] A commercial failure, the film owes much of its plot to *The Exorcist* (William Friedkin, 1973), though it is also clearly influenced by a number of other Hollywood classics, including *The Evil Dead* (Sam Raimi, 1981), *The Amityville Horror* (Stuart Rosenberg, 1979), *A Nightmare on Elm Street* (Wes Craven, 1984) and *Friday the 13th* (Sean S. Cunningham, 1980). The story revolves around a case of possession. A middle-class family moves into a house with a bad reputation. Soon afterward, Mini, the college-student daughter of the family, becomes possessed by a spirit. The film's controlled storytelling, inventive camerawork, complex sound design, non-Bollywood cast, and deliberate disavowal of song-and-dance sequences and comic routines—in short its realistic protocols and its Hollywood-inflected idiom of horror—mark it as a product that is entirely different from horror of the Ramsay school. In what follows, I offer a close reading of this seminal film to show how Varma's work can be seen as a blueprint for a new articulation of horror.

*Raat*'s desire to liberate horror from the *masala* format is diegetically captured through two crucial dream sequences. The first, set in a movie theater, depicts Mini, her college sweetheart, and another couple cutting classes in order to watch a popular film. The sequence opens with the group making its way through a crowded lobby, purchasing snacks, and settling into a massive, single-screen theater. This set of shots provides us with a glimpse into the social life of middle-class moviegoing, circa 1990. While we never see any of the film Mini watches, we can guess that it must be a *masala* movie, since spectators are shown first with serious expressions and then laughing uncontrollably. The audience is loud and boisterous, and the communal aspect of moviegoing is emphasized through long and mid-shots that show rows of moviegoers, responding similarly to the film. We cut to the first close-up of Mini, and almost immediately the ambient noises cease, and the sound of Mini's laughter is isolated. We realize, a split second before she does, that something is amiss, and almost immediately the camera pulls out and up to reveal an empty theater. It cuts to an extreme long shot of the absolutely deserted theater, and is now placed behind and above her. It then cuts to a mid-shot of Mini's growing bewilderment and next cuts to frame her from the back, now at mid-distance and slowly creeping up. She whips around with a start, and we cut to a bird's-eye view. She begins to panic and runs out into an empty lobby, rushing to the entrance only to realize that it is locked. During this segment, she is framed frontally, often in extreme long shot. She looks to the manager's office and sees that someone is in there with her back to her. She approaches slowly, the camera tracking from behind. This long take follows Mini as she walks up to and enters the office. She approaches the chair, the low camera angle emphasizing her dread, and spins it around to find herself confronted with her double. The scene finally cuts back to the theater to reveal that Mini has been hallucinating.

The movie-theater sequence in *Raat*, I suggest, has two crucial moments—the emptying out of the cinema hall while a movie is in progress, and the director's citation of *Psycho* (Alfred Hitchcock, 1960)—the chair with its back to us and a swift, swiveling revelation. At the beginning of the sequence we are in the terrain of the classic Hindi film—at the level of the product as well as the exhibition infrastructure and viewing practices. By suddenly emptying the movie theater, Varma creates a tabula rasa on which he can then inscribe his new vision of cinema and its more individuated mode of spectatorship. By referencing *Psycho*, Varma announces a radical break with Ramsay horror and posits that the genre must henceforth be thought of in psychological terms. This break is also symbolized by Varma's painstaking detailing of movie-theater architecture—luxurious seats, sparkling corridors, gleaming window panes—in short, a milieu quite the polar opposite of B-circuit movie theaters.

Varma explicitly enunciates his new approach to horror at the very beginning of the film. The opening sequence comprises three points of view: that of Mini, the impartial camera, and of the eye of horror. What is crucially important is that the source of horror is never represented—seen from an objective perspective. Instead, its presence is established by placing us in its optic space. In other words, the socially available monster that characterized the Ramsay film is replaced here by an invisible entity whose existence is never given but is apprehended by a play among the various points of view. The scene takes place in a neighborhood that is utterly deserted: the half-finished buildings, peeling walls, empty sheds, boarded fronts, spreading brambles, and a vintage car left to rust all conjure the sinister emptiness of a ghost town. As the credits roll, the soundtrack layers a woman's cries and howling wind noises with the music of dread—screeching wails, thudding percussion beats—that is the staple of horror. The frame is completely dark except for a thin, wavering crack of light through a closed door. As the credits conclude, the door swings open, and we follow the Steadicam across the courtyard as it turns into a narrow alley and then left again past some thorny bushes. The camera's itinerary suggests that each time it comes upon a clearing it prefers to veer into alleys and cul-de-sacs. We hear the faraway beep of a horn, and the camera immediately follows this sound, snakes its way through a lane, past the abandoned car, and onto a main road. It spots in extreme screen left an approaching bus—the source of the beeping sound—and as the bus approaches, the camera quickly retreats behind some branches. It is now a hidden camera. The sequence cuts for the first time to an overhead shot of a girl who gets off the bus. The next few cuts are organized by an impartial point of view: the bus speeds away, the girl looks around and starts walking down the path that we have just traversed. We cut back to the stalking Steadicam, which now follows her in a continuous take. As though sensing its pursuit, she whips around, and the scene cuts to another overhead shot. As the sequence progresses, the girl gets increasingly panicked, rushes toward the abandoned car, and we see her growing terror in a series of reaction shots. She runs through the neighborhood, banging on closed doors, darting into lanes, and finally goes through the doorway into the room from which the Steadicam had emerged. This segment shows the interplay of three points of view: those of the stalking camera, the protagonist, and the more objective third eye. At no point are we privy to what makes her afraid, since our point of view always coincides with that of the stalking camera. This is horror without objectivity—pure affect, the protagonist's and ours. Curiously, this opening segment is revealed to be a dream sequence whose various elements have no relation whatsoever to the subsequent diegesis. It is structurally similar to the prelude of the standard Ramsay films, which stage the original event that sets up the chain of horror (or, to state it in terms of the Hollywood formula, the occasion of repression that sets up the return, as in *Friday the 13th*). However, its valence is radically different, insofar as it is entirely an interior event. First, it is Mini's dream, and then it institutes a new phenomenology of horror that is predominantly psychological. This is established through technologies—Steadicam, multilayered sound design—that are novel to Hindi cinema.[27] It is worth noting that the opening credits reverse the conventions of *masala* films that give top billing to stars. Here, the Steadicam operator, stereo mixer, audio designer, and other specialists get first mention to signal their central role in creating new techniques of horror.

Why, then, are these new techniques embedded in virtual sequences and not in the actual story world? A brief survey of audience reception suggests that these scenes are among the film's most memorable—readers on fan sites repeatedly attest to this.[28] One viewer even complains that the "music and dream sequences make the film seem scarier than it is," while several note that the thrilling promise of these dream sequences is belied when the film enters the actual territory of the supernatural. One particularly astute viewer on the Internet Movie Database blog (http://www.imdb.com) suggests that the film might be a metaphor for schizophrenia, so that Mini's hallucinations and her subsequent possession might be one and the same thing.[29] Varma's own comments bear out this psychological provenance of terror:

If you are alone at home at night and you hear a moaning kind of sound from inside a room where no one is supposed to be there, the slow wary walk of yours towards the room to check the source of the sound is when you will be scared maximum. *That is because your own imagination takes over your mind.* But once you see the source no matter how dangerous or frightening it is, you will either scream for help or run or attack it depending on you as an individual. You will simply jump into a defense mode and *your fear at this time will be much lesser that what it was during the walk* [my emphases].[30]

If, according to Varma, true fear is that which is psychologically activated, it stands to reason that those sections of *Raat* where the body rather than the mind is possessed are less terrifying. While the body possessed might create visual and visceral excitement, such thrills are no innovation in the spectacle-driven *masala* tradition, where such sensations are par for the course. But fear that dwells in the imagination can only be apprehended through a private communion between the story world and viewer. Not only does this psychologically anchor the film's characters, conferring them with interiority, but, more crucially, it unequivocally *produces* the viewer as a privatized spectator and embeds him in a new regime of sensation. The stalking camera foregrounds film spectatorship as voyeurism, and in the frontally oriented Hindi cinema, where the viewer's voyeurism is far from secure, psychological horror might indeed help install the viewer as an individuated subject. In order to break with the dominant form that Hindi cinema calls the social film, society must first be dissolved. But in *Raat* this evacuation of the social can only happen in the virtual domain of a dream. As the viewer quoted above notes, "I would guess that the creepiness of such 'ghost town' isolation might hit native Indians even harder, as it's probably unusual to find such a deserted town, and especially unusual for someone to exit a bus without being met by family or friends."[31] Sponseller claims, in other words, that public life in India, indexed by a "realistic" film like *Raat*, does not support such radical isolation—not, at least, at this temporal and spatial juncture. Simply put, such sequences lack verisimilitude. Thus the film needs to naturalize such sequences as dreams. As Varma learns, for psychological horror to take hold, it has to move indoors. Moreover, it has to find the adequate social materials—a newly married couple looking for a home, a nuclear family—in order for horror to do its work. While his next film *Kaun* (Who is it? 1999) is set indoors, its protagonist is a sociopath, not a ghost. We have to wait until *Bhoot*—which fans have called "the finished version of *Raat*"[32]—for these new technologies of horror to find an upmarket sociology appropriate to it.

The preceding discussion of Varma's films points us toward what may be the most appropriate methodology for studying contemporary Indian horror. In trying to work out the logic of Varma's cinematic techniques, I am implicitly recommending that we work with a conception of horror that shifts the focus from what the text *represents* to what it *does*. This means that we pay closer attention to the materiality of the film—the bits and pieces of filmic matter like sounds, interiors, perspectives, dialogue— as well as the way it interfaces with the sociocultural matrix within which it operates. In the concluding section of this chapter, I bring such an approach to bear upon the contemporary Hindi horror film in order to bring to light the objects it is composed of and the larger world to which it connects. For the purposes of my analysis, I focus on two sets of interiors that these films vividly explore—the domestic interiors of the urban living spaces where the protagonists of these films are placed and live their lives and the psychological interior of couple-space that the texts create by means of the plotlines and the storytelling conventions that they employ. To inhabit these interiors is to claim a stake in the emerging social formations and modes of consciousness of which the genre of horror is an index.

## Rings of Fire

The preceding discussion has gestured toward the main constituents of new Indian horror. To be more explicit: New Horror is based on an individualistic psychology rather than folklore and group dynamics. It focuses on nucleated, middle-class couples rather than traditional extended families, it utilizes advanced technologies rather than kitschy art to obtain its effects, and it speaks to an emergent socioeconomic order that is beginning to replace the formation that was postcolonial India. To analyze the reformatting of horror, one must pay close attention to the objective makeup of the screen images in order to trace how horror constitutes the couple and how, in turn, this new couple-form calls up the entire network within which New Bollywood cinema is implicated. This means that the study of New Horror has less to do with an examination of monsters than with an inquiry into things, technologies, and networks.

Let us begin by comparing the respective sites of haunting in old and New Horror. The Ramsay films we have looked at begin by depicting the protagonists living in respectable, middle-class homes. What is interesting here is that the monster's powers are very weakly present in these modern locales. In *Purana Mandir*, for example, the curse that the monster Saamri had cast upon Raja Harimansingh's family—that every daughter would die at childbirth—holds true wherever the descendants of the clan reside. However, Saamri, who is interred in an old temple in the countryside, can do no harm to these city folk. In fact, the viewer is justified in asking whether he is even capable of moving in contemporary space-time.[33] It is crucial that in order to exorcise the original curse that motivates the narrative, the protagonists (Suman and Sanjay) have to journey back to the hinterland to confront the monster in its age-old dwelling. The crumbling structures that they encounter not only create an atmosphere of mystery and dread, they impose an anteriority on the monster—the "time of the monster" is bygone time, distant time. The fact that the protagonists must go *back* to encounter him establishes his temporality as essentially that of the past. Thus the monster's "place"—quite literally his residence—determines his effectivity. Since the monster is thus condemned to the past, he is rendered incapable of impinging on the present. Saamri may terrify Suman and Sanjay, but he can in no way alter their mode of being in the world. In other words, the monstrous has little bearing on the constitution of modernity and of modern subjectivity.

Horror in New Bollywood cinema makes a radical break with past cinematic tradition. In the films that characterize New Horror, spirits—who replace monsters like Saamri—dwell together with the protagonists in modern apartment buildings or bungalows. Very often, these are new accommodations, signifying an orientation toward approaching terrors rather than ancient curses. Thus, in Ram Gopal Varma's *Raat* and *Bhoot* the haunting occurs in dwellings—the first set in a single-family home in a middle-class neighborhood, the other in an urban high-rise—that the protagonists are just moving into.[34] In *1920* (Vikram Bhatt, 2008), horror strikes as the couple arrive at a large mansion that the architect husband has been commissioned to turn into a luxury hotel, while in

*Vaastu Shastra* (Feng shui, Saurabh Narang, 2004) the site of haunting is a beautiful, eco-friendly home that the family moves into to escape the heat and dust of inner-city living. Most recently, in *13B: Fear Has a New Address* (Vikram Kumar, 2009), a long-desired apartment that fulfills the protagonists desire for home ownership turns out to be peopled by the specters whose single-family home had been razed to construct this apartment building. Varma's recent film, *Phoonk* (Scare, 2008)—his third remake of *The Exorcist*—is also obsessed with habitation. The protagonist, a construction engineer entrusted with designing a mini-city project, ignores the requests of his laborers that he construct a shrine to propitiate the resident deities before commencing the project. He pays a price when these spirits take their revenge inside his own home.

In all these films, the wrath of the spirits is triggered by an action in the relative present. In the Ramsay model, the primal event occurred a long time ago, though its potency survives to the present. Saamri's curse, for example, lay on the Harimansingh family for well over two centuries. Yet it was an inert spell, in the sense that future events (except the eventual exorcising) had no effect on it. Suman is doomed to die at childbirth regardless of how she conducts her life. In New Horror, on the other hand, it is one's desire for the future that triggers horror. In a remarkable scene in *Bhoot*, Vishal, the husband, meets with a real estate agent in search of the dream apartment. As he drives Vishal around, nothing that the agent shows him catches his eye. Vishal then spots one complex that appeals to him and he asks if anything is available there. The agent says yes, and when Vishal queries him as to why he hadn't mentioned it earlier, the agent apologizes and says that he had been silent about this apartment because there had been a mysterious death in it a while back. Vishal is both amused and irritated—he cannot believe that the agent allowed superstition to get in the way of business practices. He orders the agent to show him the flat, likes what he sees, and lets the agent know that he wants to sign the lease immediately. This "point of purchase" episode is extremely significant in what it tells us about New Horror as a whole. Vishal's decision emphatically prioritizes the future over the past. From Vishal's perspective, not only does the agent bring up an irrelevant past event, but his apprehension about the mysterious death also signals an outmoded way of thinking. Vishal's vote for the future signifies a crucial truth: unlike the classic version of horror that dwelled in the retrospective mode, contemporary horror is ineluctably joined to futurity. This temporal disposition allows horror to be productive in ways that go beyond the thrilling, for it can now play a constitutive role in the formation of modernity. Thus horror, like the multiplot films discussed in the next chapter, exemplifies an upbeat, upscale style of moviemaking that works as the perfect synecdoche for the exuberant promotion of the modern typified by political slogans like "India Shining," public personalities whose signature gesture is the high-five, and endless commercials with the punch line "Let's Go!"

New Horror wants to possess the future, and this desire is played upon and literalized by means of a fixation on possessions. Films like *Bhoot* and *13B* pay an inordinate amount of attention to the material circumstances in which the protagonists live their lives. The same restless camera whose point of view will be appropriated by the spirit (and coincide, as is often the case, with that of the spectator) is first employed to orient us to their habitations. We follow the Steadicam/tracking shot from room to room, along corridors, across hallways, pausing at stairwells, ducking into corners. We stop to take in the arrangement of furniture, knick-knacks, home electronics, appliances, mirrors, and so on; we close in on objects on a side table or pull back to gaze at the arrangement of blue pottery in a shelving unit. The layout of the apartment and its contents are made so familiar to us that a critic can complain that in Ram Gopal Varma's *Phoonk*, "a lot of screen time is wasted showing us the interior designing [*sic*] of the house."[35] The covetous attention the camera confers on these spaces and objects to make them phenomenally vivid for us might be the very reason that this object world is later animated. As Varma himself notes, "When we with the whole family leave the house and go on a holiday for a few days, when we return, open the lock and step inside, a thought fleetingly might cross our minds, what the house and the various objects in the house have been up to while you were away. Can we be really sure that the various inanimate things in our house we so take for granted in the course of the day don't really come alive in the night after we go to sleep?"[36]

The central figure of the modern horror film—the nuclear couple occupying an upscale domestic space—functions as what Bakhtin calls a "chronotope" in that it places the text in alignment with the vectors of post-liberalization India.[37] As we saw in the introduction, the remarkable growth in the economy made possible by the reforms of 1991 led to two secondary processes—the growth of the middle classes and the rise of a consumerist culture—that have radically shaped the image of contemporary India. The enormous cultural impact of India's recent economic growth—between 1980 and 2002 the national economy grew at 6 percent, and between 2002 and 2006 at a "sensational" 7.5 percent[38]—is a function of the country's long history of underdevelopment. For half a century before independence, the economy was literally stagnant: it grew by 0.8 percent per year, which was the same rate as population growth, which meant that there was no growth in per capita income. It is commonly believed that the "mixed economy" model introduced by Jawaharlal Nehru and continued under the government of Indira Gandhi was responsible for this tepid pace of development. There was no significant middle-class formation during this era—the population could still be divided into traditional elites and a large mass of rural and urban poor. Given that the elite itself subscribed to a Gandhian ideology of frugality and renunciation, conspicuous consumption was limited to a small coterie of feudal landlords and industrial magnates.

The post-liberalization expansion of the economy would lead to a significant increase in the size of the middle class, especially in urban areas. According to one analyst, between 1989 and 1999 the proportion of urban, middle-class households almost doubled.[39] This triggered a concomitant growth in consumption, which by 2006 accounted for 64 percent of India's GDP, compared to 58 percent for Europe, 55 percent for Japan, and 42 percent for China.[40] This propensity to consume would in turn make possible the emergence of a full-blown commodity culture. To take three telling examples that chart the growth in possession of consumer durables: between 1985 and 1995 the percentage of households that owned bicycles rose from 31 percent to 51 percent; those owning pressure cookers rose from 11 percent to 25 percent, and those owning black-and-white television sets from 4.7 percent to 24 percent.[41] The consumer revolution and the growth of the middle classes begin to alter the landscape of the city and of interior domestic spaces. Urban geographers have documented how the past two decades have been characterized by a frenetic building boom that replaced traditional dwellings with cost-efficient, high-rise apartment complexes (fig. 13).[42] As a recent study observes, the thrust of this urban planning is toward, "a series of rehabilitation and housing policies, and parallel regimes of demolitions and upgradations" that seek to eliminate "slum housing, mixed-use economies and informal settlements" that have characterized the "blurry urbanism" of Indian cities like Mumbai (fig. 14).[43]

This urbanization involves the construction not only of office buildings but also of residential spaces that aim at gentrification. The increasing imprint of the globalizing middle classes is evident in the recent emergence of gated communities and suburban condominium complexes that have come to dominate a landscape of working-class tenements, shantytowns, slums, and two- or three-story family homes that accommodated several generations of the extended family.[44] Sociologists have pointed out that this geographic reorganization corresponds to the emergence

13   Scene of construction. (From Vikram Kumar's *13B: Fear Has a New Address*, 2008.)

14   High-rise of horror. (From Ram Gopal Varma's *Bhoot* [Ghost], 2002.)

and consolidation of the nuclear household that now functions both as an economic and affective unit.[45] These developments, once viewed ambivalently as a necessary aspect of modernization, have now acquired a high degree of glamour by being linked with an upwardly mobile philosophy and lifestyle that everyone is asked to aspire to. Elaborating on this impulse, Leela Fernandes has shown how the middle classes invest in an urban aesthetic that aspires to a spatial separation between work and home, commercial and residential zoning, and an ordering by economic class.[46] These studies also document how the drive to streamline urban space is repeatedly thwarted by unplanned growth and resistance on part of the urban poor. Thus the middle-class dream of sanitized spaces that would resemble Singapore or Shanghai remains a work in progress awaiting completion in a "possible India."

Horror facilitates the formation of this consumerist vision by depicting and addressing the couple in its new milieu (figs. 15 and 16). As we have seen, most films—*Bhoot, Raat, Hawa,* and *13B* for example—are set in urban locales. Even when the countryside is depicted, the vantage remains urban. Thus in *Darna Mana Hai* (Fear is forbidden, Prawal Raman, 2003) and *Darna Zaroori Hai* (Be afraid, J. D. Chakravarti, 2006), a frame narrative set in the country embeds six separate fragments, mostly featuring thoroughly cosmopolitan characters. Moreover, the stories in these segments all use flashbacks to relocate the narrative in urban spaces. The countryside then, in a reversal of the pastoral itinerary of Hollywood horror, becomes a gateway for an excursion into the heart of the city. To take another example, when the setting is a mansion reminiscent of a bygone feudal era, the interior space is "apartmentalized"; that is, it is made functionally equivalent to a modern living space (fig. 17). Thus in *1920* the couple chooses to stay in a huge *haveli* (a traditional mansion that housed large extended families and so teemed with people) that turns out to be as nucleated as the apartments in *Bhoot* or *13B*. This evacuation must be read along with Varma's emptying out of the movie theater in *Raat*. In both cases a space that is densely social and heterogeneous is evacuated so that we may entertain the possibility of new modes of conjugality, new life-worlds, and a new cinema.

In every New Horror film the characters, the dialogue, the mise-en-scène, the very attitude of the film itself, are unmistakably middle-class.

15 Lisa and Arjun gaze at a dream home. (From Vikram Bhatt's *1920,* 2008.)

16　Vishal and Swati gaze at a dream home. (From Ram Gopal Varma's *Bhoot* [Ghost], 2002.)

17　Lisa and Arjun moving in. (From Vikram Bhatt's *1920*, 2008.)

Lead characters are young, college-educated, and Westernized. The rural and the urban poor are depicted only in secondary roles—as domestic help, service staff, or random figures that the protagonists briefly encounter. This marginalization is in stark contrast with Mumbai cinema's foregrounding of the underprivileged in previous decades—in *Awara* (Vagabond, Raj Kapoor, 1957), *Upkaar* (Good deed, Manoj Kumar, 1967), and *Deewar* (Wall, Yash Chopra, 1979), to cite the most obvious examples. Filmic dialogue accentuates the aspiratory status of the genre—most characters speak "Hinglish," a seamless mixture of English and Hindi that is fast becoming the lingua franca of India's emerging elite. Such a strategy amounts to a willing renunciation of film's large rural public, a sentiment harshly expressed by Ram Gopal Varma: "Anyone who looks at film as a formula of one song, two comedy scenes and three ac-tion scenes . . . is lost now. . . . With my films I am targeting the urban multiplexes, the sophisticated media-savvy crowd. I couldn't give a f— for the villages."[47]

This displacement of the working classes from the filmic frame is echoed, as we have seen, by the dream of gentrifying common spaces that haunts the Indian middle classes. In fact, film may be a step ahead of reality in this instance. Contemporary urban landscape is a chaotic mix of development and decay, aesthetics and opportunism, and wealth and poverty. As the following description of Mumbai reveals, "Today, the city's image consists of strange yet familiar juxtapositions—a roadside Hindu shrine abuts St. Thomas' Cathedral, chimney stacks are dwarfed by skyscrapers, fishing villages and slums nestle at the foot of luxury apart-ments, and bazaars occupy the Victorian arcades!"[48]

In New Horror, however, the landscape is almost fully cleansed of the unruly and the unorganized, a move made possible by the privileging of interior over the exterior, aligning the spatial imaginary of horror to the NRI films discussed in the previous chapter. As pointed out earlier, horror film devotes lengthy footage to an exploration of domestic space. Ranjini Mazumdar observes that the emphasis on design and the rise of scenic in-teriors in Hindi cinema of the 1990s led to a shift from location shooting to shooting on sets. Today, "the production of the interior has acquired a systematic approach enabled by the coming together of art directors, the advertising world, fashion designers, and the film industry."[49] This concerted attempt to create what one designer calls an "aspirational" space fits exceptionally well with horror's scopic drive. In its efforts to elicit the supernatural, the horror camera meticulously details the chic interiors that define a middle-class utopia (fig. 18). The repeated zooms on cars, elevators, windows, doors, stairwells, furniture, appliances, and even kitchen utensils construct a mobile catalogue of desirable objects.[50] The inventory on display may not equal that of the classic Bollywood in-terior, which was regally sumptuous, but it is much more *real*. Here tech-nology plays a big part, cameras like the Steadicam, close-ups, pan shots, and the innovative use of sound give us a much better sense of the actual presence of things. Further, the repeated representations of humans in-teracting with objects—people using cell phones, clicking on remotes, opening and locking doors, getting in and out of elevators, stir-frying food, driving to and fro to work—suggest a lifestyle that is inseparable from its commodities. We see, then, that the domestic interior and the sum of its possessions function as the central figure in New Horror film.

The concrete world that New Horror presents us with is not merely

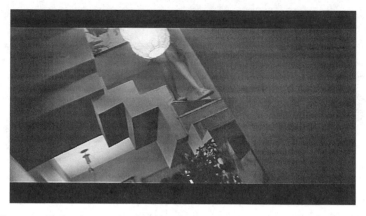

18 The camera looks askance at Swati and her domestic possessions. (From Ram Gopal Varma's *Bhoot* [Ghost], 2002.)

mise-en-scène but a composite of elements that connect the filmic space with a pro-filmic landscape of actual urban development, consumer culture, and class-formation. In other words, the movement between *Bandh Darwaza* and *Raat* is more than the shift from horrifying *masala* to horror as a distinct genre; it is simultaneously an index of the radical differences between Nehruvian and post-liberalization India. By constructing the couple-form as middle-class in its very essence, the horror film enables us to inhabit and travel in the spaces and pathways that make up twenty-first-century India. In her perceptive analysis of film noir, Vivian Sobchack observes that the scenes in noir films are often set in seedy lounges, bus-stations, hotel lobbies, and other such impersonal spaces. This is so, she says, because "lounge time in the mise-en-scène of noir is temporalized negatively as idle restlessness, as a lack of occupation, as a disturbing, ambiguous, and public display of unemployment" and because the "noir world of bars, diners, and seedy hotels . . . realizes a frightening reversal and perversion of home and the coherent, stable, idealized, and idyllic past of prewar American patriarchy and patriotism."[51] I want to argue along similar lines that the material possessions so abundantly displayed in New Horror, as well as the technology of presentation—the various experiments with camera and sound listed above—realize the matrix of tendencies that characterize contemporary Indian society. The choice of the urban, multistory apartment complex as the scene of horror, the accumulation of objects within the frame of the film, and the technologizing of the quotidian resonate with growth in new towns and cities, the burgeoning of shopping malls and luxury consumption, and the amplification of life through information and communication technologies.

I want to briefly indicate some other features of contemporary horror that reinforce my claim that the genre's distinctiveness lies in its articulation of the nucleated couple and its cinematic life-world with the "real" matrix of socioeconomic change. One noticeable aspect of all these films is the primacy of sound. While all horror films are perhaps more indebted to sound than other genres, noise plays an extraordinarily important role in new Indian horror. It operates at three levels—diegetic, soundtrack, and "social acoustics." At the diegetic level, the text continuously depicts machines that emit sounds—cell phones, blenders, television sets, elevators, buses, and bulldozers. The imposition of these soundscapes is nondiegetic: these mechanical noises constitute the voice of consumerism and modernity. At the level of the soundtrack, we are constantly bombarded with cascades of horror sounds that do more than terrify; they refer back to the pure materiality of sound,[52] and thus they take us to the third level, that of social acoustics. By this I mean that what becomes implicated here is not merely textual or affective events but also the entire apparatus of exhibition and screening: modern multiplex theaters with advanced Dolby sound systems that can effectively deploy the loud, multi-tonal sounds that characterize these films. By shading off into sheer volume and frequency, horror is positioned within the aural grid of modernity.

There is yet another interiority, that of the couple-form, whose modulations are of equal significance in understanding the significance of New Horror as a genre. A fundamental feature of New Horror is its representation of the couple as an isolated and autonomous dyad that is not subsumed by the social in the way that couples in classic Bollywood were. I want to suggest that this move serves the purpose of providing a model for a citizen-form that is demanded by the emerging globalized era. Such a project is enabled by the genre's intrinsic features; indeed, one can argue that horror is the post-liberalization genre par excellence because its formal properties are ideally suited for positing a new mode of subjectivity. It is worth noting here that horror is the only contemporary genre that predates liberalization. The other new forms that are emerging now—comedies like *Mujhse Shaadi Karogi?* (Will you marry me? David Dhawan, 2004), action films like *Dhoom* (Uproar, Sanjay Gadhvi, 2004), and science fiction works like *Koi . . . Mil Gaya* (I found someone, Rakesh Roshan, 2003)—are new inventions that have devolved from *masala*'s demise and do not have horror's extended genealogy. And while these new genres participate (though not equally) in the formation of new modes of subjectivity and sociality, horror's role in this process has greater heuristic value. As we have seen, horror coexisted with *masala* for two decades or so and then transformed itself at the turn of the century. This evolutionary path allows us to compare two distinctly different forms of horror and thus get a more precise fix on cinema and subjectivity in the contemporary period.

Horror as a genre operates through a strategy of individuation. In order to find its victim, the horrific must isolate the individual from the social order.[53] That is why the typical slasher film is based on a series of unconnected excursions in which the curious victim in each case leaves the security of the group and pays for this act of individual deviation at the hands of the monster-in-waiting:

After a drowning scare, a snake in a cabin and visits from both the law and Crazy Ralph, *Ned goes to investigate a noise in one of the cabins*, and doesn't come out. . . .

Jack is then stabbed through the neck with an arrow, and the killer leaves for the camp restroom. *Marcie goes to investigate a sound in the showers*, and the killer splits her face open with a vicious axe swing.

From her cabin, *Brenda hears a child crying in the woods and braves the storm*. As she slogs through the driving rain, the archery range is suddenly illuminated, with Brenda standing in front of the targets [my emphases].[54]

As the above plot summary for *Friday the 13th, Part 1* illustrates, horror beckons the individual away from the group and toward doom. However, it is not Ned or Brenda who is being individuated but the monstrous itself. All the victims in the horror film are indistinguishable from each other—who wants to remember Tina Gray or Steve Christy?[55] On the other hand, we are not allowed to forget Freddie Krueger or Jason Voorhees. In other words, Hollywood horror divides its cast into a set of interchangeable victims and one "abnormal" hyperindividual who is evil, potentially eternal, and, most important, unique. What we have here could qualify as a "universal law" of horror: in the Ramsay films for example the memorable characters (and hence the true individuals) are Saamri and Nevla.

New Indian horror enacts a reversal of this logic of individuation.[56] *Raat* inaugurates an alternative paradigm that differs from classic horror in almost every respect: The monster vanishes, to be replaced by an invisible spirit (*Raat, Bhoot, 1920*); this spirit has no substance, for it is merely the residue of a human who was unjustly killed (in *Bhoot* the spirit that haunts the apartment is that of a divorced woman murdered by a spurned lover); the horrific expresses itself by possessing the female protagonist and making her demonlike; and none of the lead characters die; rather, it is the spirit that is exorcised and released. The essential difference between these two paradigms boils down to the fact that whereas Western (and classic Hindi) horror focuses on the monster, New Bollywood focuses exclusively on the protagonist-couple. One could restate Robin Wood's seminal thesis by observing that Western horror creates the prototype of the "abnormal" individual so that it may threaten normality.[57] New Indian horror, on the other hand, is given the charge of producing normality itself in the form of the modern nucleated couple.[58]

Being "possessed," I argue, is as much a chronotope as domestic possessions. If horror's task is to delineate the citizen-couple appropriate for a post-liberalization economy, then it needs to identify and foreground the couple in the starkest possible manner. It makes sense, then, that horror dispenses with romantic love and focuses on the couple's postnuptial state—its point of departure *needs* to be the already married couple. Recall that the central concern of the social film (and the *masala*) was to portray the prenuptial state and offer the means by which a couple could be produced out of two lovers. This prenuptial love was acted upon by a variety of intervening forces, some that inhibited and others that facilitated the couple's goals. The former category included the unyielding patriarchal father; impediments of class and religion; and a second, more acceptable suitor, who was often a villain. The latter group usually consisted of an understanding mother, a helpful sidekick, and a wise guru. So urgent was this project of couple-formation that all other genres—gangster, comedy, and horror—had to be situated within the matrix of romantic love. New Horror and other genres of contemporary film, as we have seen, treat marriage not as end but as a premise. New Bollywood asserts that romantic union is no longer an issue, thus dissolving the foundational problem of the social film. Its protagonists are typically recently wed and about to inaugurate their lives in a new job, a new apartment, and a new city. At the same time, however, it acknowledges the existence of another problem, one that can serve as its own raison d'être. The social film, as many commentators have pointed out, enacted a compromise solution between the demands of feudal patriarchy and bourgeois love.[59] The conjugal pair that it held up to view in the closing shot may have emerged as a consequence of individualized romantic longing, but it subsequently has to be subsumed into the feudal extended family in order to be legitimate. The problem for new cinema is to start with this mixed mode of the couple-form and remold it into the heterosexual, nucleated unit we associate with modernity.

Of the many varieties of contemporary filmmaking, horror is best equipped for the task of redefining the couple. Owing to its formal structure, horror is able to put the couple under a spotlight and circumscribe it by a "ring of fire" that keeps the couple isolated from the rest of society. In every New Horror film, the couple must leave kith and kin in order to set the story in motion. In other words, the couple *must* be alone before the disaffected spirit that haunts them can show itself. Freed in this manner of its social moorings, the couple is presented in its purest form, as that which carries the potential to build a life. This new couple-in-the-making can now begin to construct its future—hence the detailed accounts of leasing, moving furniture, remodeling, decorating, and entertaining. The couple realizes itself through these lifestyle choices, and through their creation of a life, the abstract form of bourgeois conjugality is given an actual instantiation. The couple enacts itself through a plentitude of materials, but they remain utterly alone. The mystery as to why the "realism" of New Bollywood can be so unrealistic—why in *Bhoot* we never see other family members or friends until the very end, or why the mansion in *1920* is so deserted—is solved if we understand that its central concern is to project the metaphysical reality of the new couple-form. This theoretical commitment to a higher realism justifies New Horror's lack of fidelity to the purely empirical.

If empty apartments symbolize the ring of fire that horror institutes around the couple as a social unit, possession by a spirit is a second circle, this time around the individual psyche. Traditional Bollywood cinema (including Ramsay horror) disavowed psychology, for it represented a world in which the psyche was subsumed by the social. In this regime, an individual's role—father, son, daughter, servant, landlord, priest—determined his or her behavior; the psyche was a "black box" that remained inscrutable and therefore irrelevant. In order to postulate the nucleated couple-form, however, cinema must also introduce the level of psychology into its conception of character. If classic Hindi cinema always remained in the realm of social identity, New Bollywood had to delve into depth psychology, which alone can provide the ontological ground on which the new dyadic formation can stand. Recent cinema's use of technology illustrates how filmic technique serves a philosophical purpose. The increasing use of the point-of-view shot must be understood as a method that enables depth perception and thus signals the very possibility of psychology. The seeing camera has analogues in the cast of characters—hence the proliferation of psychologists, therapists, and psychiatrists in recent *hat-ke* film, as well the spate of movies about mentally and physically disabled people (e.g., Aparna Sen's *15 Park Av-*

*enue* [2005] and Sanjay Leela Bhansali's *Black* [2005]). It is also striking how the camera in the New Horror film shoots the couple and its habitat from a large number of angles and distances, announcing, as it were, that this couple is a specimen that needs to be cognized from an infinite number of perspectives. The camera's constant play of composition-decomposition-recomposition, suggests that the object it seeks to portray (the couple-form) is so nascent that it needs to be captured incessantly so that it cannot elude our grasp. The multiple angularity of vision in New Horror is a function of its creative role—it glances askance in order to produce the multifaceted couple.

I turn, finally, to the matter of possession. In Hollywood horror and in the Ramsay films, the monster demands that all humans be his victims. In New Horror, the spirit selects only one body to possess: Swati in *Bhoot*, Lisa in *1920*, Mini in *Raat*. In each of these instances, the spirit is entirely invisible to the male partner in the couple. In other words, New Horror builds *two* circles or rings of fire, one around the couple and the other around the female spouse. In each case, the male partner displays a high degree of skepticism about the existence of the spirit—in *Bhoot* for example, Vishal explains Swati's claim that there is someone else in the apartment as a case of misperception. When Swati's behavior becomes more extreme, he is convinced that she has developed some sort of psychological disorder and so takes her to a psychiatrist. Dr. Rajan confirms Vishal's hypothesis but is unable to effect a cure. At this point we have an unbridgeable distance between husband and wife: each spouse's belief system (and hence behavior) is incommensurable with the other's. Thus horror' s first move via possession is to radically separate the couple-form into its constituent parts. Horror's first appearance helps to posit the individual (here the female subject) as individual, unsupported by any other social relation, including marriage. Horror's second moment is conjugative: as the spirit gets more possessive, through bouts of convulsions and fits, female subjectivity is annulled as the woman becomes pure body. This is the juncture at which the husband "converts" from scientific rationalism to a helpless ecumenism that will grasp at any straw in search of a cure. That the exorcism is conducted through the agency of a shamanlike figure (often a woman) merely signifies that reconjugation—for at this moment the couple is reconstituted and (figuratively) retakes its vows—needs to be sanctified by the sacral order. We can now see New Horror's entire trajectory: it begins with a couple-form that is in question because it potentially is insufficiently independent of the extended family; it then bisects the couple into two autonomous elements through the agency of the horrific; through the process of exorcism, which leads

19  Lisa and Arjun post-possession (1). (From Vikram Bhatt's *1920*, 2008.)

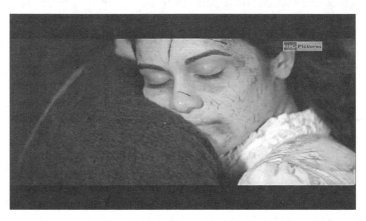

20  Lisa and Arjun post-possession (2). (From Vikram Bhatt's *1920*, 2008.)

to greater understanding, the couple-form is soldered back into a unitary structure that is now fully nucleated and autonomous. The journey into the realm of the supernatural thus produces the couple as the basic unit of capitalist reproduction (figs. 19–23).

This analysis explains why New Horror—a movement launched in the year of liberalization with the release of Ram Gopal Varma's *Raat* (Night, 1991)—has shed the stigma of B filmmaking and emerged as an A genre, as these newspaper articles note:

Indian film directors are no longer scared of making horror movies. For years the genre here has been associated with B-class Bollywood flicks. Made mostly under Ramsay banners, these films would be full of neon lighting and fake skeletons. But of late, with the making of films like Vikram Bhatt's *1920*, Mahesh Bhatt's *Raaz 2*, . . . the scenario seems to have undergone a change.[60]

Can Bollywood cope with a sudden change from its boy-meets-girl amid color, song and dance formula? The answer is keeping everyone—especially audiences—in suspense. After all but ignoring the suspense and thriller genres for some time, Indian helmers are suddenly scrambling to churn out production after suspense-filled production.[61]

The "next wave" has several key characteristics that distinguish it from Ramsay-era horror. First, production budgets are now large. Though the

21  Horror ends and leads to the formation of the post-nuptial dyad. (From Vikram Bhatt's *1920*, 2008.)

22  Vishal and Swati embrace while the social steps to the side. (From Ram Gopal Varma's *Bhoot* [Ghost], 2002.)

23  Horror concludes with the formation of the nuclear family. (From Vikram Kumar's *13B: Fear Has a New Address*, 2008.)

smash hits *Raaz* and *Bhoot* were made for only $833,000 and $1 million respectively, these figures were significant compared to previous outlays on horror films and enabled the directors to incorporate A-grade production values. Following the success of these films, budgets have increased substantially—it is rumored that the Bhatts spent close to $10 million on *Raaz 2*. Second, this financial freedom, itself a consequence of the capitalization of the film industry, enables horror's "technological turn." The use of sophisticated equipment is not only widespread but is advertised as an achievement: consider, for example, *Raat*'s top billing of the Steadicam operator, the extensive press coverage of the men behind the VFX effects in Vikram Bhatt's *1920*, and Varma's much touted turn to 3-D horror in his forthcoming *Warning*.

Third, New Horror films are mainly released in upscale, urban, multiplex exhibition theaters. Like the multiplot films discussed in the next chapter, horror sees itself as belonging almost exclusively to the middle classes. The economic logic of the multiplex—higher ticket prices, shorter runs, a greater number of releases—means that horror films do not need to draw a large, heterogeneous audience in order to be financially viable. Thus filmmakers can focus on producing a type of film that can be marketed as a highly differentiated product. New Horror is predicated on a "genre ideology": the directors of the movement see themselves as trailblazers who are fighting to create a pure version of horror that needs to distinguish itself sharply from classic Hindi film:

A Bollywood film without songs is like chicken tikka *masala* without the spice. But, if you listen to some people, the Bollywood film song, is on the way out. . . . The leader of the sans-song movement is director Ram Gopal Varma who believes that nonmusicals are "the way of the future." It cuts cost, allows for a variety of subjects and reduces the length. Last year, Varma's *Bhoot* (Ghost), a taut, songless horror film, became a sleeper hit . . . in India.[62]

Like the couple at the center of the New Horror story, the genre itself is forward-looking. Commenting on *Click* (a remake of the Thai film *Shutter*), Pritish Nandy, owner of a production company named after him, sums up the programmatic aspect of New Horror very concisely when he observes that "horror is a very interesting genre. Bollywood has not been able to (effectively) tap this genre so far. With, *Click*, we have tried to capture the deepest of fears in a rather blunt manner."[63]

This self-reflexivity speaks to the successful production of horror as a New Bollywood genre. The couple in *Raaz 2*, 2009's first big hit, is also highly self-aware. In fact the film thematizes the very process of upward mobility that has been a condition of the possibility of horror's emergence. In this ecologically themed horror film, the protagonist, Nandita, realizing that her desire for a middle-class lifestyle is complicit with the appetites of rogue capital, notes, "In my rush to secure my own domestic space I had neglected to think of those I am dispossessing." We might read this as horror's developing social conscience or simply as the couple's social consciousness. The next chapter elaborates on the way horror's solitary couple reenters the social by means of another contemporary genre—the "multiplex film."

# Conjugal Assembly: Multiplex, Multiplot, and the Reconfigured Social Film

New Bollywood emerges by reworking the conjugal couple in Hindi cinema. This project is realized, as the first three chapters have shown, in a variety of ways: in relation to the symbolic politics of kissing versus song-and-dance, within the fold of the auteur film, and by means of a radical reconstruction of an already existing genre. This chapter argues that the reformatting of the celluloid couple can also be linked to shifts in modes of exhibition and film-viewing. The emergence of a unique narrative form—the multiplot story featuring multiple couples—can be seen as coincident with a new type of exhibition space—the multiplex theater. What the multiplot does at the level of narrative construction, I suggest, works in tandem with how multiplex exhibition re-imagines the constitution of the audience. In the era of the massive, single-screen theater, Hindi popular cinema solicited a mass audience that cut across social divides. The recent transition to multiplex exhibition coincides with the gradual erosion of this cinema's status as a populist medium addressed to "the people." It now appears to seek a middle-class audience primarily located in urban areas. This phenomenon, I argue here, leads to a new conjugation of the screen couple, narrative form, exhibition space, and audience logic.

The multiplex theater—an exhibition space designed for multiple screenings—is about a decade old in India. Franchised, built to standardized specifications, and frequently anchored in malls, multiplexes generate 30 percent of all movie revenues, even though they account for a mere 4 or 5 percent of India's twelve thousand screens.[1] This disproportionate statistic generates two plausible inferences. First, the enormous economic clout currently enjoyed by the multiplex sector suggests that it will dominate the shape of the film industry in the future. Although a vast majority of the Indian viewing public—especially in the rural areas—does not yet have access to multiplex screenings, all indicators point to its growing importance as a mode of exhibition. Current investment trends bear out this prognostication—more than four hundred multiplexes have been built since 1997, and another three hundred are under construction now, many of them in small cities and towns.[2] For many analysts of the industry, this revolution in retail, based on the multiplex, is perhaps the most radical dimension of the restructuring that Bollywood is currently undergoing.[3] The second inference concerns the nature of the movie audience. The fact that multiplexes currently constitute such a small percentage of all movie screens points to a fundamental difference between New Bollywood and Hindi film. Whereas the latter sought to win as large an audience as possible with national blockbusters like *Deewar* (The wall, Yash Chopra, 1975) or *Sholay* (Embers, Ramesh Sippy, 1975), multiplex retailing targets a very specific segment of Indian society: the urban, globalized, middle class. It does so, as we shall see, by means of an aesthetic form that uniquely addresses the growing multiplex audience.

While multiplexes exhibit a wide range of films, from Hollywood blockbusters to regional films, they have given rise to a unique, low-budget, nonformulaic genre known as the "multiplex film," sometimes referred to in the vernacular as *hat-ke* (lit., "eccentric," or "offbeat").[4] The affinity between the exhibition infrastructure offered by the multiplex and the form and content of this emerging genre is widely acknowledged by industry practitioners. According to the film journalist Derek Bose, these are films where "the story-line, treatment, production schedules, even budgeting, distribution and pre-release promotions are tailored towards multiplexes."[5] Madhur Bhandarkar, the *hat-ke* filmmaker par excellence, whose films include the hit *Page 3* (2005), and *Corporate* (2006),[6] notes that "exhibitors would never run my films in a 1,000-seater hall; . . . they would never recover their money."[7] Rakesh Omprakash Mehra, who directed the hugely successful *Rang de Basanti* (Color of spring, 2006), points to the same link when he observes that "the distribution platforms have changed in the country and that has helped new age story lines to develop and deliver."[8] In other words there is a growing perception among industry professionals that the multiplex and the genre associated with it have more in common than mere nomenclature.

A number of scholars have investigated how exhibition infrastructure is intimately tied to the cultural status of cinema at different historical junctures and how the physical space of a theater can shape audience dispositions and how spectators engage the film product.[9] Less attention has been directed, however, toward the extent to which film form participates in the phenomenology of exhibition.[10] The "multiplex film"—a genre eponymous with a structure of exhibition—provides a fertile site for investigating how film aesthetics articulates with exhibition architecture to immerse audiences in new modes of moviegoing. I focus on a specific type of multiplex film, one that I term the *multiplot film*. Typically released only in multiplex theaters, multiplot films feature several pairs of couples loosely connected by place or circumstance. Such a treatment of conjugality, I argue, becomes a powerful strategic tool for rethinking the notion of couplehood and its relations to the social in modern India.

I begin by investigating how the formal properties of the multiplex film reprise the spatial and social logic of the multiplex theater. The relation between film form and exhibition architecture needs to be historicized, and so I look briefly at the 1940s Hindi social film—a "master genre" that includes comedy, drama, spectacle, and thrills—to suggest that it might be seen as a response to the challenge of creating a national film audience under the conditions of single-screen exhibition. I then outline how the multiplex theater is redefining film audiences and moviegoing in India by tracing two phases in the formal development of the multiplex film. The genre began as an exclusively metropolitan phenomenon, and the first wave of multiplex films were characterized by extreme formal experimentation that exploited the technological capacities of the new theaters. Here, aesthetic inventiveness serves as an analog for emerging conditions of exhibition. But as multiplexes have been transformed from an exclusive to a more generalized space for film viewing, the multiplex film has had to find a more expansive address that encompasses a demographic broader than that of first-generation films. I argue that the recent slew of multiplot films marks a second moment in the evolution of the genre, in that they habituate film audiences in India to the re-imagination of the social body that is ongoing in the multiplex theater. Multiplot films typically consist of a number of loosely allied story arcs and resemble what David Bordwell has called "network narratives."[11] One of the crucial achievements of this narrative device, I suggest, is to construct a more capacious and internally diversified conception of the middle classes that corresponds more adequately to the broader audience being solicited by the multiplex. I look closely at a group of multiplot films—*Honeymoon Travels Pvt. Ltd.* (Reema Kagti, 2007), *Just Married* (Meghna Gulzar, 2007), *Salaam-e-Ishq* (Hail to love, Nikhil Advani, 2007) and *Life in a . . . Metro* (Anurag Basu, 2007)—that center primarily on courtship and marriage. Heterosexual couple-formation in Hindi cinema, as we have seen, has always served as a site in which to imagine a model of the ideal citizen. In classic Hindi cinema, it was the task of the lead romantic pair to exemplify society's capacity for negotiating differences of class, caste, and ethnicity, as well as to define the limits of such couplings. A single love story therefore became the object of identification for a large, heterogeneous audience, putatively fusing the diverse population inhabiting the theater into one desiring subject. The underlying thesis of Hindi cinema was that diversity had to be overcome if the nation was to succeed. Multiplot narratives are diffused; they feature a plurality of couples from all parts of the social spectrum; yet these couples share habits, attitudes, and dispositions that enable them to navigate the same spaces. Sociological differences notwithstanding, they are anchored in a shared milieu and, *taken together*, produce the social. In other words diversity and difference in the multiplot are enabling factors that are crucial for the construction of a new version of society and the citizenry.

## Exhibition and Film Form

On the basis of the assumption that most audiences construe their relationship to cinema not through particular film texts and their meanings but "through the social experience of cinema-going,"[12] cinema studies have, in recent years, expanded the scope of their inquiry from a study of the historical development of forms and the politics of representation to include cinema's inscription in social and cultural activity. Consequently, an increasing number of scholars have turned their attention to the particular histories and phenomenologies of moviegoing in different local contexts and examined how diverse modes of distribution and exhibition have conditioned both the production and reception of cinema.[13] This research has demonstrated that one of cinema's effects has been to democratize entertainment.[14] Historians of early American cinema have shown how this new art form was enthusiastically embraced by disenfranchised populations.[15] Similar trends appear to emerge in the case of early film exhibition in India, though the country's colonial status and the particularities of caste- and region-based ethnic identity complicate the democratizing narrative.[16] The colonial authorities were certainly aware that cinema's exhibition format instituted an egalitarian space full of perils.[17] Thus, the Indian Cinematograph Committee Report of 1928—commissioned by the colonial administration with a view to rationalize film censorship—repeatedly testifies how exhibition space, the composition of the audience, and film form articulate each other. Anxieties surrounding on-screen sexuality, for instance, are directly linked in the report to the nature of theater architecture and the egalitarian mode of film exhibition, which allow the literate and the illiterate, the working classes and the bourgeoisie, men and women to be dangerously proximate. As William Mazzarella notes, "the spatial arrangement of the audience in the cinema halls was itself imagined on a sliding scale from rabidity to reason."[18] Multiple accounts construct the "frontbenchers" as noisy, riotous, and entirely overwhelmed by the moving image.[19] There is recognition here that, given the nature of colonial exhibition space, the image itself—the putative source of such excitement—needed to be regulated. Thus, as we have seen in chapter 1, respondents repeatedly stress the need to curtail on-screen intimacy, especially the kiss, in order to keep the masses under control, even as others acknowledge that such prohibition compromises the mimetic competence of cinema and thus its appeal to a middle-class audience, forging thereby an enduring connection between the middle-class spectator and a realist aesthetics.[20] In these ways, the conditions of film viewing begin to articulate with film form. The obsessive focus on the social identities of the audience and the multiple attempts to categorize responses to the moving image along the demographic lines of caste, class, and ethnicity is itself one of the effects of a mode of film exhibition that makes these groups occupy the same public space.

The democratic space that so troubled colonial keepers of morals was a direct consequence of the mode of film exhibition. A version of the movie palace arrived in major Indian cities in the first few decades of Indian cinema. As Manishita Dass and Amit Rai have shown, the movie theater, with its art deco style, neon-lit marquee, winding staircase, and glittering foyer, was very much a component of the early Indian cinema experience, especially in urban areas. While these thousand-seat theaters no doubt sought to attract a predominantly elite audience, in order to be financially viable, they were compelled to admit patrons from all the social classes.[21] The very architecture of film exhibition meant that the upper classes would have to share space with the whistling, cheering, coin-throwing frontbenchers. Thus popular cinema never quite became an exemplary bourgeois entertainment form, and, as scholars like Ashis Nandy and Madhava Prasad have suggested, post-independence Hindi cinema continued to retain a distinctly populist address.[22] In Nandy's vivid phrase, film form and aesthetics had to incorporate a "slum's eye view."[23]

It is in the light of this need to accommodate a variety of viewing populations and aesthetic agendas that we can best understand the predominant form of post-independence Hindi cinema—the social film. As we noted earlier, this general form—known in later years as *masala*—held its own into the 1980s. It is evident that such a complex form, which was quite distinct from the internally coherent narrative that characterized classical Hollywood cinema, had to accommodate the multiplicity of viewing vantages immanent in the thousand-seat, single-screen theaters where films were typically screened.[24] The architecture of the single-screen theater where these different populations could attend movies together was intimately linked to the hopes and anxieties surrounding moviegoing as a democratizing experience. We could go further and ask to what extent the all-encompassing social film (and the *masala* format that it gave way to) is tied to the dominance of the single screen and its need to appeal simultaneously to various socioeconomic segments of the audience. In other words it is possible to link the textual heteronomy of Hindi film form and what Prasad has called its "heterogeneous form of manufacture" to the composition of the audience as well as the space that housed them.[25]

A recent essay by Ashish Rajyadaksha provides a rich account of the relationship between Hindi film's formal heterogeneity and the process of democratic politics in India.[26] His analysis sheds considerable light on how form might indeed connect to the conditions of single-screen film exhibition. A striking difference between Hindi film and classical Hollywood cinema lies in the fact that the former does not prohibit the exchange of looks between the screen and the audience—its images are more frontal in relation to the audience, so that the apparatus openly solicits the viewer. Rather than framing such "lack of realism" as a sign of Indian popular cinema's backwardness, Rajyadaksha suggests that this "baseline frontal address" acknowledges the paying viewer's *right* to receive images, thus iterating the contract between the apparatus and the viewer. As such, the act of moviegoing reprises the democratic pact whereby every citizen, by voting, is identified by the state. Rajyadaksha builds his reading on the insights of Partha Chatterjee, who has recently proposed a distinction between civil and political society in postcolonial

India. While the former is grounded in abstract notions of individual sovereignty and modernity, political society is composed of those who vote—and thus participate in democracy—but do not enjoy the privileges of civil society, and are therefore not fully vested citizens.[27] Frontality, as well as the attraction-driven presentational format of Hindi popular cinema, can therefore be viewed as a formal reflex of the two societies that comprise the moviegoing public in India.[28] The "baseline frontal address" can be read as an accommodation of the claims made by political society to be included in the narrative contract of cinema, while the partial accommodation of realist norms speaks to the disciplinary project of cinema as a classic bourgeois form.[29]

I would like to triangulate Rajyadaksha's alliance between film form and democracy by recalling the spatial arrangement of theaters in India. The seating in the large, single-screen theater was typically differentiated by ticketing price: those with expensive tickets sat at the back of the hall or in a balcony, whereas those who paid less were placed up front, near the screen. It is legitimate to ask to what extent both frontality and the package of thrills that came with the social film/*masala* were functions of the phenomenology of perception of the frontbenchers. In other words, could film form be responding to its subaltern audience not only by providing them with the sensations deemed appropriate to their needs but also by admitting them to the party by looking them in the eye? There is an interesting connection here between filmic morphogenesis and exhibition space: the vectors and intensities of film form replicate the political constitution and energies of the front-row audience.[30] On the other hand, the citizen who can afford to sit further back is in one sense left out of the picture; she apprehends the image less viscerally and thus consistently demands a more realistic route to identification. This relationship between viewer positioning and cinematic form partly explains the dissatisfaction expressed by the elite toward Hindi cinema throughout its history. The persistent criticism of Hindi film's "escapism" can be understood as a response to a democratic form of exhibition that imposes the aesthetics of political society upon those who occupy the civil sphere. There is good reason, therefore, to posit a link between the spatial politics of single-screen exhibition and the development of omnibus forms like the social film/*masala*. Further, the constitution of the couple, as I tried to show in chapter 1, through the dual mode of narrative and performance accommodates these different stakes. We must thus inquire into the fresh transactions that occur among an emerging architecture of exhibition, film form, and social relations.

## The Retail Revolution in Indian Cinema

As research and market reports note, the exhibition sector in India is witnessing a major boom, with annual growth rates in the region of 10 percent.[31] This is a significant development when we consider that, for most of its history, this sector of the film industry was very slow to expand. This was partly due to government land use and licensing laws that discouraged the construction of theaters (for example, between 1950 and 1956, Prime Minister Jawaharlal Nehru announced a freeze on theater construction, claiming that it diverted capital from more useful types of investment). Further, theater owners considered exhibition revenue as though it were rent on land rather than capital that should circulate and expand.[32] Thus, in the fifty-year period from 1948 to 1997, the exhibition sector grew at an annual rate of less than 5 percent, causing the screen-to-viewer ratio in India to be among the lowest in the world.[33] The watershed moment came in 1997 when the Priya Village Roadshow (PVR) Anupam, considered to be India's first commercially owned multiplex, opened in New Delhi.[34] Soon after, the government made multiplex theaters tax-exempt, fostering the multiplex boom that is still, according to most analysts, in its first phase.[35] The sector is dominated by large corporations, the five largest are PVR, Cinemax India, Inox Leisure, Fame India, and Adlabs Films (recently renamed Big Cinemas). The last, owned by one of India's largest industrial groups, Reliance, is a conglomerate with investments in all segments, from film production to retail and home video. It owns about one hundred and fifty screens and a popular Imax theater in Mumbai, and is in the midst of an acquisition spree aimed at boosting its holdings to more than five hundred screens in the next few years.[36] As of 2007, there were 480 multiplexes in India,[37] and the multiplex boom has recently been acquiring a global dimension. Reliance has been buying up US multiplexes in such Indian diasporic markets as New York, Los Angeles, Chicago, and Washington, DC, and currently owns two hundred and fifty screens in twenty-eight North American cities. Not surprisingly, film retail has attracted some of the best valuations in the media business, and as of 2004–2005 this sector was capitalized at around Rs. 35 billion.[38] There is tremendous growth in ancillary industries as well—India is billed as the emerging "digital cinema laboratory" of the world, and the home video market is expected to grow at an astonishing 25–30 percent in the next decade.[39]

Before I analyze how multiplex exhibition in India is affecting film form, it may be instructive to invoke a comparative framework and briefly review the history of the multiplex in the United States. The first twin theater in America was built in 1964, and by 1978, only 10 percent of screens were multiplexed. An explosion in theater construction took place in the 1980s—with the number of screens added becoming the dominant statistic. In architectural terms, the generic multiplex was a far cry from the grandeur of the movie palaces, but its retail strategy, allied to TV channels and department stores, emphasized variety under one roof—the main selling point being its access to the suburbs.[40] The emergence of the multiplex form of exhibition meant that "the diversity aspect of film consumption shifted from the conglomerate program running on one screen to the multiscreen exhibition," where there were multiple features to choose from (as many as twenty), but each required a separate ticket.[41] Variety in the multiplex, according to Ina Rae Hark, delivers the "unconsumed narrative experience" and satisfies the "sensation of novelty." Thus we have Marcus Loew's credo: "We sell tickets to theatres, not to pictures."[42] Programming techniques likewise shifted. The notion of regular changes and normal runs disappeared, and "opening wide" emerged as a strategy to ensure quick profits in the opening days of a highly promoted and, therefore, highly anticipated film.[43] Likewise the revenue model changed as the proportion of profits from concessions became larger than ticket revenues. Initially, the high prices of food and beverages were meant to help "sleeper" films remain in the theater longer, but soon this strategy was generalized for all products, so that "films serve[d] as loss leaders to drive the profitable sale of concessions."[44] The multiplex developed retail synergies in other ways as well. Theaters located in malls received preferential leases. They were usually placed at one end of a mall, and they were hard to find—necessitating a trip through the mall and thus extending opportunities for all retail businesses.[45] Most recently, the arrival of the megaplex, where film offerings are supplemented by a full range of entertainment options like food courts and video-game stations harkens back, in a sense, to the movie-palace era. Megaplexes are becoming architecturally significant, offering multiple attractions and an increasingly immersive experience.[46]

The Indian multiplex is a hybrid of the earlier multiplex and the more recent megaplex models of exhibition. While screens are not quite as numerous, the Indian multiplex shares the latter's vision of being a family-oriented entertainment complex, where films are screened in the context of several other leisure activities, including game parlors, restaurants, retail stores, and so on.[47] Intimately tied to the retail revolution in India during the last two decades, multiplex exhibition is tightly folded into new modes of consumption. As a recent study notes, the multiplex in

India has emerged as the bulwark of a new infrastructure of leisure targeting a "consuming class" that aspires to belong to a "global middle class."[48]
Almost invariably anchored in malls (also a new phenomenon), the multiplex is intended to maximize retail synergies, especially via lucrative
ties with extensive food and beverage offerings that go far beyond the
standard popcorn, candy, and soda. What is on sale is much more than
the movie ticket and refreshments. The common spaces inside, including the box office, lobby, and corridors, are designed to host advertising
displays of consumer goods, including those offered by other vendors in
the mall. These spaces also serve as sites for special events, contests, and
promotions, with celebrities in attendance, of commodities like watches,
jewelry, and electronics. Other products—tied-in merchandise, video
games, ringtones—are sold here as well. In marketing parlance, it is an
environment created to interact with the consumer at multiple "touch
points." Thus Saurine Doshi, partner at the consulting firm A. T. Kearney,
sums up a major survey of the movie industry by noting that "we expect
non-box-office revenues to increase three to four times in the next five
years driven by multiple customer touch points. Box-office revenues are
expected to decrease to nearly 75 percent by 2010 and further to 60 percent by 2020 from 84 percent in 2006."[49]

What is perhaps most significant about the multiplex is its phenom-
enological singularity. The multiplex is a hermetic space that is radically
discontinuous with the environment outside. Clean, shiny, climate-
controlled, and technologically state-of-the-art, it is a world apart from
the heat, dust, and crowds of urban India. The mall-multiplex as an urban
form is a city unto itself and as such resembles what architect Rem Koolhaas has called the "generic city" that consists of endlessly reproducible
modular structures.[50] To walk through its doors is to pass into an other
India, continuous with the smooth spaces of global capitalism. The multiplex is thus an urban form that "liberates the city from the captivity
of the center, from the straightjacket of identity."[51] Though India's elite
might feel perfectly at home here, the multiplex remains an object of awe
and wonder for the country's growing middle classes. This might explain
why 97 percent of urban youth, most of whom are not affluent, prefer to
watch films in multiplexes.[52]

The multiplex cinema, an accessory to middle-class formation, thus
functions within the larger matrix of liberalization that has characterized
the Indian economy and culture since the early nineties.[53] If the single-
screen theaters with their thousand-plus seats, fixed showtimes, and hierarchical pricing relied on a heterogeneous product—the social film and
the *masala*—that sought to weld multiple populations into an audience,

the multiplex utilizes a homogenizing milieu to advertise a wide spectrum of products and subjectivities. The multiplex film, I suggest, is energized by a similar architectural imagination. It seeks to replace the diverse audience of the social film with a homogeneous, middle-class one, even as it celebrates the range of options that middle-class life allows. In doing so, the multiplex film, quite consciously, narrows the film audience and marginalizes the poorer segments of the viewing public. Filmmakers whose works are shown at multiplex theaters admit as much. Thus Jaideep Sahri, who wrote the script for the multiplex hit *Khosla ka Ghosla* (The troubles of Khosla, Dibakar Banerjee, 2006), says, "On the one hand, I get to track my revenues better and my audience gets a better-presented movie but—while multiplexes helped movies like *Khosla ka Ghosla* and *Bunty Aur Babli* [Bunty and Babli, Shaad Ali, 2005]—families portrayed in those movies will not have been able to afford a multiplex ticket."[54] Such a process of middle-class formation, I argue, is accompanied by the creation of a new formal device—the "multiplot film." The socioeconomic vectors induced by liberalization ask that both exhibition and film form develop a homogenous frame within which to display the multifaceted aspects of middle-class ethos. The next two sections examine the evolution of the multiplex film to illustrate how this end is achieved.

## The First Generation

Though the multiplex theater provides the ideal staging ground for multiplex film, there is more here than mere tautology. The multiplex film predates its brick-and-mortar analogue and has been long in the making. A proper genealogy would begin with the middle-class cinema of late 1960s and 1970s, as evidenced in the work of directors like Basu Bhattacharya, Hrishikesh Mukherjee, and Rajinder Bedi, for example, as well as that of the closely allied Indian "parallel cinema."[55] This precursor cinema had two aesthetic impulses—toward indexical realism and formal innovation—that identify it as an art form that sought to access the contemporary from the vantage of the nascent middle class.[56] If this "middle cinema" did not quite take off, this was in some measure due to the absence of suitable exhibition venues. Some attempts were made by government-sponsored agencies like the National Film Development Corporation to finance theater construction, but such efforts remained sporadic. During the 1980s and the 1990s this mode of filmmaking would migrate to the small screen; and in an example of a feedback loop, we now see that many of the "multiplex films" bear the formal traces of television aesthetics. To take one example, the ensemble cast and multiple story arcs that characterize the multiplot film, which I discuss later, owe something to TV serials that were popular in the eighties. The works of directors like Mahesh Bhatt and Kalpana Lajmi, regional filmmakers like Aparna Sen, as well as auteur-directors like Vidhu Vinod Chopra, Mani Ratnam, and Ram Gopal Varma revealed a fresh, technologically slick approach to the contemporary. These films carry an aura of "liveness"—not only in their choice of up-to-the-minute subject matter, but also in their narrative rhythm and cinematography, which show the effects of television news reporting.[57] Moreover, the protocols of television's genres (soaps, sitcoms, game shows, and MTV) as well as television's linguistic medium (a fast-paced hybrid of Hindi and English) were not only a big influence on middle cinema but would also prove immensely generative for the multiplex film. One of the most salient characteristics of the multiplex film is its constant featuring of other communication technologies—radio, television, telephony, and new media. This depiction frequently acts as shorthand for detailing the contemporary in various ways—it might thematize media, activate plot movements, or affirm cinema's capacity to encompass other media. More than any other type of cinema, the multiplex film has most keenly registered the momentous communications revolution in India.

The first generation of multiplex films (1995–2004 approx.) reprises the phenomenology of the multiplex itself. This first wave occurred at a time when India was in the grip of a collective euphoria about the coming economic "miracle"—perhaps best exemplified by the now infamous slogan "India Shining." Though multiplexes constituted, at this time, a negligible fragment of the exhibition sector, they entirely dominated the media discourse. The very *form* of the multiplex that I have described above excited both audiences and commentators; it symbolized for them the dream of development in which they were eagerly participating. The multiplex film, in the first generation, was concerned primarily with the aesthetic consequences of the transformations unleashed by liberalization. These films are characterized by kinetic forms that seem to run far ahead of their content. Thus they are often cognitively bewildering—familiar formulas are casually jettisoned, but little else is offered in their place to moor the frantic and frenetic representation of the new. Consider Sriram Raghavan's *Ek Hasina Thi* (There was a beauty, 2004). Produced under the aegis of Ram Gopal Varma's Factory—a production house dedicated to modernizing Hindi film—*Ek Hasina Thi* starts out as a stalker film, then turns into a prison procedural (i.e., focusing on the process of imprisonment) for a while, then shifts gears to conclude as a woman-centered revenge saga. Generic conventions are consistently applied in each segment, but the transitions between segments are abrupt, pronounced, and quite arbitrary. While it is tempting to interpret this proliferation of genres as muddled and inept filmmaking, I would argue that we need to see it as a strategic revision of the *masala* principle. Lalitha Gopalan has theorized classic Hindi film as a "cinema of interruptions" characterized by sudden twists and leaps that take the form of song-and-dance sequences, comedy routines, fight sequences, and an intermission. The sharp generic turns that we see in *Ek Hasina Thi* can be read as a continuation of this tradition, though here the shifts occur in the realm of viewing protocols and of spectatorial relations and expectations. Analyzing Rajat Mukerjee's *Pyar Tune Kya Kiya?* (How have you loved? 2001), Madhava Prasad observes that the film takes a hairpin turn from a conventional Bollywood romance to a thriller in the style of *Fatal Attraction*.[58] At this point, according to Prasad, the spectator has a simple choice: either to get on board or get left behind, not just by the story but by the very flow of modernity itself. There are good reasons that such convulsions of form are an intrinsic part of the first-generation multiplex film. If the global modern is a bewildering collocation of disparate entities and processes, then an art that aspires to be contemporary must struggle to find a form that is adequate to this complex reality.

At the level of content, these films are characterized by similar convulsions of the conjugal relation. In films such as *Jism* (Body, Amit Saxena, 2003), *Murder* (Anurag Basu, 2004), and *Market* (Jay Prakash, 2003), sex hijacks the entire domain of couple-formation, becoming a "thing-in-itself." Other films, such as *Ek Choti Si Love Story* (A small love story, Shashilal Nair, 2002), whose tagline reads "I am 15, she is 26," and *Dansh* (Snake bite, Kamika and Kanika Varma, 2005), an odd remake of Polanski's *Death and the Maiden*, take us to strange and perverse relationships hitherto unexplored in Hindi cinema. The couple-form is experimented with and "de-formed," in these extreme situations. There is no attempt, as there is in New Horror, to install new forms of conjugation. Rather, the couple is stranded between the conjugal models of old and New Bollywood.

This experimental mode is at play in the constant application of techniques new to Indian commercial cinema (dissolves, jump-cuts, split screens, voiceovers, accelerated and parallel editing). These may often seem semantically gratuitous, yet they serve to fold the spatio-temporality of the multiplex and its adjacent reality into film form. Consider the intense attention paid to sound design in the multiplex film. The phenomenology of sound becomes more complex in the multiplex environment and begins to supplement and even supplant visual effects. Since theaters are now equipped with surround sound, the experience of cinema has become more immersive. For example, audiences are now able to hear low-frequency sounds previously inaudible in the large, single-screen theaters that lacked multichannel sound projection. Consequently, audio design in the multiplex movie has become much more intricate and layered, relying far more on ambient sounds. Not only does this allow greater sonic realism in Hindi cinema, but films can also explore sound situations that go beyond the song-and-dance sequence. As I have argued in chapter 3, the upward mobility of a genre like horror from the B to the A category—as evidenced by the multiplex release of films like *Bhoot* (Ghost, Ram Gopal Varma, 2003) and *Darna Mana Hai* (Fear is forbidden, Prawal Raman, 2003)—is linked to the technological capacities of multiplex exhibition that enable the film to create its affects through sound.[59] As multiplex theaters encourage the use of more elaborate sound design, the signature audio event of Hindi popular cinema—the song sequence—also undergoes changes, as discussed in chapter 1. Increasingly, we are witnessing the disappearance of the song-sequence or its absorption into the soundtrack, where songs combine with other elements in a multilayered sonic environment. We also see radical shifts in song composition—especially the relation of voice to accompaniment— as multichannel sound projection and digital composition deemphasize the primacy of the voice.

The rise of the first-generation multiplex film indicates a major departure from the traditional social film/*masala* format that dominated Hindi film for almost four decades. Available only to an affluent, urban audience, multiplex films signal Bollywood's decision to forego a comprehensive national public in favor of a middle-class target audience that is securely enmeshed in the consumption economy. This change in the delivery system has been accompanied by an equivalent shift in the nature of the product being purveyed. As I have described, the multiplex film in its initial phase was characterized by reckless genre-mixing and code-switching, by novel uses of state-of-the-art technologies, and by the creation of a narrative and audiovisual style and sensations that anticipated to the life-world of the emerging middle classes. The couple, as I have briefly tried to indicate, is not yet a viable construct in these films; rather, conjugality is the site for exploring all manner of psychic variations like masochism, obsession, voyeurism, and erotomania. As the multiplex theater becomes more widespread, it gives rise to a second generation of films that is less concerned with formal experimentation, focusing instead on the new sociology of the couple. To this end, it adopts a formal template—the multiplot film—that is the focus of the remainder of this chapter.

## Second-Generation Multiplexes and the Multiplot Film

The second half of the 2010s witnessed the formation of what I call the second-generation multiplex film. Characterized by a novel narrative technique—the multiplot—these films belong to an era when multiplex exhibition in India had entered its second phase of growth. The single most important development in connection with the multiplex has been its spread from metropolitan to small urban centers. While multiplexes have rapidly transformed moviegoing in major cities like Mumbai, Delhi, Chennai, Hyderabad, Bangalore, and Kolkata, the sector is now expanding into virgin territories. Urban multiplexes comprise only 5 percent or so of the total film screens in the country. Most film viewing—70 percent of total film revenues in fact—takes place in medium-size cities and smaller towns, where films are screened in old-fashioned and dilapidated single-screen theaters. Surveys show that 75 percent of the moviegoing population of these towns prefers to watch movies at home; usually on pirated DVDs.[60] The public in these smaller towns yearn for multiplexes to show up in their neighborhoods. Further, the average proportion of an Indian film's domestic revenues generated by ticket sales is between 85 percent and 90 percent.[61] Compare this to revenues in the United States, where box-office returns make up only 15.7 percent of film revenue for Hollywood studio pictures. These figures demonstrate that in order to become the primary mode of exhibition, the multiplex had to expand into the new urban India.[62]

In the last few years, "urban" India has indeed come to encompass an area far greater than that of the six biggest cities listed above. As recently as 2001, a third of India's urban population lived in India's largest metropolitan areas, and this market also had 40 percent of the country's disposable income. There was thus a strong overlap between metropolitan life and consumer culture. By the end of 2007, however, that percentage had declined by 10 percent, while that of smaller cities and towns began to rise. The balance between the two has shifted quite radically; currently, 70 percent of the Rs. 74 trillion consumer market is located in key urban towns (KUTs) and the rest of urban India (ROUI). More important, most growth is now centered round this secondary sector. Consider one telling statistic—the subscriber growth in telecom products was 58 percent in the six largest cities, but an astounding 93 percent in the KUTs and ROUI.

A recent report by Ernst and Young entitled *The Dhoni Effect: The Rise of Small-Town India* discusses this new trend and argues that these newly emerging urban areas will be the new drivers of consumption and present rich opportunities for businesses. Not surprisingly then, the second phase of the multiplex boom is focused on these new urban consumers, with almost all the building activity concentrated in second- and third-tier cities like Lucknow, Indore, Nasik, Aurangabad, Kanpur, and Amritsar, as well as in B- and C-class towns like Pimpri, Latur, Kochi, Bhatinda, Madurai, and Jalpaiguri. This endeavor has a lot of potential since it is feasible to "multiplex" any well-populated urban area. As Alok Tandon, chief operating officer of Inox Leisure, Ltd. reveals, "Our plan is to have an Inox in every city having a population of between 700,000 to a million."[63] Multiplexes in smaller towns are not as glamorous as those in the larger metros (the term used in India to denote a large city, a metropolis). Thus, ticket prices, though much higher than those for single-screen theaters, are lower than in the metros, and certain features like seat-size and lobby décor are downscaled to correspond to a lower-income audience. Thus the exhibitor chain PVR has launched a new division called PVR Talkies that offers a no-frills multiplex concept for smaller cities. Ajay Bijli, PVR cinema chief, comments, "We have nine theatres operational now, but we will be taking this number up this year. About 20 percent of the planned new screens will be PVR Talkies."[64] These budget cinemas minimize investment on interior design: foyers are air-cooled rather than air-conditioned and traditional paper posters are still used for promotion instead of LCD screens. The theater complex acts as the top-floor anchor in malls and drives consumer foot traffic ("footfalls" in marketing terminology), and multiplex chains frequently set up alliances with major retailers like Pantaloons. As is typical, profits largely come from food and beverages, though the fare offered in these smaller markets is not Coke and popcorn but Indian snacks like *pakodas* and *vada paav*. The spread of the multiplex has also been aided by digital and satellite delivery of the film product. The shift to digital has accelerated the modernization of existing venues. The advent of digital prints means that theaters in smaller markets can buy titles the moment they are released—thus becoming less susceptible to the challenges of video piracy—and at a fraction of previous cost.[65]

The next generation of multiplex films is born precisely at the moment when the multiplex transforms from an elite venue to a general form of exhibition that I have described above. The most significant corpus of this second wave is a series of multiplot films released in the second half of the decade: *Yun Hota to Kya Hota?* (What if . . . ? Naseeruddin Shah,

2006); *Honeymoon Travels Pvt. Ltd.* (Reema Kagti, 2007); *Hattrick* (Milan Luthra, 2007); *Just Married* (Meghna Gulzar, 2007); *Delhii [sic] Heights* (Sanyukta Varma, 2007); *Life Mein Kabhi Kabhi* (Sometimes in life, Vikram Bhatt, 2007); *Salaam-e-Ishq* (Hail to love, Nikhil Advani, 2007); *Life in a . . . Metro* (Anurag Basu, 2007); and *Mumbai Meri Jaan* (Mumbai, my love, Nishikant Kamat, 2008). If the first-generation multiplex film was concerned with the creation of a film grammar that would make possible the enunciation of a new middle-class cinema, these films are entrusted with broadening the audience of the multiplex film to include the proliferating middle classes in all of urban India.

I contend that the form of the multiplot is one that is most adequate for the task of reassembling a film public in the age of liberalization. As I have indicated throughout this book, the emergence of New Bollywood is characterized by a double movement—a deterritorialization and then a reterritorialization. In the first instance, New Bollywood negates the notion of an organic whole that lay at the bottom of Hindi film's narrative logic. It can therefore no longer locate itself in a continuous though contested sociological terrain that provided the ground for such classics as *Shree 420* (Mr. 420, Raj Kapoor, 1955) and *Deewar* (The wall, Yash Chopra, 1978). In other words new cinema views the social as a collection of discrete elements that are only connected at optimal moments. Nor, however, can New Bollywood refuse the task of reterritorializing, that is, of providing an integrative account of the autonomous and disparate aspects of social life. It thus cannot stay content to inhabit the murkier realm of more recent Hindi cinema, where the moral order is barely restored and social conflicts remain unresolved as, for instance, in *Parinda* (The pigeon, Vidhu Vinod Chopra, 1989) and *Satya* (Ram Gopal Varma, 1998). The imperative placed on the multiplex film is, then, that of conjoining all the different fractions of the middle class together as a viewing public in such a manner that each retains its particularity even as it partakes of the ethos of a generalized consumerist culture. To pose it in a contrastive manner, classic Hindi film sought to erase real differences (in class, caste, religion) by subsuming them under the logic of romantic love and social justice; the multiplex film seeks to preserve differences (which are essential to the modern marketplace) within an indifferent, and therefore homogenizing, plane of modern capital.

The structure of the multiplot film enables the realization of New Bollywood's goal of reconstituting its public. In the typical multiplot, we follow several protagonists, each representing a different sector of the burgeoning middle classes. The digressive, subplot-heavy, attractions-driven *masala* form that described the broadest possible sociological arc makes way for "network narratives."[66] The plotlines in the multiplot run alongside each other with very weak links—they may intersect but they usually do not. These narratives of adjacency (rather than conflict) habituate us to new forms of social diversity that resemble the spatial logic of the multiplex. Just as the multiplex affords a *multiplicity* of events to occur within its domain, the multiplot allows for the simultaneous representation of multiple character types who together signify the middle class as a differentiated collective. The total field of the multiplot is constituted as a network—even though characters are situated on a common plane of interaction, they in fact connect with each other quite randomly. The textual layout of the multiplot resonates with the rise of "network society"—a new configuration of the social where invariant and largely self-enclosed social groupings have been replaced by mobile mappings of individuals and information in cyberspace.[67] This concordance explains the extraordinary popularity of network narratives in a variety of global cinemas in the past decade. Though numerous instances of such narratives can be found in earlier periods of film history, their proliferation in the past decade is remarkable. Network narratives make a very different sort of demand on the viewer than the traditional form of storytelling that features a single (or sometimes paired) protagonist placed within a causally determined plot. In order to make sense of how all the various plot threads fit together, the viewer is forced to reach for the bigger picture. The diegesis provides a few anchors by way of a common milieu, a singular event, and social or kinship ties, but it is the viewer's task to hold these threads together and submit to this more contingent and evolving narrative structure. Building on Bordwell's suggestion that these films embody an "expanding social network,"[68] I suggest that in the case of New Bollywood, the network narrative helps to constitute an internally differentiated, rapidly expanding middle class as the ideal multiplex audience. While the multiplot design can capture demographic and cultural diversity, the overarching network structure—analogous to the architecture of the multiplex itself—contains and manages this heterogeneity. In what follows, I look at a number of recent multiplot releases in order to demonstrate how they reconfigure the social by means of narrative strategy. While I provide brief plot summaries, my main purpose here is to shed light on the mechanisms employed by these network narratives in pursuit of this goal.

In the 2007 film *Life Mein Kabhie Kabhi* (Sometimes in life, Vikram Bhatt, 2007; hereafter cited simply as *Life*), five college friends celebrate graduation night with excessive carousing, only to find themselves in jail. The group, differentiated by gender and socioeconomic backgrounds, collectively decides to reconnect five years later to take stock of the extent to which they have reached their personal goals. After this initial sequence, the film turns into a five-pronged bildungsroman in which each protagonist is tried, tested, and taught life's lessons. Halfway through the movie, each story arc reaches a climax as its protagonist is faced with crucial decisions or deals with the consequences of past actions. A vertical split screen (see fig. 24) summarizes the story up to this point, and as it freezes, the film breaks for the intermission. As Lalitha Gopalan has pointed out, the interval is a narratologically significant interruption in traditional Hindi cinema, for it marks the midpoint between conflict and resolution.[69] *Life* deploys this conventional narrative caesura to reassemble its plot lines, but this coming together is a merely visual device, a simultaneous enlargement and splicing of the frame, produced for the spectator. Each story line remains distinct, adjacent to the others. The five friends meet from time to time, but these encounters are not significant in narrative terms. Their subjectivities and destinies do not press against each other; rather, they follow their own vectors of disillusion and redemption. In marked contrast to films like *Crash* (Paul Haggis, 2004) or *Babel* (Alejandro González Iñáaritu, 2006),[70] whose multiple plots are meant to exemplify the inescapable interconnectedness of the social, here the social is imagined as a weakly connected multiplicity.

*Hattrick* (Milan Luthria, 2007)—released at roughly the same time as *Life*—exemplifies how the connection between plotlines can be even more arbitrary. The three story arcs in the film are as follows: a terminally ill patient gives a sentimental education to his emotionally stunted doctor; a newlywed couple navigate the perils of domesticity; and an immigrant responds to his racial marginality by oppressing the women in his family. The first two are set in Mumbai, the third in the United Kingdom. These plots are united by the fact that each features a protagonist who is a cricket fanatic, and in each plotline sport spectatorship becomes an affective flashpoint. Thus their relationships to each other are far more tenuous than those of the five friends in *Life*. These characters form a community only insofar as they consume the same media images of cricket—beamed into each plotline via television screens—and thus participate in similar rituals of fandom. The plotlines never intersect, and there is no expectation that they will. The film plays with this expectation by having characters from different story lines cross each other's paths at a sports bar, but this convergence is not developed in any way. The characters remain unaware of each other, and the adjacency principle is strictly followed. The same graphic arrangement used in *Life*, a vertically split screen, recapitulates this parallelism (fig. 25).

changing belongs to life!

24   The split screen captures the weak connections between different social subjects. (From Vikram Bhatt's *Life Mein Kabhie Kabhiee* [Sometimes in life], 2007.)

25   The split screen depicts the adjacent yet nonintersecting social formation of the multiplot film. (From Milan Luthria's *Hattrick* [Three in a row], 2007.)

The cross-cutting between plotlines in both *Life* and *Hattrick* functions somewhat like the conjunction *meanwhile* in a nineteenth-century novel. This *meanwhile*, as Benedict Anderson famously observed, helped the novel visualize the nation as an imagined community progressing through "homogeneous empty time."[71] Here, the "omniscience" of the network allows it to simultaneously navigate different plotlines, and such a movement conjures up the multiplex audience in that it too is composed of adjacent collocations that are differentiated by taste and choice, yet connected at the more abstract level of class and consumption. Parallel editing, typically used to generate suspense in cinema and create a sense of impending collision between the different storylines, performs a very different function here. The frequent cuts help establish a formal equivalence between the plotlines, thus undoing the older arrangement of main and subplots, major and minor characters. This putative (and formal) "democratization," as I have argued above, is central to the social and fiscal logic of the multiplex.

The last film in the current group of titles I am discussing—*Mumbai Meri Jaan*—is of special significance because it exemplifies in a striking way the multiplot film's abstract formalism, which reduces politics and social conflict to pure quantitative difference. The film's story line is standard multiplot: we are introduced to five different story arcs involving a large and motley cast of characters—an ambitious journalist and her idealist fiancé; an underemployed malcontent; a corrupt police officer and his partner; an upright businessman and his pregnant wife; and a street vendor. The opening sequence captures the various sites and sounds of a large, unnamed megalopolis (that strongly resembles Mumbai), and as we alternate between story arcs, the crisply edited exposition of each plot unfolds more like an extended montage than parallel editing. And then a bombing occurs—as has actually happened several times in Mumbai in the period 1993–2008. Some of the film's characters are more directly implicated in this event than others—the journalist's fiancé is a victim, the businessman's friend is gravely wounded, the malcontent helps in the rescue efforts—while others merely hear about the attack. After playing and replaying the bombing through time-lapse photography, the film begins to track the effects of the event on the lives and psyches of its characters. As in *Life* and *Hattrick*, the development of each story arc occurs relatively independently of other segments.

The film works by mapping the catastrophic event onto a socioeconomic grid, specifying social distinctions by speech and mise-en-scène. The journalist and businessman, who are from upper-middle-class backgrounds, are affected psychologically by the event, while the lower-middle-class policeman and malcontent are shown as reacting more viscerally. These class-specific responses are contrasted, interestingly, with that of the street vendor. Not directly affected by the bombing, the struggle of daily survival leaves him little leisure to contemplate the political/psychosocial implications of terrorism. However, as we see below, he uses the event instrumentally. A poor migrant from the south of India, he aspires to the consumer pleasures available in the modern metropolis. In one scene, he takes his wife and child to a glittering indoor mall (anchored by a multiplex!). While sampling some perfume at a cosmetics counter, he is forcibly evicted by security guards. Wracked by humiliation, he seeks revenge on the mall by calling in a bomb hoax. Many are injured in the stampede that follows. This "act of terror" on the street vendor's part raises the tantalizing prospect that such senseless violence might indeed become the instrument of the disenfranchised, thus rhetorically aligning the street vendor with the terrorist. But this dangerous alliance is neutralized as the street vendor, remorseless at first, realizes the error of his ways. He sees, through the sufferings of one family, the human cost of his actions. Initially framed as an observer, and then as an outsider, in the film's final scenes he is touched by the event. This affect interpellates the street vendor into the middle-class structure of sentiment that the film has been detailing thus far.

In the closing montage, as the song "Bombay Meri Jaan" from the 1956 noir classic *CID* (Raj Khosla) plays on the soundtrack, we witness each plot reaching its resolution. The use of this celebrated soundtrack, which also gives the film its title, is indeed inspired. This song, like many others from the 1950s Hindi cinema, explores the egalitarian potential of the city. In *CID* the two lower-class characters become a fully enfranchised romantic couple in the space of this song, energized by the danger and pleasure of urban life. But only in song—for the city remains in 1950s cinema a highly stratified space comprised of *bangla* (grand house) and *sadak* (the street); *amir* (the rich) and *gareeb* (the poor). Here, the narrative consigns the lower-class characters to minor roles as comic foils to the lead romantic pair. The multiplot film, in contrast to 1950s Hindi social film, undoes this hierarchical relation between urban spaces and populations, between main and subplots, thus delivering, putatively, that more "democratic" social imaginary provisionally glimpsed in the song from *CID*. But democracy here is merely a formal matter, conjured through a montage that, in splicing together the various plotlines, resembles the many offerings at the multiplex theater, all catering effectively to the same class of viewer. Further, these synchronous plots have the effect of spatializing time, thus flattening the multiple temporalities that characterized the social world in India.[72] The category of the middle class expands, and each segment gets both its own story and the full weight of spectatorial attention. The film deliberately stages the terrorist attack as a traumatic core around which different segments of the middle classes can cohere, while the multiplot structure preserves the specificity of individual responses, anchoring them in particulars of psyche and circumstance, yet granting to each roughly equal time.

As the above discussion shows, multiplot films use the network narrative in order to construct a diegetic space that represents the middle class as a self-defining and self-contained formation whose values and practices define the shape of modern India. They do this, as I have shown, by cataloguing a set of differences that previously would have denoted real social division in order to make them equivalent within the field of capitalist social action. These films depict the coming-into-being of a dominant social group, but they do not give much attention to the process by which *individuals* reformulate themselves as middle-class subjects and citizens. In other words they are more concerned with the externalities of middle-class existence than with its inner life. As I have argued in the introduction, cinema has always relied on romance and conjugality in order to trace the contours of selfhood and subjectivity, and so the task of probing the nuances of middle-class individuality is taken up by a subgenre of the multiplot film that is concerned with the vicissitudes of love and marriage. In films like *Salaam-e-Ishq, Honeymoon Travels Pvt. Ltd.* (hereafter cited as *Honeymoon*), *Just Married*, and *Life in a . . . Metro* the diversity of the social body is imagined through manifold instantiations of the middle-class couple. There is a natural fit here between subject matter and generic form—romantic stories structured around chance encounters and coincidences lend themselves ideally to the temporality of the network narrative. Interlocking sexual histories, the unbidden comings and goings of desire, and the contingencies of city life help create the social web required in the network narrative. Degrees of knowledge and ignorance between different players evoke ironies and the potential for dramatic confrontations. The first three films listed above—*Salaam-e-Ishq*, which is a loose adaptation of *Love, Actually* (Richard Curtis, 2003); *Honeymoon*; and *Just Married*—explore different types of couples varied by age, ethnic background, romantic history, socioeconomic status, and even sexual orientation. Elective conjugality is contrasted to "love marriages," and the limits of each mode are tested against the other so as to unsettle this enduring cultural binary; young love coexists with mature romance, while love-at-first sight is explored alongside the extramarital fling. In *Just Married*, for example, a couple who have had an arranged marriage go on a honeymoon and encounter a wide variety of couples—the young, the old, the shy, and the bold—and these other stories develop alongside their own delicate interpersonal negotiations.

Films like *Just Married* produce a conjugal panorama and use the multiplot structure to give us different takes on the process of coupling. Such a gathering of heterosexual, middle-class couples marks a break with the conjugal conventions of classic Hindi cinema. In that space, the romantic couple's sovereignty was far from secured. As Madhava Prasad has argued, the couple, though a harbinger of modernity, was always subject to the disciplining gaze of tradition.[73] Its coming-into-being involved serious clashes with authoritarian figures, and most films ended with the couple capitulating to the demands of the extended family and the broader social world. Though free choice and nuclear conjugality were evoked as desirable, such a "modern" couple-form was rarely realized; in fact, death was the price of the truly autonomous couple's transgressions. While the agony and ecstasy of romantic love were sensuously experienced, especially in the flights of song and dance, the couple remained an ideal. Since the obstacles to romantic fulfillment were ideological, the couple was thought of as a fused and indissoluble entity, and the individuals comprising the pair were rarely distinguished by the particulars of psyche, biography, or sociology. This generic couple gives way in the multiplot film to a multiplicity, thus positing a difference between couples. More important, dramatic conflict is psychologized and becomes anchored in the dynamics of couple-formation. Thus in *Honeymoon* we glimpse the couples as they appear to each other in public and then in private as they work through the travails of married life: Mili, who appears as the demure wife of the domineering Partha in public, struggles for autonomy in private, while the movie-crazy, stereotypically Punjabi Pinky tries unsuccessfully to seduce her husband Vicky, whose sexual orientation seems unclear. One wife runs off with a former lover, while another discovers that her new spouse is gay. An older couple, both on their second marriage, navigate their troubled pasts and imperfect presents. The one perfect coupling, it turns out, is a union of superheroes! The private/public alternation as well as the intercutting between scenes present each couple as unique, confronting particular challenges, and none as ideal. In a climactic party scene, the couples engage in a collective dance. The choreography is at odds with the synchronized, show-style dancing that has characterized the Bollywood song-and-dance spectacle. Each body moves in its own particular way and simultaneously announces its stake in a universal conception of middle-class citizenry.

Unlike Hindi cinema of the past, these films assume the right of the couple to form a private union based on romantic love. The multiplot structure is used to generalize this liberal-democratic model of union across a certain band of the socioeconomic, demographic spectrum. This concerted extension of an emerging conjugal model into a norm goes hand in hand with the establishment of the multiplex as the typical form of exhibition in India.[74] A tour bus in the case of *Honeymoon* and a vacation resort in *Just Married* provide the mediating milieus for this exercise. It bears noting that these milieus typify the lifestyle of the proliferating middle classes and resemble the multiplex environment in that they too are discontinuous with the real conditions of life. The India that is excluded by these narratives is referenced by stock characters such as the bus-driver and the tour guide in *Honeymoon*. These figures, who clearly do not belong to the middle classes, stand for the voice of tradition, espousing regressive views that the text tolerates in a patronizing manner. Older modes of film romance are also nostalgically evoked through snippets of Hindi film song whose unabashed romanticism contrasts ironically with the vicissitudes of couple-formation in the multiplot. If romantic duets once functioned to consolidate the couple in Hindi cinema, in *Honeymoon* they help us take the measure of new modes of conjugality. Thus they guide us through a flashback or are incorporated into the soundtrack for whimsical effects.

I turn, in conclusion, to Anurag Basu's *Life in a . . . Metro*—one of the most complex and assured instances of a network narrative that brings together the diverse aesthetic tendencies of the multiplex film that I have been documenting. The first generation of multiplex films jettisoned the established idioms of Hindi cinema in pursuit of new forms that were more congruent with India's emergent reality. This avant-gardism resulted, as we have seen, in a degree of semantic and cognitive unintelligibility. The task of the second-generation multiplex film has been to widen the address of the multiplex, and it does so by using a formal innovation—the network narrative—to evoke a new social imaginary. *Life in a . . . Metro* is a hybrid text in that combines some of the aesthetic innovations of the first generation—off-kilter framing, a densely textured, realistic mise-en-scène, and expressionist lighting—with the network construction that characterizes the multiplot films I have discussed above. At the same time, the film returns to two enduring features of classic Hindi cinema—the urban milieu and the song sequence. This repurposing of older modes and motifs of representation makes *Life in a . . . Metro* a striking instance of the evolution of Hindi cinema that historicizes the older form while retroactively claiming it as the cultural archive of the middle-class viewer.

The title of the film, *Life in a . . . Metro*, is a succinct description of its content. It explores middle-class life in contemporary metropolitan India through the romantic adventures of several characters linked to one another through bonds of kinship, friendship, and work. Interestingly, though the film is obviously set in Mumbai, the text refers to the locale only in general terms—as a *metro*. The erasure of specificity—the "unnaming" of familiar iconic landmarks like the Marine drive, Victoria Terminus station, the Mahalakshmi Temple, Juhu Beach, and the Dharavi slums—serves a crucial function. We are no longer in the historical space of Mumbai, which has been meticulously archived in Hindi cinema as a stratified space, but in the sociological milieu of the metro—typically inhabited by the upwardly mobile middle classes. Evoked through highrise buildings, commuter trains, the ceaseless flow of traffic, glittering malls, office cubicles, neon signs, and rain-drenched streets, the word *metro* connotes an environment that encompasses and connects human lives in specific ways.

In keeping with the conventions of the 1950s Hindi city film, *Life in a . . . Metro* features several characters who happen to be migrants. But these are migrants with a difference; they come not from the village but from other metropolises and towns—the sisters Shivani and Shruti are from Kolkata, Monty and Rahul are from provincial towns, and Neha's origins are never disclosed. Further, the city is both a place of arrival and a point of departure. Akash is awaiting a job offer in Dubai, Ranjeet is forever traveling out of town, and many other characters have globally dispersed ties. The city is thus a node in a mobile network and not, as it had been in Hindi cinema, a fixed locale that connoted modernity and served as village India's "other." What *Life in a . . . Metro* does is to take Hindi cinema's stock image of the city and re-imagine it as a site where new modes of subjectivity can be compiled. At the same time, the film portrays the city—in a way that Hindi cinema always has done—as a heterotopic space that connotes anomie and alienation while offering the potential for subjective freedom. Thus, in the climactic scene of the film, the resolutions of all the different plot threads, some happy, some not, unfold in public places—streets, trains, and stations. The film is premised on naturalism, evoking an urban milieu that constantly presses against these human subjects, shaping their behaviors and limiting their agency. This finds frequent expression in a graphic scheme where frames are bisected at a diagonal. The human subject is squeezed into a corner, while the cityscape dominates the frame. This sense of entrapment is highlighted by a mise-en-scène in which characters are limned against windows of high-rise buildings, enclosed in cars, hemmed into hivelike office spaces. The composition of shots, though deep, rarely places the human subject in the foreground. Our view is repeatedly obstructed by storefronts, pillars, crowds, and multiple frames. The vertical lines of the split screen described above have now been folded into the mise-en-scène as an aspect of the milieu that the characters inhabit, so that verticality now emerges as part of the experience of cinema (see figs. 26–29).[75]

The city is imagined as a mobile space that facilitates contingent encounters, yet the framing and mise-en-scène suggest the difficulty of achieving real intimacy. Thus, while the stress and speed of the environment encourage ephemeral relations, it is the subject's charge to find enduring love and establish authentic connections. Characters must transcend this milieu and fight the dehumanizing effects of the city. In one sequence this takes the literal form of a character, Shruti, going to the

26 The shots from the opening montage shown here and in figures 27 and 28 graphically incorporate the split-screen effect to convey the multiple narrative arcs; shown here are Shikha and her son. (From Anurag Basu's *Life . . . in a Metro*, 2007.)

27 Shruti in the opening montage. (From Anurag Basu's *Life . . . in a Metro*, 2007.)

28 Rahul and Neha in the opening montage. (From Anurag Basu's *Life . . . in a Metro*, 2007.)

29 Night life in the city, showing Neha and Ranjeet. (From Anurag Basu's *Life . . . in a Metro*, 2007.)

roof of a high-rise building, taking in a bird's eye view of the city (a view reserved until now for the camera), and then letting out into the sky a primal scream. In another sequence, Rahul, the provincial boy on the make, finds redemption by going to the very edges of the city, a wasteland littered with abandoned construction sites and broken dreams. Further, each resolution, though it occurs in full public view, is quite private—the result of actions or inactions on the part of characters.

Conjugality becomes problematic in this mobile landscape: Shruti's roommate, Neha, is having an affair with Shruti's boss, Ranjeet, who also happens to be the husband of Shruti's sister, Shikha. Ranjeet's assistant Rahul is in love with Neha. The lonely and neglected Shikha is attracted to Akash, an aspiring actor who happens to rehearse in the building in which her dance teacher Shivani lives. In order to keep the web of connections tightly wound, the film makes greater use of chance and coincidence than the network narratives discussed earlier. Thus Shruti, who is looking for a partner, first meets Monty via an online dating service, rejects him, and then meets him again at a job interview just after she has walked in on her boyfriend having sex with another man. It is also Shruti who realizes, by chance, that Neha's abusive lover is her own brother-in-law, Ranjeet. Rahul lets his boss, Ranjeet, use his apartment for assignations, only to realize that the boss's girlfriend is none other than Neha. A misplaced cell phone is the agent of his discovery. A cell phone is also instrumental in Shikha's accidental realization that her husband, Ranjeet, is having an affair, and this knowledge frees her to explore her feelings for Akash. The cell phone, which keeps an electronic record of these illicit connections, takes on the role of the vigilant community whose historical task in Hindi cinema has been to police desire. Since the scenes of discovery are private and individuated rather than public and social, characters have control over their own responses. They must act of their own accord rather than be compelled by social interdictions. For instance, though Shruti finds out about Ranjeet and Neha, she does not alert Shikha about this. Ranjeet confesses to the affair, and the couple must decide, in the privacy of their kitchen, what to do with this knowledge. Similarly, when Shikha returns to her marriage at the end, she is motivated by her own ideological conditioning—she is a mother—rather than by a social prohibition. Characters no longer occupy a preconstituted social world but are encompassed by a milieu, the city. The networks they form—by cell phone, e-mail, and chance encounters—take the place of collectivities like the family, community, neighborhood, and workplace. Their capacity to create networks within which issues of conjugality are relayed and reconfigured mark them as subjects of India's new middle class.[76]

The metro is the medium that holds this network together, and the film uses song sequences as another device that assembles the different plot threads. Songs are inserted at narrative turning points. A song occurs, for instance, at the first complication in each story arc. The song serves to synchronize these various strands by playing over a montage of images from each story arc. As such, it functions as the sonic equivalent of the split screen. In addition, the song affectively aligns the story arcs. While it transcribes subjective states—joy, sorrow, pain—the song belongs to no one character but expresses, as it were, a network of emotion. The songs function analogously to a soundtrack, since the characters on-screen are not lip-synching. However, they are not entirely nondiegetic either. The

associate producers
ram mirchandani
alpana mishra
siddharth roy kapur

30  The playback singers are present in the diegesis. (From Anurag Basu's *Life . . . in a Metro*, 2007.)

actual singers show up on-screen but are not acknowledged by the story world (fig. 30). These sequences strongly resemble music videos, in which a band's performance is accompanied by a narrative that "picturizes" the song. At the same time, they recall and deconstruct the convention of playback singing in Hindi cinema. Here, the star on-screen lip-synchs to a song recorded by another artist, thus setting up what Neepa Majumdar has called "the dual star system," whereby the song sequence is received as a composite of two performances—one aural and the other visual.[77] In the interests of realism, the multiplex film, as noted above, typically dispenses with the song sequence, which either disappears altogether or is incorporated into the soundtrack. *Life in a . . . Metro*, in contrast, retains, in Majumdar's words, the "embodied voice" by giving us an on-screen image of the singer while at the same time eschewing the artifice of the "all-singing, all-dancing" Hindi film. *Life in a . . . Metro*'s invocation and repurposing of two of the most enduring features of Hindi cinema—its representations of the city and its use of song and dance—make it an especially interesting example of the multiplex film. The film's assured citation of the conventions of classic Hindi cinema speaks to the multiplex film's emergence as a dominant form.

The multiplot films discussed in this chapter vividly exemplify the changes in cinematic form induced by the rise of multiplex exhibition in India. The multiplex, I have argued, is not merely a different brick-and-mortar arrangement of movie screens and seats, but one element in a network of practices and institutions that is constitutive of Indian modernity. By providing a viewing space that is simultaneously *exclusive* (self-consciously sealed off from the distresses of urban reality) and *linked* (symbiotically connected to other mercantile practices), the multiplex is a node that is crucial to the project of middle-class formation. It is entirely appropriate that the configuration of material practices embodied in the multiplex is paralleled within the textual domain of the multiplex film. We saw in chapter 3 how cinematic form in New Horror is congruent with the new sociology of the middle classes. The multiplot film is another instance of the convergence of aesthetic form with adjacent reality. The network narratives that structure films like *Honeymoon* or *Life in a . . . Metro* are concerned with how different populations inhabit the same space—a tour bus, an apartment building, or, for that matter, a city—and they stabilize at the level of content the new social relations and bodily habituations that characterize the middle-class habitus. And, as I have also pointed out, these multiplot essays in subject-formation turn repeatedly to the conjugal couple in their portrayal of middle-class individuality. The "realism" that both viewers and critics note in these films is thus no more than an aesthetic reflex that points to the social body's accommodation of the multiplex and the genre of cinema with which it is synonymous. Contrasting cinema to the classical arts, Jean Mitry has observed that "cinema must express life with life itself,"[78] thus drawing into a tight loop lived experience and its rendering as cinematic form. As the multiplex produces new phenomenologies of exhibition and shapes the moviegoing public, so the multiplex film reforms the spectator so that she may now properly inhabit this phenomenal realm.

My discussion of the multiplex film has continued and developed the mode of analysis employed earlier in the book. The first two chapters examined how New Bollywood cinema's emergence is tied to a repurposing of the conjugal and textual forms of classic Hindi film. The previous and present chapters have demonstrated that New Bollywood's staging of the postnuptial couple has gone hand in hand with modifications in genre-formation and modes of exhibition. In each of these cases, New Bollywood works through the figure of the couple to articulate connections between emerging industrial structures and filmic morphogenesis. In the final chapter, we go beyond Hindi-language cinema to see how these techniques of figuration patented in New Bollywood can reorient the aesthetic affiliations and conjugal arrangements of regional cinema.

# Bollywood Local: Conjugal Rearrangement in Regional Cinema

In the Bengali film *Bariwali* (The lady of the house, Rituparna Ghosh, 1999), the protagonist rents her crumbling mansion to a crew filming an adaptation of Rabindranath Tagore's 1902 novel *Chokher Bali* (Sand in the eye). It is clear that this fictional, low-budget production belongs squarely to the genre of the literary film that has been a mainstay of Bengali *bhadralok* (i.e., middle-class) cinema.[1] The protagonist's maid, an avid fan of Bollywood movies, assesses the film's prospects in these grim terms: "It is going to flop. No stars, no songs and dances, story of a widow from a 100 years ago, . . . it has no chance."[2] When auteur-director Rituparna Ghosh made his own version of *Chokher Bali* (2003), he took the critique of this Bollywood fan very seriously. Though his subject matter remained true to the theme of Tagore's celebrated story—the trials of a widow caught in an erotic quadrangle comprising her best friend, the friend's husband, and the husband's friend—Ghosh's film broke significantly with Bengali *bhadralok* cinema's long-standing commitment to a "tradition of quality."[3] Ghosh cast a Bollywood superstar of global repute—Aishwarya Rai—as the widow Binodini, and this adaptation completely reimagined the conjugal plot of Tagore's novel. Moreover, the film's sumptuous production values bore little resemblance to the austere and understated aesthetics of Bengali cinema. *Chokher Bali* represents a morphing of classic Bengali film into what I call the "new *bhadralok* cinema," a movement that is paralleled by larger trends in Bengali society and culture. This transformation is accomplished by a very specific strategy—one that involves turning to and selectively appropriating the production techniques, aesthetic criteria, and narrative protocols of New Bollywood cinema. This turn enabled Ghosh, as I will show, to significantly reorient the figuration of heterosexual conjugality in Bengali cinema. Following an introductory section that elaborates on what I mean by New Bollywood as technology, I first examine the conventions and practices that constituted Bengali *bhadralok* cinema and then discuss the material and cultural configurations of contemporary Bengali society that call for a new cinematic imagination. The second half of the chapter offers a close reading of *Chokher Bali* alongside Sanjay Leela Bhansali's 2002 Bollywood blockbuster *Devdas*, which was an adaptation of Saratchandra Chatterjee's Bengali novella of 1917.[4] Ghosh, I argue, draws on Bhansali's techniques of representation to reorder the conjugal plot of Bengali *bhadralok* cinema, especially the couple's relation to the outside world. By tracking *Chokher Bali*'s citations of *Charulata* and *Ghare Baire*–two of Satyajit Ray's celebrated adaptations of Rabindranath Tagore—I show how Ghosh's film rethinks the conjugal relations of Bengali *bhadralok* cinema. New Bollywood functions here not as a model to be imitated but as a technology—a way of doing things—that facilitates the birth of a new *bhadralok* cinema. In the process, Bengali cinema is reoriented from a vernacular product with a regional address to a local form—emanating from Kolkata—but fully aligned with the cultural and economic parameters that constitute globalization everywhere.[5]

## Bollywood as Technology

The word *technology* has two distinct meanings. In its narrow or restricted sense, it refers to the tools and artifacts that are employed in material processes of labor. In this usage, technology is part of the *forces of production* (Marx) or *factors of production* (neoclassical economics). The term, however, encompasses much more than the mechanics of physical energy. Thus McLuhan's assertion that the "medium is the message," declares that technology is not merely a form of labor but a form of mentation. Other philosophers and theorists, such as Martin Heidegger, Jacques Ellul, and Harold Innis, also remind us that technology always exceeds its material instantiation by virtue of being simultaneously an attitude, a calculus, a stance, and a practice that constitutes the socioeconomic complex within which it is located.[6] More recently, Michel Foucault subsumed the concept of technology within that of a "technique of self"; consequently, for him, "technology is not simply an ethically neutral set of artifacts by which we exercise power over nature but also always a set of structured forms of action by which we also inevitably exercise power over ourselves."[7]

My notion of New Bollywood as a technology derives from this latter usage. New Bollywood, as I have been arguing, is not simply a list of movie titles made in Mumbai and elsewhere; rather, it incorporates a set of cinematic and extra-cinematic techniques that render the world as a particular and distinctive effect of this disciplinary matrix. The entire range of practices that characterize contemporary Bollywood—Dolby sound, digital projection, multiplex exhibition, mobile downloads, diasporic audiences, the DVD market, niche marketing, event management, tie-ins with Indian Premier League cricket, soundtrack releases, a style of dancing, "India Nite" on college campuses,—together constitute a technology for telling stories, disseminating culture, and intersecting with the market. This profusion of "touch points" suggests that New Bollywood is plugged into multiple channels of contemporary consumer capital, and, as technology, it is charged with fully monetizing these connections. Its function, therefore, far exceeds celluloid storytelling insofar as it is a practice that is fully integrated with a capitalist media ecology.[8] Consequently, New Bollywood has emerged as one of the major interfaces for staging India's encounter with economic and cultural globalization. A crucial measure of New Bollywood's effectivity as a technology of the global pertains to the know-how that it offers other cinemas that are attempting to globalize.

Whereas Bengali *bhadralok* cinema historically constructed itself as a regional cultural form not entirely motivated by commerce, its current version has equally self-consciously turned to New Bollywood technology as a means of updating and reformatting itself. The effects of "Bollywoodization" are evident across multiple levels of cinematic practice. For example, much greater attention is being paid to state-of-the art equipment and techniques of production. The national award for cinematography was presented in January 2010 to Avik Mukhopadhay for his work on the film *Antaheen* (Endless, Aniruddha Roy Chowdhury, 2009). It was Mukhopadhay's third trophy—a remarkable feat when we consider that normally the more advanced production centers in Chennai or Mumbai tend to garner awards in these more technical categories. We witness, as well, a new emphasis on post-production, where digital special effects—especially DI (digital intermediary) and VFX—are employed to manipulate the "look" of a film, from the glossy finish of a *Poran Jai Joliya Re* (The heart burns, Ravi Kinnagi, 2009) to the gritty authenticity of *Madly*

*Bengalee* (Anjan Dutt, 2009). The idea, says director Suman Ghosh, is to give an "international look to a regional film."[9] This growing concern with the look of a film is also reflected in the obsession with fashion and fitness. It is now common for fashion designers and trainers to work with stars to build a look appropriate to a film. The industry is incorporating New Bollywood–style merchandizing and modes of exhibition. Films regularly tie in with local musicians and designers in an attempt to presell the soundtrack and fashion accessories across multiple retail platforms. The jewelry designer "Anjali" rose to prominence designing the pieces for *Chokher Bali*, and many Bengali bands get equal billing with lead actors.[10] The opening of a new multiplex that will exclusively exhibit Bengali films (multiplexes usually show hit Bollywood or Hollywood titles) suggests that, as in New Bollywood, there is a focus on niche marketing that targets the middle-class audience through exhibition spaces that are articulated with the new yuppie lifestyle. The glamorization of filmic content has entailed the creation of a celebrity culture that was once anathema to the *bhadralok* sensibility.[11] The leading English-language daily in Kolkata, the *Telegraph*, now regularly features Tollywood gossip in its pages, an indication that star-talk—once associated with lowbrow Hindi film—is now seen as integral to the consumption of Bengali cinema. The fact that noted actress-director Aparna Sen's recent *The Japanese Wife* (2010) received both praise and blame for reverting to the classic style of Bengali filmmaking—slow-paced editing, realistic mise-en-scène, deliberative camerawork, the foregrounding of dialogue—indicates that the frenetic and highly technologized film apparatus associated with New Bollywood is fast becoming the norm in Bengali cinema.[12]

The film I am concerned with here—*Chokher Bali*—was arguably the first Bengali movie to adopt all of the technologies of New Bollywood filmmaking and marketing detailed above. Its lush cinematography, meticulous sound and art design, and exploitation of adjacent consumer economies, as well as its success at multiplexes and among the Bengali diaspora mark the film as a successful instance of the Bollywoodization of a regional cinema. These overt borrowings, I suggest, are less noteworthy than a more *implicit* mode of "technology-transfer" from New Bollywood to Bengali cinema that *Chokher Bali* exemplifies. Put simply, the film imports from Bollywood a historiographic technique—a practice *and* a stance toward the past that break with the tradition of quality that has characterized Bengali *bhadralok* cinema. This allows contemporary Bengali cinema both to claim its *bhadralok* past and to turn it in a new direction. As many commentators have pointed out, recent Mumbai productions are notable in enunciating a distinct and original historiography with regard to Bollywood's own history.[13] Where Hindi cinema up to the 1990s had been relatively oblivious to the cinematic past, Bollywood films in the last two decades are self-referential and exhibit a widespread tendency to cite earlier Hindi films. We must see this retrospection not merely as postmodern citation but as a concrete attempt to rethink standard historical accounts of Indian cinema that started with *Pather Panchali* (The song of the road, Satyajit Ray, 1955) and ended with parallel (i.e., art) cinema, giving short shrift to popular film. Current Bollywood rewrites this historiography and legitimizes itself by designating as its ancestor the popular Hindi cinema of the postwar period. This counternarrative ignores both art films and those produced in the preindependence era, and begins instead in the fifties, when Hindi cinema made its bid for national dominance.[14] This revisionist move serves two purposes. First, it supplies New Bollywood with a recognizable genealogy and thus allows it to define itself as the repository as well as the mold of national culture. Second, as noted in chapter 2, the fact that Hindi films show up in New Bollywood cinema as citations—nostalgic special effects—directs our attention to what is new about Bollywood. Though originating in New Bollywood, this historiography is a discursive technique that can be abstracted from its original site and applied to the making of new cinemas in other contexts.[15]

Ghosh's *Chokher Bali* is a paradigmatic instance of a new Bengali cinema precisely because it returns to and reworks—aided by a Bollywood toolbox—the terrain of *bhadralok* culture, the cinema it gave rise to, and the conjugal ideal expressed by this cinema. The film is not only set in a time period when the Bengali *bhadralok* were emerging as a distinct sociological group, but it also adapts a novel by Rabindranath Tagore—a figure central to *bhadralok* culture. In addition, as an adaptation, it returns to the literary roots of *bhadralok* cinema. Further, *Chokher Bali* widely references the films of Satyajit Ray, another *bhadralok* icon and Tagore's most eminent adapter. Yet Ghosh's recuperation of *bhadralok* culture and its cinema are deeply informed by historiographic techniques patented by New Bollywood. The film reinflects Tagore's themes of gender, desire, and colonial modernity to project a vision of Kolkata's past that is entirely congruent with the consumerist fantasies of a newly resurgent, rapidly globalizing present. However, *Chokher Bali*'s treatment of its historical setting is not anachronistic but revisionist. While *bhadralok* historiography indexes the cultural and intellectual ferment of this era, Ghosh's film is more attentive to material culture and bodily life.[16] This is captured not only through mise-en-scène and cinematography but also in the film's focus on the body, its polymorphous desires, and the carnal satisfactions of conjugality. Here the casting of Aishwarya Rai—a New Bollywood brand par excellence—as the widow Binodini is key. Ghosh uses Rai's glamour to connect with consumerism in the present and render the past more seductive. I demonstrate how Ghosh constructs this *new* historiography by examining the film's treatment of two intertexts— Rabindranath Tagore and Satyajit Ray.[17] New Bollywood furnishes Ghosh with a new way of approaching Tagore and Ray's reading of him, thus providing the technological means by which Bengali cinema can move forward by reimagining its relation to tradition. What *Chokher Bali* does is to reconceptualize "Bengaliness" by means of a longer and different historical arc; in the process, it lays the foundation for a new *bhadralok* cinema.

## *Bhadralok* Cinema

### *Colonial Bengal and the Literary Film*

To grasp the significance of *Chokher Bali* as a cultural intervention that forges a new relationship to Bengal's past, we must first examine three interrelated contexts: Kolkata past and present, the Bengali literary film, and *bhadralok* culture. The capital of British India until 1911, the Eastern Indian city of Kolkata emerged in the course of the nineteenth century as the primary economic and political node of British India and the nerve center of the nationalist movement, its prominence rivaling that of other imperial cities like London, Paris, and Shanghai.[18] The rise of the *bhadralok* (sometimes referred to as the "new middle classes") coincided with this rise of Kolkata, and *bhadralok* culture constructed and represented itself as urban, literary, progressive, refined, and disdainful of materialism. It was simultaneously an aesthetic and moral stance constitutive of Bengaliness as an ethnic identity. The Bengali film industry's affinity for the literary was connected to a *bhadralok* mindset that saw literature as paradigmatic of cultural modernity. The Bengali practice of using the same word—*boi*—to refer to both books and films tells us that, for the *bhadralok*, the literary signified more than "literature"—it connoted a realist and rational stance associated with the modern.[19] Bengal had the largest English-speaking population of all the British provinces and was at the forefront of the nationalist movement in the late nineteenth century. Gopal Gokhale's alleged remark, "What Bengal thinks today, India thinks tomorrow," captured the prevalent view that Bengali and Indian modernity were somehow synonymous. The valorization of the literary by the Bengali *bhadralok* can thus be seen as an expression of a regional modernity that combined pride in the vernacular, Westernized notions of the aesthetic and a liberal politics of progress.

The unfolding of Bengali cinema must be understood within the context outlined above. Sharmistha Gooptu's recent study of New Theatres—the most influential Bengali studio between the 1920s and 1950s—convincingly argues that the iconicity of this studio is linked to its embrace of *bhadralok* culture.[20] Of the ninety or so films produced by New Theatres between 1931 and 1939, about forty were mythologicals, melodramas, and formulaic socials. Many were in Hindi and Urdu, yet New Theatres came to be associated with the "literary" film that puta-tively appealed to "cultured, intellectual *bhadralok*" and a fiscal ideology that was less commercially oriented.[21] In short, the aesthetic vanguard-ism associated with literature combined with technological modernity to confer a unique and enduring legitimacy on this industrial product that lasted through the 1960s. Interestingly, *bhadralok* cinema emerged as Hindi popular cinema's "other." Throughout the 1930s and 1940s, film journals like the Mumbai-based *FilmIndia* and *Filmland*, and the Kolkata-based *Varieties* and *Bangla Bioscope* contrast popular Hindi cin-ema's investment in melodrama and spectacle to Bengali cinema's lit-erariness and realism.[22] This ideology persists to this day. In the words of Anglophone writer Amit Chaudhuri, the "idea of the Bengali is con-comitant with modernity—a modernist sensibility that is attached to high culture and disdainful of low culture and bad taste. *A sensibility that would not watch Hindi films*. . . . We have not found a language to describe Bengalis apart from that."[23] As I hope to show below, as postcolonial modernity makes way for globalization, a new *bhadralok* cinema emerges by breaking through this opposition between Hindi and Bengali cinemas and the cultural identities they subtend.

### The Post-Independence Period

Even as Bengali cinema flourished and gained international recognition, the film industry and the *bhadralok* culture it was based on went into rapid decline. The Partition of India in 1947 into West Bengal in In-dia and East Pakistan (subsequently Bangladesh) dealt a heavy blow to the film industry, for it meant the disappearance of nearly two-thirds of the market for Bengali films. Despite this loss and an ongoing crisis in the studio system exacerbated by World War II, the 1950s and 1960s marked the golden years of both commercial and parallel cinema in Bengal. Bengali cinema successfully fought off the threat from Mumbai. As Bhaskar Sarkar notes, during these decades of economic decline and social unrest brought on by the Partition, one's *bhadralok* origins assumed a special significance. Thus the films of this era anxiously iterated *bhadralok* mores, especially in matters of love and marriage, and cinema celebrated the pleasures of bourgeois life. The extraordinary draw of the star duo Uttam Kumar and Suchitra Sen was owing to their ability to project an intense yet de-eroticized romantic plenitude that symbolically managed rapidly changing class and gender relations.[24] As Uttam Kumar's obituary in the eminent magazine *Filmfare* noted, "[They] were a romantic pair that not only had few equals in Indian, even world, cinema but also was the most effective answer that Tollygunge could offer to the more lavish Hindi productions."[25] Kolkata—home to Satyajit Ray, Ritwik Ghatak, and Mrinal Sen—was also one of the epicenters of new film movements that sought a meaningful alternative to the formulaic, box-office-driven commercial fare.

By the late 1960s though, Bengal suffered an extended period of political turbulence that led to an unrelenting flight of capital to other parts of the country. The *bhadralok* middle classes also fled the state, either to the West or to booming urban centers like Delhi or Bangalore. By the 1980s the city had gone into economic and cultural freefall; when Rajiv Gandhi, then prime minister, declared that "Kolkata is a dying city,"[26] he was echoing a sentiment commonly held in the rest of India. In these changed circumstances Bengali commercial cinema began to lose its appeal and ceded considerable ground to the Mumbai film industry. Local producers responded by importing the *masala* format along with stars and technicians from Mumbai to upgrade the vernacular product.[27] Satyajit Ray commented on the bind that the local industry found itself in by observing that "at the present moment, if Bengali films have to compete with Hindi ones, we need many more films of the kind that were made by Nirmal Dey [a director from the 1940s whose commercially successful, well-made films Ray greatly admired]. Pure art will never be enough for the industry to survive; at the same time, if Bengali cinema simply [tries] to imitate Bombay it will fall flat on its face."[28] Ray was both right and wrong. While Mumbai-inspired *masala* films failed to hail the middle classes, this new formula—a kind of "lumpen" cinema that married the spectacular conventions of the Mumbai product to vernacular performance idioms like "Jatra" (folk theater)—made considerable inroads among rural and semi-urban audiences.[29] In the next two decades, the reception of Bengali cinema would become increasingly spatialized along a city-country axis. Though directors like Anjan Chowdhury, Swa-pan Saha, and Haranath Chakravarty routinely churned out "hits" and "superhits," the urban middle classes resolutely stayed away from the Bengali *masala* movie. The state of Bengali cinema at the end of the eight-ies can be summed up as follows: a profit-making rural/semi-urban sector aimed at a lowbrow audience and a moribund *bhadralok* cinema that had lost its urban base.[30]

### The Globalized Present

Starting in the late 1990s, Kolkata's fortunes began to turn.[31] Taking a leaf out of China's book, the left-wing government began to court global capital, touting Kolkata as the "new" Bangalore or the "Gateway to the Asian Tigers." This economic resurgence was underwritten by a more wel-coming attitude to capital that marked a significant break with *bhadralok* ideology. In keeping with what Fredric Jameson identified as "the cul-tural logic of late capitalism,"[32] the entrenched opposition between cul-ture and the economy had been rapidly breaking down as different actors (newspapers, magazines, media old and new, and celebrities) engaged in redefining Bengali identity so that it now incorporates fiscal progress and the pleasures of consumerism.

Bengali culture's embrace of global consumerism provides the context for *Chokher Bali*, as does the regeneration of the Bengali film industry that began with the new millennium. In 2003 for example, when only 6 of the 150 films made in Mumbai could be counted hits, Tollywood's output of 45 films yielded 6 megahits, 5 hits, and a total of 20-odd films that proved to be profitable.[33] *Chokher Bali* led the charge, running for months in the upscale Kolkata multiplexes usually reserved for Hollywood and A-List Bollywood films, and creating an unprecedented media and merchandiz-ing frenzy. Produced for an extravagant Rs. 25 million, it recovered all its costs in just ten days.[34] Unlike the typical Bengali film, *Chokher Bali* was distributed outside the state. Its dubbed Hindi version had a two-month run nationwide, which producer Shreekant Mohata judged "decent" for a regional product.[35] It was also shown at several film festivals, includ-ing Cannes and Locarno, where most international critics compared it to *Devdas* and noted its tasteful if subdued pleasures.[36] While the film was a phenomenon in Kolkata and a big draw with the Bengali diaspora globally, its more modest national and international career suggests that, despite Ghosh's wish to "approach markets strategically and be global by design rather than by default," *Chokher Bali* is best understood as a local product that represents an effort to create a new market for Bengali film. Like other regional industries—those of Tamil, Telegu, and Malay-alam—Tollywood is now courting diasporic markets. To quote producer Bijay Khemka, "Let's face it—more Bengalis live abroad than in India."[37] This overseas audience of ethnic migrants is not the one consisting of cosmopolitan cineastes that patronized the record 226-day run of Satyajit Ray's *Pather Panchali* at the Fifth Street Playhouse in New York. When the male lead of *Chokher Bali*, reigning superstar Prosenjit, says that he would like his company, IDEAS, to "build an international market for main-stream Bengali cinema," the emphasis on *mainstream* marks a substan-tial shift from *bhadralok* ideology.[38] In an era when revenues are driven by high-gloss production values, even the literati are forced to concede that Bengali cinema's frugal aesthetics will no longer suffice. Thus Bud-dhadeb Dasgupta, the noted art-house director, confesses that 50 percent of his budget now goes into the technical aspects of production because "global quality determines a global market."[39] Goutam Ghosh—another cult figure—reasons that even independent films need to reflect the tech-nological state of the art and, like Khemka, identifies the "untapped" Bangladeshi and diasporic Bengali market as the audience of the future.[40] This assessment is on target, since Bengali films are gaining audiences in the United Kingdom and the United States among the second-generation immigrants who had no interest in the 1960s melodramas favored by their parents. Leading this charge are the films of Ghosh, for they supply the right blend of ethnic content and world-class production values that appeal to the global Bengali.[41]

The reinvention of Kolkata and its cinema involves a dual process: a wholehearted embrace of global consumer culture on the one hand and the simultaneous production of an ethnic identity that serves to neutralize the deracinating effects of globalization on the other.[42] While the new "Bengaliness" is not tied to locality (it includes Bengalis in In-dia and in the diaspora, and also Bengali-speaking Bangladeshis), it is produced, nonetheless, by a turn to history. *Chokher Bali* illustrates this quest for a common historical ground that will unite emerging cultural identities at the same time as it creatively realigns the past to make it cleave more closely to Bengal's recent insertion in a global present. Since the existing representational resources of Bengali cinema are not quite adequate to this task, Ghosh has to borrow the tools of New Bollywood to fashion a new cinema. In the remainder of this chapter, I compare the techniques of figuration in *Chokher Bali* to the films of Satyajit Ray on the one hand and Sanjay Leela Bhansali on the other to trace the impact of New Bollywood. As elsewhere in the book, I focus on the changing form of the couple to access the aesthetic and industrial alignments of new *bhadralok* cinema.

## The New *Bhadralok* Cinema

Most reviewers of *Chokher Bali* compared it unfavorably to the canonical cinema of Satyajit Ray. Thus, the novelist Amit Chaudhuri contrasted Ghosh's citational practice to "Ray's own homage to Jean Renoir," which lovingly translated "the astonishing scene with a woman on a swing in *Une partie de campagne* (1936) into the one in *Charulata*." Ghosh's quotations of Ray—the shots of Binodini on a swing or staring through binoculars—"are not homage, really. They are more like a domestication, a taming, of some of Ray's most liberating moments in the extravagant and slightly wild palace of *Chokher Bali*."[43] What Chaudhuri's perceptive review misses is that in the new *bhadralok* cinema the web of filiations has been rewoven. In keeping with Ghosh's adoption of the historiographic technique of New Bollywood, director Sanjay Leela Bhansali is Ghosh's Renoir. Thus *Chokher Bali* is not a "loving translation" but a turn away from Ray's cinematic style. This revaluation of Ray has been long in the making in Ghosh's career. His earlier films, particularly *Utsab* (The festival, 2000) reflect critically on what Ray signifies for the Bengali middle classes. Starring Madhabi Mukherjee—Ray's muse and the star of many of his best-known films—*Utsab* documents the transformation of *bhadralok* culture in a rapidly globalizing Bengal. The repeated references to the films of Ray are less an act of homage than an ironic way to mark the disappearance of a mode of cultural subjectivity. In *Bariwali*—a film about the making of a film—Ghosh repeatedly comments on the representational and moral limits of the art film exemplified by Ray, and explores the growing irrelevance of the *bhadralok* aesthetic. The implication is that "new" Bengali cinema needs to update this tradition in order to address a global Bengali audience. *Chokher Bali* appears to have fulfilled this charge. Consider its reception in Bangladesh, for example. The Dacca *Daily Star* commended Ghosh for providing the visual pleasures of Bollywood cinema in a familiar language and setting, listing in great detail how *Chokher Bali* improves on Bhansali's *Devdas* by combining technological finesse and glamour with authenticity and local flavor.[44]

While this turn to Bollywood is indeed an unusual one for Bengali middle-class cinema, it is nonetheless Bhansali's remake of *Devdas* that imagines Bengal at the turn of the nineteenth century as one of the *originary* sites of *global* modernity and serves as the immediate precursor to Ghosh's film, also set at this historical juncture.[45] *Devdas's* attitude toward history crucially influences Ghosh and his citations of Ray's literary films, among them *Charulata* (The broken nest, 1964) and *Ghare Baire* (The home and the world, 1984). As Moinak Biswas reminds us, Ray's skill at augmenting the idioms of international cinema—the cosmopolitanism that critics applaud—is due to his "confidence in the value of a modern tradition as it negotiated a vernacular cinema as *part* of a world idiom."[46] Ghosh's task, however, is to craft a *new* cinema that will engage a globalized Bengali middle class and express cultural identity as *difference* during a phase of rapid social and economic transformation in Bengal. While Ray's citations connect the vernacular *to* the world, Ghosh's task is to produce identity *for* the Bengalis of the world. Thus *Chokher Bali's* references to Ray congeal cinematic history into nostalgic images, while the very different milieu they inhabit illuminates how the new *bhadralok* cinema is shaped by New Bollywood's take on "history," "culture," and the "cinematic past."

Set in 1899, Bhansali's *Devdas* is not driven by the notion that the past as loss can enable us to reflect dialectically on the present, a historiography that shapes Ray's *Charulata* and Bimal Roy's version of *Devdas* (1955). For Bhansali, the historical setting of his film supplies a cultural genealogy for the present. The past is no longer a potentially irretrievable "other"; it is not lost but waiting to be refashioned on celluloid.[47] Ghosh's review of *Devdas* draws attention to how the film's specific historical location—colonial Bengal—becomes the occasion for a bravura display of Bollywood's technological prowess.[48] So mesmerizing are the visuals that we can hardly focus on the tragic fates of Devdas and the two women—Paro and Chandramukhi—who love him. If the novel and earlier film versions documented the impasse of romantic love in Bengal at the turn of the nineteenth century, where characters—trapped between feudalism and modernity—are driven by desires that they can neither repress nor act upon, Bhansali's *Devdas* turns the encounter with modernity into an audiovisual spectacle that leaves little space for mourning. This vision of colonial modernity captures the nation and the film industry's romance with globalization, and turns the past into a repository of materials for producing the cultural particularity of the present.[49] The film's reception globally as a glittering instance of "brand India" testifies to the success of the project.[50] Like other such films, including *Lagaan* (The tax, Ashutosh Gowarikar, 2002) and *Asoka* (Santosh Sivan, 2001), *Devdas* imagines a past that is more closely aligned to the consumerist exuberance of the present. These films seem to bear out Ackbar Abbas's description of globalization as a remake, "a shot by shot reworking of a classic, with a different cast, addressed to a different audience, not 'Back to the Future' but 'Forward to the Past.' "[51]

In these "remakes," intertextuality emerges as a key aesthetic technique that enables Bollywood to use the history of popular Hindi film as an archive for images and narrative codes to be repurposed and mined for film effects.[52] Thus the opening sequence of *Devdas* establishes the film's historical setting and heralds the entry of megastar Shahrukh Khan in the lead role. The credits inform us that Bhansali's film is a tribute to Pramathesh Barua and Bimal Roy—both of whom had made celebrated film versions of the novel—but the opening sequence recalls not these classics but Karan Johar's *Kabhie Khushi Kabhie Gham* (Sometimes happiness, sometimes sadness, 2001).[53] By citing Johar's blockbuster, *Devdas* self-consciously takes its place in the emerging New Bollywood canon and its star system rather than in a longer cinematic lineage that includes Barua and Roy. Though this lineage is referenced and superficially recuperated through visual conceits, Bhansali is clearly breaking with—rather than inserting himself in—this historical trajectory.[54] The references to Ray in *Chokher Bali* serve a similar function. The film's reflexivity enables new *bhadralok* cinema's project of creating a contemporary Bengali identity that can be disseminated globally. As I show below, *Chokher Bali*'s citations of Ray make possible a new spatial imaginary that is driven by the globalizing imperatives of present-day Bengal and its cinema.

Set in Kolkata, in 1905, *Chokher Bali* is best described as a love quadrangle. The voluptuous, self-absorbed Mahendra and the ascetic, self-sacrificing Bihari are close friends. Mahendra marries Ashalata, though Bihari carries a torch for her. At first, Mahendra seems captivated by his simple, if ill-educated wife, but he soon becomes obsessed with Binodini, a beautiful, English-educated widow who lives in the extended household. Binodini, however, is attracted to Bihari, but she starts an affair with Mahendra to punish Ashalata for commanding Bihari's affections. A pregnant Ashalata discovers the relationship and leaves the household. Binodini promises to give up Mahendra if Bihari will have her. Bihari accepts the proposal, but at the appointed hour, Binodini disappears, leaving a letter of explanation for Ashalata. Though set almost entirely in the rooms and corridors of Mahendra's Kolkata mansion—what Chaudhuri calls Ghosh's "extravagant and slightly wild palace"—the film opens with a long shot of rural Bengal—a color-drenched, pastoral landscape made familiar to the Bengali viewer by a poetic tradition that dates back to the nineteenth century. As in *Devdas*, the film's opening shot pointedly establishes its vernacular setting by evoking certain iconic sights (hyacinth ponds, paddy fields) and sounds (the call of palanquin bearers, conch shells).[55] This exposition immediately cuts to a mid-shot of the film's star—Aishwarya Rai—as a voiceover by Mahendra's mother, Rajlakshmi, introduces her as Binodini. Styled and framed as an old portrait, the shot invites us to linger on the limpid-eyed, bejeweled Rai, whose casting as Binodini in a regional-language film had obsessed the media and dominated the film's prerelease publicity for months. This sequence—where a local setting heralds the appearance of a global star—follows that of Bhansali's film, in accordance with the star-centered logic of Bollywood cinema. At the same time, the high ethnographic content of this opening segment (widows in white saris with close-cropped hair, marriage rituals, English missionaries, domestic architecture) is not easily translated. It activates a cultural archive of Bengaliness that is more particular than Bhansali's "vernacular drag" and hence more localized in its address.[56] The non-ethnic reviewer of the film draws repeated attention to this semiotic intransigence. This might well account for its lukewarm reception among non-Bengali audiences.[57]

If the film produces a thick description of Bengali culture, it is equally invested in the history of Bengal. In an interview, Ghosh said that he chose Tagore's novel for the web of relationships and "the period flavor I could invest the film with."[58] Thus a meticulous attention to dress, jewelry, props, furniture, and paintings evokes a fin-de-siècle milieu, but the film also discursively reprises the "history" of Bengal during a particularly eventful period.[59] Therefore the film is set—as the novel is not—between 1902 and 1905. Published in 1902, Tagore's novel dates to the last decades of the nineteenth century. Ghosh's backdrop is the first phase of anticolonial nationalism leading up to the Partition of Bengal along communal lines into East Bengal (predominantly Muslim) and West Bengal (predominantly Hindu) in 1905. This temporal shift enables him to work into the film events that happened after the publication of the novel—the death of Vivekananda, for example, who, as an exemplar of ascetic Bengali masculinity, frames our understanding of the two male leads between whom Binodini shuttles. Vivekananda's struggles with sensuality, well-known to Bengali audiences, are the "historical" text that thickens our reading of Mahendra's hedonism and Behari's moral panic. The assembling of other references—to the scientist Jagdish Bose, who demonstrated that plants are animate; to the nationalist Bipin Pal; and to the religious reformer Ram Mohan Roy—flesh out the historical setting. The film ends with the Partition of Bengal in 1905 that marked a turning point in the nationalist movement in Bengal. If Ghosh deliberately summons the grand narrative of nationalism as a historical context, he does so to render this backdrop irrelevant to the private drama of repression and sexual longing that occurs within enclosed spaces—houses, carriages, gardens. And here lies the crux of Ghosh's turn to Bhansali and his turn away from Ray and the *historiographic* ambition of the new *bhadralok* cinema. Like Bhansali's *Devdas*, in which the outside—either in the form of space, time, or historical determination—impinges hardly at all on characters and their actions, *Chokher Bali* undoes the mutual relation of inside and outside, the private and the public, the home and the world, that has shaped both literary and cinematic representations of Bengali nationalism. Historians have argued that though nationalist discourse putatively fashioned an inner world protected from the incursion of colonial modernity, insofar as this world served as the creative ground for the making of a nationalist subject, it marginalized other enunciations of personhood. As such, the "home" was constantly oriented toward the world, and "private" matters like child-rearing, women's education, and conjugal relations were central to debates over what form Bengali modernity would take.[60] Tagore's novel confronts historical change in the Bengali household by exploring the struggle between two visions and versions of conjugality and selfhood, but in Ghosh's film history turns into a "period setting." This setting, invoked through signs and objects, costumes and props, only congeals the separation between inside and outside.

The disarticulation of inside and out is expressed through *Chokher Bali*'s evocation of film history.[61] Let us illustrate this through Ghosh's citation via Bhansali of a crucial and celebrated sequence from Satyajit Ray's *Charulata*. This film, based on a Tagore short story, *Nashtanirh*, (The broken nest—published the same year as *Chokher Bali* and serialized in the same journal, *Bangadarshan*) is also an exploration of a troubled marriage. Charulata is married to Bhupati, who, preoccupied with the publication of an English-language nationalist newspaper, neglects his young wife. Charulata develops a bond with her brother-in-law Amal through a shared love of literature. When Amal discovers that Charu's feelings for him are romantic, he distances himself from her. The film concludes with Bhupati's discovery of his wife's secret and an uncertain reconciliation between husband and wife. Early in the film, we see Charu wander listlessly from room to room in a mansion not unlike the one in *Chokher Bali*. This sequence, in which Charu goes through a series of actions only to leave each unfinished, establishes with great delicacy Charu's loneliness. When she lifts a pair of opera glasses to her eyes and watches the street below, her enforced separation from the world outside is emphasized (fig. 31). The scene concludes as she turns these glasses

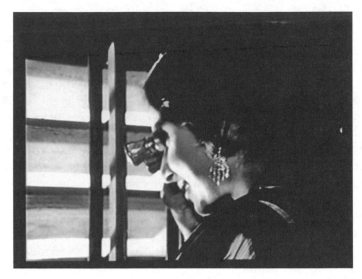

31  Charulata looks at the world outside through an opera glass. (From Satyajit Ray's *Charulata* [The lonely wife], 1964.)

onto the retreating figure of Bhupati, subjecting him to a similarly exteriorizing gaze. This sequence has been read as setting up the thematics of interiority and exteriority, home and world, that run through the film. Ravi Vasudevan, in a suggestive reading of the scene, proposes that the two looks be considered dialectically—by first looking out onto the street, Charu adopts the look of the world, and this animates her satirical look at Bhupati and the *bhadralok* world that he represents. However we read the sequence, two things are clear. The opera glasses play a figurative role—first, they are *meant* to be read, and, second, inserted as they are between inside and outside, this mechanism of vision brings the home and the world into a constitutive relation that the film thematizes.[62]

When these opera glasses return in Bhansali's *Devdas*, they are the same instrument but now emphatically literalized. Paro uses them so she might gaze at Devdas more closely. This is a citation emptied of all rhetoricity—the opera glasses are just opera glasses. As such, it emblematizes the film's disinterest in exploring the relation between the home and the world. Unlike previous adaptations of Chatterji's novel that connected the private drama with the historical experience of modernity in colonial Bengal,[63] Bhansali's *Devdas* is noteworthy for its almost claustrophobic focus on the inner world—what Ranjani Mazumdar has called New Bollywood cinema's unfolding of the "panoramic interior."[64] Not only does this focus provide opportunities to show spectacular real estate and the consumerist displays of family life, including rituals, songs, and dances that are the hallmark of Bollywood cinema, but the increasing focus on the private also indexes the disappearance of the social that characterizes globalization processes, while allowing for the emergence of a new narrative of the interior (fig. 32).[65]

When we encounter the opera glasses once more in *Chokher Bali*, they have become an instrument of voyeurism—Binodini looks through them so she can see more clearly Ashalata's and Mahendra's conjugal play in the marital bedroom (fig. 33). The scene renders literal the following passage in Tagore's novel where the narrator recounts Binodini's libidinal investments in the couple: "Her love hungry soul was now deprived of the

32 Paro looks at Devdas. (From Sanjay Leela Bhansali's *Devdas*, 2002.)

33 Binodini peers into Asha and Mahendra's bedroom. (From Rituparna Ghosh's *Chokher Bali* [Sand in the eye], 2003.)

vicarious thrill of watching and instigating the drama of conjugal love. Though the game was painful to watch—it roused dormant, frustrated longings—it held a sinister fascination for her."[66] The glasses allow her to look into those spaces inside the home typically forbidden to a widow. In this citation, the opera glasses, rather than connecting the outside with the inside as they had done in Ray's film, mark a spatial order of the interior that Binodini will subsequently transgress. As Binodini turns the opera glasses inward, the film captures—while citing—the rupture between the old and new *bhadralok* cinema. If the former posited the constitutive relation between the home and the world, the private and the public, the individual and the social in the construction of a specifically Bengali modernity, *Chokher Bali*, pace *Devdas*, undoes these articulations. Since the new *bhadralok* cinema's ideal addressee is a globally dispersed—rather than a regionally situated—Bengali viewer, ethnic particularity (Bengali-ness) is indexed here through shared cultural habits (dress, food, language) and idioms of intimate life rather than through evocations of a concrete but ever-changing spatio-temporal location (Bengal). *Bhadralok* cinema addressed to a regional audience could assume a shared conception of place and then explore the relation between subjects and their sociohistorical determinations. By contrast, new *bhadralok* cinema, targeted to a deterritorialized Bengali, follows New Bollywood and focuses on the private—locating cultural particularity in what happens inside homes, families, marriages, and relationships.

If Satyajit Ray's modernist adaptations of Tagore had faithfully tracked how female desire (Charu's in *Charulata*, Bimala's in *Ghare Baire*) is asymptotic to but ultimately subsumed by the narrative of nationalism, in Ghosh's film no such tragedy ensues from the confrontation between gendered desire and the nationalist project. This paratactical relationship between the inside and outside, the individual and the social, in which the one never quite enters into a productive tension with the other, is central to the spatial imagination of New Bollywood cinema, and Ghosh's absorption of this technique of figuration becomes clear if we compare a scene in *Ghare Baire* to its citation in *Chokher Bali*. Perhaps the most crucial scene in Satyajit Ray's adaptation of Rabindranath Tagore's 1917 novel of the same name is the one where Bimala, along with her husband Nikhilesh, crosses for the first time the threshold between the inner and outer quarters of their home to meet Nikhilesh's nationalist friend and her future lover, Sandip (fig. 34). This passage from the home to the world is the most lyrical scene in the film—staged in stately slow motion, so that screen time stretches out to imbue this "journey" with iconic significance. Shot in brilliant color from complex angles, the scene visu-

34  Bimala and Nikhilesh emerge from the home into the world. (From Satyajit Ray's *Ghare Baire* [The home and the world], 1984.)

alizes the articulation of the home and the world, of love and politics, that will lead to a series of tragic consequences—riots between Hindus and Muslims, Bimala's betrayal, and Nikhilesh's death.[67]

Once again, this symbolic passage is literalized in Bhansali's film as Devdas walks across a similar stained glass corridor with Paro and delivers her to her husband. Ghosh's citation—where we see in rapid mid-shot Binodini and Mahendra's scampering feet as they rush to their assignation in Mahendra's carriage (fig. 35)—is not only speeded up, but Binodini's journey outside the home is evacuated of all meaning. This sequence cuts to the interior of the carriage (fig. 36) where Mahendra and Binodini's lovemaking is punctuated by a single and symmetric cut to a street scene in which a band of nationalists brushes past the carriage chanting slogans (fig. 37). The montage captures the strict parallelism of the inside and the outside.

This parallelism is enforced in a more sustained fashion by *Chokher Bali*'s use of sound and background music. The film's score includes the cries of vendors, street noises, nationalist chants, snippets of recorded song, but most frequently loud singing, heard in snatches behind the conversation. This musical paratext is no doubt a citation of Satyajit Ray, who often used nondiegetic segments of sound and music to signal the "world" outside the frame—an aural supplement to the mise-en-scène.[68] Ghosh's paratext functions, however, like the catalogue of historical and cultural details that he assembles in the opening sequence discussed above. The background score runs along with the story world but is quite remote from it. Like the song-and-dance sequence in contemporary Bollywood cinema, which appears for its own sake—an additional source of value and commodity pleasure—and can be removed with no great loss to the narrative, music in *Chokher Bali* enforces the separation between the inside and outside that I have suggested is the historiographic intervention of new *bhadralok* cinema. In contrast to *Charulata* and *Ghare Baire*, where female desire imperils both the home and the world, in *Chokher Bali* adultery is a private matter.[69] In Ghosh's words, the film is about a woman's "intrinsic desire for personal liberty *while* the drone for national sovereignty grows around her."[70] The two issues—"personal liberty" and "national sovereignty"—while mutually and tragically implicated in Ray's explorations of Bengali modernity, have been pried apart by this film. The breakdown of this relation between the personal and the political, the private and public, so that nationalist history functions not as an agent but as a *setting*, also mediates the film's relation to its other intertext—the novel by Rabindranath Tagore.

## Resurfacing the Body

Ghosh approaches Tagore's widow Binodini from a different and lesser-known historical vantage. This rereading is putatively authorized by Tagore's own admission: "I regret the ending of this novel, I should be censured for it." These words serve as the opening title of the film and, as such, energize Ghosh's adaptation of the novel. In this cinematic rendition, Ghosh recovers another account of the widow as an embodied subject that we find in the theatrical archive of the nineteenth century. While social reformers sympathetically documented the physical sufferings of the widow, dramatists of this era based their argument that widows should remarry on material grounds, foremost among them the widow's dangerous sexuality—her thwarted passions and drives. The first hint of this rereading is to be found in Ghosh's curious subtitle, "A Passion Play." Indeed, Tagore's novelistic exposition of the widow Binodini in *Chokher Bali* served to exemplify his contention that the modern novel "no longer simply delineates events in the right order, it analyzes them in order to extract stories about the inside of human beings."[71] Working in a medium like cinema, less adept than the novel at revealing the inside, Ghosh rematerializes the widow by drawing on the historical

35 Binodini and Mahendra scurry to their assignation. (From Rituparna Ghosh's *Chokher Bali* [Sand in the eye], 2003.)

36 Binodini fulfills her desires within the carriage. (From Rituparna Ghosh's *Chokher Bali* [Sand in the eye], 2003.)

37 The nationalists march on the streets. (From Rituparna Ghosh's *Chokher Bali* [Sand in the eye], 2003.)

authority of another medium—nineteenth-century Bengali theater. The theatrical mediations on the widow drew attention to the widow's body—to the widow as body—for theater is indeed more closely allied to the techniques of display central to cinema. Thus plays carry suggestive titles like *Bidhaba Bishom Bipad* (The widow is trouble, Anon., 1856); *Bidhabamanoranjan Natak* (The amusements of a widow, Radhamadhab Mitra, 1857); *Bidhaba Shuker Dasha* (The peril of a widow's pleasure, Anon., 1961); and they refer repeatedly to the widow's *joubonjontrona* (the bodily agonies of youth) and *joubonjvala* (the fires of youth) as problems that remarriage will redress.[72] In seeking to "translate" the widow, cinema reaches back into another performance mode—theater—to find historical authority.

While Tagore explores with trenchant irony the problem that female desire poses to the family and the collectivity until it can be disembodied and harnessed to the public good, Ghosh wants to reinstate the widow as a subject whose desires are not only embodied but legible on the surface. This material account of desire is precisely what had to be renounced to accomplish the novelistic production of Bengali modernity. While Tagore's novel enacts this bourgeois disavowal of passion, Ghosh is committed to reversing the marginalization of the physical that has been so central to *bhadralok* (middle-class) self-constitution. By reinvesting the material domain, Ghosh aligns the contemporary global to the Bengali modern, even as he draws out of Bengali modernity certain competing modes of representing the subject. In so doing, this adaptation breaks with the tradition of the "literary" film that attempted to reproduce the novel's interiorized "vision" of the subject. The new Bengali cinema, of which *Chokher Bali* is exemplary, has no qualms about representing the subject as sheer exteriority. If Tagore—working within the verbal medium—was entrusted with imagining the widow's interior, Ghosh is invested in "widowhood" as a form of subjectivity that emerges through a series of bodily practices—she must wear white, she may not covet jewelry, she must not eat fish, she may not drink tea. For Ghosh, Binodini's rebellion takes the form of transgressing ritual interdictions and of bodily display. By linking subject formation to *visible* acts of consumption, Ghosh hollows out the interiorized subject of Bengali modernity. Binodini's desires are now written on her body. The choice of Aishwarya Rai, a New Bollywood brand, to star in the film immediately connects Binodini to a regime of commodities. This technique of figuration, in itself a rereading of the historical archive of the widow, is informed by the historiographic technique of New Bollywood. It reprises, in addition,

New Bollywood's immersion in other consumer economies and media worlds.

Interestingly, many of the film's inventions (its departures from the source) accrue around the topic of consumption. In the opening scenes of the film, Binodini appears to us as a photograph, and then we view her, alone, eating a chocolate given to her by her English teacher. In the film, Mahendra's first two encounters with Binodini are mediated. First, he encounters Binodini as an alluring image and then via her English orthography. As he reads a shopping list that Binodini has written for Ashalata, he is struck by her modern ways of home management. She knows, for instance, that naphthalene protects against termites more effectively than homegrown remedies like tobacco! This scene cuts to one that contrasts Binodini's rational, secular worldview with the ritualized life-world of the older women—Rajlakshmi and Annapurna. At issue is the consumption of afternoon tea, forbidden to widows as a habit-forming British indulgence. While Rajlakshmi drinks tea in secret behind closed doors, Annapurna is afraid that this transgression might compromise her ritual status. Binodini undermines their arguments through a modern synthesis of Enlightenment reason and Hindu philosophy, with the result that all three women now ignore dietary codes and enjoy this forbidden beverage in exquisite bone-china teacups.

Binodini's most spectacular transgression occurs when she wears Ashalata's jewelry and shows herself thus bedecked to Mahendra and Bihari. In Tagore's novel, memories of Binodini reading a novel (a dangerous enticement in Tagore's Bengal) had provoked Mahendra into taking a decisive and adulterous step. In the film, he is unraveled by the sight of Binodini decked in ornaments. The contrast between how she usually appears—in a widow's white weeds—and all that glittering gold overpowers Mahendra. Tagore dematerialized the widow even as he provided a less material account of reading, thus turning the novel into a medium of the interior and addressing social anxieties surrounding the gendered consumption of novels. Working in a visual medium, Ghosh has to find an object that generates similar social anxieties. Jewelry takes the place of the novel in Ghosh's film. It is the object through which the story world makes contact with commodity culture in a rapidly globalizing Bengal and confronts the cultural unease surrounding consumerism. Jewelry now stands in for the "novel" and captures the link between female subjectivity and the fashion of the times, but whereas the novel turned this subject inward, jewelry inscribes gendered consumption on the body. If jewelry connects Ghosh's adaptation to the social world, it also functions as an index of contemporary cinema's emergence as a platform for displaying and producing new relationships to commodities. Thus the film's jewelry designer, Ananya Chowdhury, notes, "Aishwarya Rai isn't one of the most sought after models for nothing. Everything she touches seems to turn to gold. First, Paro's precious adornments ruled the most-wanted list. Now, the gold-plated copper ornaments [that] Binodini borrows and bedecks herself [with] in one memorable sequence, are set to stun and sell this Puja, from Shyambazar to San Francisco."[73] The transformative power of gold jewelry in a globalized Bengal when displayed on Rai's frame is the means by which Tagore's Binodini is made vivid again, but this time as a body that glitters. If this glittering surface flashes with the commodity dreams of the present, it also allows a momentary glimpse into the hidden archive of the body in Bengali modernity. Ghosh's interest in exploring the exterior forms of desire through the infinitely malleable body of Aishwarya Rai enables him simultaneously to make contact with the past and the present. Further, it allows him to imagine through the past a different future for a new Bengali cinema.

Having resurfaced the widow's body, *Chokher Bali* then proceeds to follow its desires along vectors entirely new to Bengali *bhadralok* cinema. Though Tagore's novel scarcely explores such desires, it nonetheless provides the possibility for them. To grasp more clearly Ghosh's complex relation to his source, we must turn again to Bhansali. One of the most radical departures that Bhansali's *Devdas* makes from the source text and its best known remakes is that Devdas's childhood love, Paro (now married to someone else), and Chandramukhi, the prostitute he consoles himself with, meet. The dramatic potential of an encounter between former lover and current mistress is heightened by the fact that this scene brings face to face two Bollywood divas—Aishwarya Rai and Madhuri Dixit. The scene where Paro and Chandramukhi stand with their backs to one another at a graphically pregnant 45-degree angle restages a similar meeting of wife and mistress in Yash Chopra's landmark film *Silsila* (The affair, 1981), remembered for bring together two actresses—Jaya and Rekha—who were supposedly reprising their real-life roles as wife and mistress to then superstar Amitabh Bachchan. Such self-referentiality is constitutive of Bollywood. However, Bhansali is careful to authenticate this revision of the source text. He revives here an old Bengali tradition according to which a religious ritual must be consecrated with the dust from a prostitute's door, since it was believed that men leave their virtues here as they enter. Paro visits Chandramukhi on this pretext, and Bhansali's textual flight is authorized by extratextual tradition. This first meeting prepares for a more extended encounter when Bhansali picturizes an elaborate dance number, "Dola Re Dola," with Paro and Chandramukhi. The synchronized dancing of wife and whore, Madhuri and Aishwarya, is not only a high point in the film in terms of star-driven spectacle but, in and through performance, it momentarily bridges the social difference that separates these two women. From erotic adversaries, Paro and Chandramukhi become devotees of the mother Goddess Durga, and the pleasure the women take in dancing together contributes to the scene's visual charge. That this spectacular glimpse of a female space undisturbed by a hetero-patriarchal gaze happens in the diegetic context of a religious festival speaks to the paradox of the performance sequence in Bollywood cinema, which is simultaneously a site of commodity pleasure and political critique.[74] The scene ends with a reestablishment of the norm. A jealous male relative whose advances Paro had once spurned breaks up this utopic space by revealing Chandramukhi's identity. Bhansali's textual departure, then, strategically uses tradition to stage alternative gender and sexual arrangements, thus releasing the "progressive" energies of Saratchandra's novel even where it most diverges from it.

Ghosh's approach to his source adopts this revisionist technique. In a literal sense, novel and film have the same ending—Binodini leaves, thus dissolving the erotic matrix that she has created, while Mahendra and Ashalata undertake an uneasy reconciliation. Yet Binodini's retreat in Ghosh's film carries a radically different valence. In Tagore's novel, her actions are apparently prompted by self-sacrifice. Not wanting Bihari to be disadvantaged by an alliance with a disgraced widow, she chooses to serve him vicariously by dedicating herself to one of his philanthropic projects. Though we might view this as a conformist ending, and it is no doubt that, we must also recall that Binodini has begun to question the viability of a romantic relationship that has no anchor in the social. Having shared an unsanctioned domestic space with Mahendra, Binodini begins to view conjugality as confinement. She muses, "Her life had all along been narrowly circumscribed, but even then there was enough room for her to turn on the other side when one side became sore. But by now even the bare elbow-room had shrunk further."[75] Rather than risking the potential constraints of married life with Bihari, who understands her so little, Binodini opts to move on as a free agent. The novel's view of nucleated conjugality is indeed very bleak—neither the faithless Mahendra nor the morally paranoid Bihari are quite worthy of the women who love them—and women seem to fare better when left to their own devices. Thus Ashalata comes into her own *after* Mahendra abandons her, drawing strength from other kinship ties, "This Asha knew her rightful place and stood her ground firmly without having to lean abjectly on

Mahendra. He could ignore her as his wife but could not help respecting her as the daughter-in-law of the house."[76]

The novel provides other glimpses of female ties outside the conjugal circuit. When Mahendra's mother Rajlakshmi falls ill, her estranged sister-in-law Annapurna's "anguished heart immediately opened its door to welcome and reclaim a lost friendship. The two sisters-in-law had lived together in the same house in friendly intimacy long before Mahendra was born, sharing each other's joy and sorrow, participating in the same festivities, sacred or secular, and facing shoulder to shoulder their common responsibilities and misfortunes. This old intimacy was almost instantly restored in Rajlakshmi's heart."[77] If Tagore's novel documents the attenuation of such modes of female alliance under the sign of modernity with its focus on heterosexual conjugality, in the film version these *traditional* kinship arrangements become the vantage from which Ghosh explores relations that fall outside the heteronormative matrix. Tagore's critique of the gender arrangements of the modern nuclear household, which deny women the multiple affiliations possible in the traditional feudal family, authorizes Ghosh's challenge to sexual norms in *Chokher Bali*. The film takes the quadrangle—two men, two women—and traces same-sex vectors of desire between Bihari and Mahendra on the one hand and Ashalata and Binodini on the other. While the former—everywhere in evidence in the director's cut—is edited out of the final version of the film, the latter is left in and is the focus of what follows.[78]

Ashalata and Binodini come face to face for the first time on the roof of Mahendra's mansion. The two women, freshly bathed and partially clothed, stare at each other across a clothesline that horizontally bisects the frame. The shot/reverse-shot sequence alternates between Binodini's face and Ashalata's half-exposed back, and vice versa. Four quick cuts accompanied by a progression from mid-shot to close-up build tension even as the rapid alternation between point-of-view shots makes the emotional responses hard to read. This sequence, obscure at the semantic level, establishes a powerful affective relation between Ashalata and Binodini. The next sequence breaks up this dyad by first semantically differentiating these two women—one is educated, the other not; one knows English, the other does not; one is modern, the other traditional—and then introducing a male figure, Bihari, at whom both women will gaze, thus instituting the first of the multiple heterosexual triangles that comprise this mutating web of relationships. The first time Ashalata and Binodini meet is the only time that they will encounter each other unmediated by a male figure, and therefore it is particularly significant that the film ends with Binodini's letter to Ashalata, in which she mourns the loss of this originary bond. I return to this ending below, but let us look first at another sequence that pulls Ashalata and Binodini into a queer plot.

Mahendra, following the fashion of the times, brings Ashalata a red velvet "blouse." This garment, constructed like the bodice of a Victorian gown, was just coming into vogue in Bengali households in the late nineteenth century, and its adoption soon became the mark of the *bhadramahila* (gentlewoman). Until this time, the Bengali woman typically draped herself in a sari that left her arms and shoulders bare. Since middle- and upper-class women were in purdah—confined to the inner chambers, away from the public gaze—this mode of dress was not considered immodest. But with greater mobility and the weakening of purdah rules, the need for sartorial reform became pressing. Mahendra's gift of a blouse to his wife must be viewed as an instance of the sumptuary experiments that reform-minded men performed on "captive household females,"[79] a process that led to the eventual desexualization of the *bhadramahila*. Ashalata is initially reluctant to don a garment that she associates with "shameless" Englishwomen and only agrees when Mahendra requests that she wear it for his viewing pleasure, thus subtly recoding the very rationale for modest female dress—her emergence to the outside.[80] Ashalata, unschooled in modern ways, turns to Binodini for assistance. This sequence is remarkable in two respects: first, it inscribes the blouse with a sensual charge entirely at odds with its historical emergence; second, it eroticizes the Ashalata-Binodini relationship. The scene is bracketed by two specular exchanges that recall the earlier scene on the terrace, only this time the looks are fully invested with desire. It opens with a medium shot of Binodini and cuts to one of Ashalata, who now occupies the same space in the frame. We watch Binodini looking at Ashalata, who stands in front of a mirror, struggling to fasten the blouse. As Ashalata and Binodini chat, this shot sequence repeats. By eschewing the single shot/reverse shot, the scene blocks our unmediated access to Asha. At all times, Binodini's gaze is firmly kept in view, and the distance between them is emphasized in each frame. In the next sequence of shots, as Binodini walks up to Ashalata, traversing this distance, her movement takes on a particular charge. As Binodini proceeds to disrobe Ashalata in order to teach her how to wear a blouse, the camera is positioned behind her so that she, once again, partially blocks our view of Ashalata's bare breasts (fig. 38). She notices with shock and anger that Ashalata's body bears the traces of Mahendra's rough love and orders Ashalata not to allow him such liberties. This segment, comprised of fairly long takes, is objectively narrated.

38  Binodini teaches Ashalata how to wear a blouse. (From Rituparna Ghosh's *Chokher Bali* [Sand in the eye], 2003.)

The final third is composed again of a series of quick, alternating shots, only this time Binodini becomes the object of Ashalata's gaze. It commences as Ashalata leaves the frame and, at Binodini's insistence, shuts the door. We cut to a midshot of Binodini, her back to the camera, disrobing and then cut back to Ashalata, who turns around from the closed door, her face in shadows, and looks with wonder at Binodini's bare back. A series of rapids cuts follow as we move back and forth between Binodini trying on the red blouse (fig. 39) and the growing rapture on Ashalata's face as she slowly moves out of the shadows and into the light, mesmerized by Binodini's beauty (fig. 40). This sequence ends with an extreme high-angle shot, at a sharp diagonal, accompanied by soaring music. This sudden turn to a melodramatic idiom heightens—turning it into a tableau—the impossible play of desires we have just witnessed (fig. 41). Bollywood's focus on the inner world of the family—that common ground between the national and diasporic subject—has been justly viewed as a symptom of globalization.[81] While this retreat from the social can indeed be politically conservative, it is not invariably so, since the "inner world" is often a site of contestation, especially in the domain of gender and sexuality. Like Bhansali's, Ghosh's exploration of alternative gender relations is validated by tradition. But this inward turn also challenges the heterosexual norms of colonial and postcolonial modernity privileged by *bhadralok* cinema and allows *Chokher Bali* to explore other vectors of desire.[82]

We must view the film's strange close in the context of these "impossible desires."[83] The film ends with a pregnant Ashalata wandering the

39 Binodini wears a blouse. (From Rituparna Ghosh's *Chokher Bali* [Sand in the eye], 2003.)

40 Asha looks at Binodini in wonder. (From Rituparna Ghosh's *Chokher Bali* [Sand in the eye], 2003.)

41 Impossible desires. (From Rituparna Ghosh's *Chokher Bali* [Sand in the eye], 2003.)

empty rooms and corridors of her house. She fingers a jar of perfume that Binodini had used to scent Ashalata's hair; she leans against the bedpost recalling the "red blouse" scene described above; and she gazes at the wooden box that had once held the jewels that Binodini had decked herself in. Ashalata walks through the spaces where Binodini had once dwelled, caresses objects that carry her imprint, and all the while Binodini's disembodied voice accompanies her. This lingering reverie, where day darkens to dusk, concludes with Ashalata reading aloud to Bihari Binodini's last letter. Binodini writes (and I paraphrase),

> You and I, though entirely unlike on the surface, lived together in a household that was tantamount to a "nation" and became close friends. We were not the first women to do so; many women throughout history have co-habited thus. Was there no inner connection between us? There was—the desire for domesticity. Having never ventured outside, we used the same man to fulfill our desires. While those desires remained unfulfilled, the nation broke apart. If Lord Curzon [the highest colonial administrator in India] has his way, then Bengal will be partitioned [into Hindu West and Muslim East], and we will live in two different "nations." If while separated, we think only of our insults, sorrows, and injuries, than we have lost the battle at the start. But a nation is a mental concept. If there is anything that still connects us, if the vows of friendship we had taken have any power, than Curzon cannot harm us. . . . I have read in the *Mahabharata* that Abhimanyu became a brave warrior in his mother's womb. Your unborn child has bathed in the holy Ganges with you. When he grows up, set him free. He will one day help you grasp what a nation means.

When Ashalata wonders what nation Binodini is referring to, Bihari responds, "Binodini is not referring to Kashi but to India. Maybe she has gone in quest of some other India." As the scene fades to black, the soundtrack repeats the muezzin's cry with which the film had opened. The closing title reads, "Forty-two years later, despite all opposition, India was partitioned."

I have reproduced this letter at length because it suddenly, unexpectedly, draws a parallel between the personal and the political, although the film has sought so carefully to keep these realms apart. The same Binodini who had once told Bihari that the "the nationalist struggle cannot to be compared to the struggle inside a woman's heart," now compares her ruined friendship with Ashalata to Curzon's willful Partition of Bengal. But Bihari also reminds us that the nation that Binodini has gone in quest of is not the geopolitical entity that Hindu nationalists like himself are clamoring to bring into being. Unlike Tagore's Binodini, who committed herself to Bihari's philanthropic projects, thus taking her place in a "real" outside, Binodini goes in search of a nation whose politics are yet to come. It is thus Ashalata's unborn son—allied to a mythic hero—who in the future will bring to his mother news of this dream-nation. The closing title lets us know that this hoped-for future— where the "friends" are still together, and Curzon is powerless against them—did not come to pass. In the Partition of 1947, Hindus and Muslims were violently sundered. By aligning female friendship with an undivided India, Binodini imagines a politics of inside and out that is quite at odds with *bhadralok* nationalism and its heterosexual arrangements, which Tagore and Ray had traced for us. To redraw the borders of the nation, it seems one needs to bring other conjugal relations into being. It is this as yet virtual map that the new *bhadralok* cinema begins to sketch for us.

Taking *Chokher Bali* as a paradigmatic instance of the new *bhadralok* cinema, I have tried to demonstrate how contemporary Bengali cinema draws on technologies of representation codified by New Bollywood. First, and superficially, Ghosh rids Bengali *bhadralok* cinema of its vernacular (in the sense of "provincial") flavor by presenting Bengali mores of dress, speech, and manner; referring to Tagore and Ray; and placing myriad ethnic paraphernalia in an aesthetically pleasing, capital-intensive package that meets the technical standards of global cinema and provides cultural satisfactions to Bengalis everywhere. In other words, *Chokher Bali* transforms Bengali cinema in much the same manner that New Bollywood transforms Hindi film. But, such technical upgrades apart, Bollywood also supplies Ghosh with a historiographic technique that allows *Chokher Bali* to claim a *bhadralok* legacy while reminding us that its time is past. The citational capture of *bhadralok* iconography only sharpens our perception of the new.

# New Bollywood and Its Others

Let me conclude, as I had begun, with another film that exemplifies New Bollywood cinema and the couple's place in it: Dibakar Banerjee's *Love, Sex, Aur Dhoka* (Love, sex and betrayal, 2010). Anurag Kashyap's *Dev D* returned to the one story that has been told and retold through the history of Indian cinema to play it again with a new twist, but Banerjee's *Love, Sex, Aur Dhoka* goes where no Bollywood film has been before. It is perhaps the only Hindi film with the word *sex* in its title, and it is certainly the first mainstream feature to be shot entirely using spycams, camcorders, and closed-circuit television (CCTV) cameras. While we typically encounter these techniques of filming in genres like horror (e.g., *The Blair Witch Project*, Ed Sanchez, Dan Myrick, and Daniel Myrick, 1999, and *Paranormal Activity*, Oren Peli, 2009) or science fiction (e.g., *District 9*, Neill Blomkamp, 2009, and *Cloverfield*, Matt Reeves, 2008), *Love, Sex, Aur Dhoka* consists of three tales of love, sex, and betrayal that together present a cross-section of relationships in urban, globalized, middle-class India. While the construction of the multiplot films explored in chapter 4 connected with the architecture of the multiplex, here narrative content is aligned with technologies of reproduction. Not only does *Love, Sex, Aur Dhoka* thematize the diffusion of such filming apparatus in everyday life and its effects on social relations, particularly love, but it also uses this very apparatus to narrate its stories. For instance, the second segment, set in a twenty-four-hour convenience store (itself a new phenomenon in India), is staged from the point of view of the store's surveillance camera. Further, the presence of this camera determines the course of the romance between a salesgirl and the store's security supervisor. This technique is employed in the other segments as well, so that the type of camera used is perfectly suited to the relationship being depicted. It is hard to imagine a more perfect union of the conjugal form and film aesthetics. The couple once again functions as the node that articulates changes in the social world with shifts in the techniques of filmmaking.

In the first segment, set in one of the many private film schools that have mushroomed in provincial towns across the country, the hero Rahul is making a student film—an all-out homage to his favorite movie of all time, the 1990s blockbuster, *Dilwale Dulhaniya Le Jayenge* (The brave heart will take the bride, Aditya Chopra, 1995). Rahul, who belongs to a lower caste, falls in love with the rich, upper-caste Shruti and tries to—*pace* Raj in *Dilwale Dulhaniya Le Jayenge*—placate her irascible father. This segment, entirely shot with Rahul's handycam, concludes with the brutal slaying of the lovers by Shruti's family. If this ending proves that life never imitates art, the film as a whole emphatically declares that New Bollywood never imitates (old) Bollywood. With a script constructed from real-life incidents like "honor killings,"[1] "MMS scandals,"[2] and "sting operations," Banerjee's aesthetic—found-footage-style cinematography, unknown actors, meticulously detailed mise-en-scène, lifelike dialogue sensitive to local dialects and inflections—is hardly the stuff of mainstream cinema. But to call it independent or experimental film would also be inappropriate. Distributed by Balaji Films (brainchild of the same Ekta Kapoor who revolutionized Indian TV with reactionary soap operas celebrating the patriarchal joint family—see chapter 2), the film had a hit soundtrack, was shown exclusively in multiplexes, and turned a profit in its first week. Its critical and commercial success suggests that a niche, but committed, urban middle-class audience—so long an elusive demographic—is rapidly becoming a reality in New Bollywood.

In 1980, the Working Group on Film Policy published a report assessing the state of cinema in India. It determined that the state-sponsored parallel cinema, while prolific, had not enjoyed any widespread commercial success, while the popular film industry continued to be blighted by illegal funding sources, the scarcity of theaters, the stranglehold of exhibitors, and obsolescent technology. This diagnosis echoed almost verbatim the findings of the Patil Commission of 1951, despite the fact that in the three decades since the 1950s, most of that commission's recommendations for the improvement of cinema had been implemented, including setting up state-based institutions for training, financing, and preserving film. The 1980 report found that while state support and investment in infrastructure had created a minority cinema addressed to the elite, it had little impact on "big cinema"—defined as a commercially successful product, aesthetically accomplished, socially responsible, and addressed to the masses. I turn now to a couple of responses to these findings. The first is from Chidananda Dasgupta, a lifelong advocate for "good cinema" in India. He asks,

Can the mass cinema become anything until it sheds its load of song and dance and the character of the variety show? Perhaps forums for popular song and dance can be created outside the cinema? Perhaps some form of social dancing, borrowed from tribal people, can be devised for disciplined mixing among young men and women, with respect for each other? With women studying and working in such large numbers, the need for such social mixing is becoming apparent every day. In its absence, the dreams of wild romance spun by cinema become instruments of frustration and end in brutality.[3]

For Dasgupta, the aesthetics of Hindi cinema and its fantastic figuration of the couple are closely aligned with the social demands placed on it. The absence of spaces and practices where men and women might freely mix and safely channel their desires explains not only film form but also the presentation of conjugality onscreen. Society's inability to provide an infrastructure for the conduct of romance—including the pleasures of singing and dancing—means that the celluloid couple is the only locus for the satisfaction of these needs. Dasgupta's logic then circles round to suggest that since romance onscreen is unreal, its social effects are detrimental. He proposes that new social formations that allow people to sing and dance in real life might indeed enable cinema to pursue more realistic itineraries.

The second response is from Bharat Rungachary:

Perhaps one percent of our audience understands cinema. Perhaps twenty percent follow what happens on the screen. But to the bulk of our people, even in the urban areas, cinema is magic, pure and simple, an alien world unrelated to their own. To further educate the one percent elite is unnecessary. To attempt to revolutionize the tastes of the bottom layer, the seventy-nine percent, is impossible. The target is, or should be, the middle section, the twenty percent. . . . To instruct and educate this section and help enlarge it should be the primary goal of the directors of the new cinema movement.[4]

Dasgupta believes that cinema will only be reformed when society changes, but Bharat Rungachary's response suggests that the line of influence might flow in the other direction. Since film, unlike the other arts, is an enormously expensive business, a new cinema can only establish itself by reconciling its aesthetic ambitions with the bottom line. One way to do this is to rethink the market for popular film. Rather than trying to address all the people all the time, cinema should identify "the middle" as its target audience and then proceed to shape its tastes.

Whatever their differences, Dasgupta and Rungachary agree that popular cinema is in need of reform and that the creation of a state-supported parallel cinema addressed to a minority is not the answer. The year is 1980, and economic liberalization and the concomitant social and technological transformations it will bring are more than a decade away. We have to wait until the 1990s for this cinema that I have called New Bollywood to take shape. Dasgupta and Rungachary might not have imagined the network of social and industrial developments that would allow for a new cinema to emerge, but New Bollywood cinema appears to have attended to their proposals for reform. While tribal-inspired forms of dancing might not have taken hold in society, it is true that New Bollywood cinema is fast shedding the song-and-dance sequence and the variety-show format. With the multiplication of media options and the spread of consumer culture, the film song picturized with the couple is no longer the sole source of sensuous pleasure. The celluloid couple is not required to present "wild romance," and couple-formation is no longer such a public matter. Rungachary's proposal that cinema abjure its mass address and focus on expanding its middle-class audience has also been adopted by New Bollywood cinema. If phenomena like urbanization and multiplex exhibition have aided this process, the sovereign, nuclear, postnuptial couple instructs this growing audience in the habits, mores, pleasures, and challenges of bourgeois life. Further, the aesthetic and political energies of the state-sponsored minority cinema have emerged again in New Bollywood as *hat-ke*.

This book has sketched the lineaments of New Bollywood cinema using the couple-form as a locus for tracking the resonances between aesthetic form, industrial structure, and a rapidly mutating socioeconomic environment, noting connections, lines of influence, and "feedback loops." Chapters 1 and 2 looked at new Bollywood cinema's reconstitution of the aesthetics of classic Hindi film and its derivative—*masala*. Chapter 1 showed how popular cinema's contemporary transformation as corporate entertainment allows the celluloid couple access to privacy without the intervention of song and dance. As a consequence, the song-and-dance sequence is presented as an asynchronous object, whose time has already passed or is yet to come. Thus the performance sequence now attaches to couples that are out of joint—the poor, the old, the queer. The second chapter developed the theme of reappropriation by means of the couple-form. I looked at the NRI films of Karan Johar to examine how their figuration of conjugality and the Hindu-extended family is motivated by a desire to convert the narrative protocols of Hindi cinema into "film effects" that memorialize the conventions of Bollywood. The heterosexual couple at the heart of classic Hindi film melodrama is an object of nostalgia in the Johar movie—affecting but outmoded. This connects, I suggested, with an industrial scenario in which a family-based mode of production is making way for huge media conglomerates. Chapter 5 explored yet another use of Bollywood "film effects," this time by vernacular Bengali cinema. New Bollywood as a technology, I have argued, helps to install commodity logic within the field of Bengali *bhadralok* (middle-class) cinema and thus articulate it with global culture at large. A historiographic technique adopted from New Bollywood also allows contemporary Bengali cinema to express conjugal desires that lie outside the heterosexual matrix. Chapters 3 and 4 are linked insofar as they highlight two stages of the couple in New Bollywood. In the horror film, the genre's basic dynamic—the need for the victims to be isolated—enables the couple to emerge as fully nucleated. The fourth chapter elaborates on how horror's solitary couple reenters the social by means of another genre—the multiplex film.

To sum up, the book is a study of the couple-form and its various modes of conjugation in New Bollywood cinema. By tracing the couple's transition from a romantic pair that embodied the ideals of the nationalist project to a postnuptial dyad that encodes multiple formulas of contemporary living, this work demonstrates how cultural artifacts manifest the contemporary order's effects on intimate life. It also shows how emerging social relations expressed through the couple-form articulate with industrial, commercial, and social structures that characterize the post-liberalization era. If the classic period was marked by an overarching filmic paradigm ably summed up by scholars such as Sumita Chakravarty, Lalitha Gopalan, Madhava Prasad, Ashish Rajyadaksha, and Ravi Vasudevan, the current moment is witness to a variety of competing genres and styles: *hat-ke*, NRI, gangster, multiplot, horror, and science fiction, as well as multiple modes of retailing and exhibition. I have conducted my investigations by examining how the three levels of new cinema—technologies and structures of production and distribution; emergent audiences and retail practices; and aesthetic form and content—are interrelated. Further, the book offers an expanded account of the highly debated notion of "Bollywoodization," the process by which classic Hindi film changes from national cinema to global product. The scholarship on Bollywood cinema has mainly looked at the extensive aspects of this process by reporting on its spread and influence in different parts of the globe. This monograph analyzes contemporary Bollywood as an *intensive* phenomenon; that is, it attempts to theorize the internal changes in the form of Hindi cinema that make it a thing called New Bollywood.

Focused on the "middle" in the nation and its diaspora, New Bollywood by no means constitutes the sum total of cinema in India. If anything, it represents a narrowing of the address of classic Hindi cinema and its subsequent avatar—the Bollywood *masala* movie. Its urban, middle-class, cosmopolitan imaginary conjures, as I have tried to indicate, a possible India of malls, multiplexes, and other such manifestations of capitalist modernity. As such, it remains, to quote Amit Rai, "untimely."[5] In concluding, I briefly allude to some of the itineraries that Indian cinema pursues outside of New Bollywood. To take just one example, the same period that has witnessed the rise of New Bollywood has also seen a tremendous growth in Bhojpuri cinema. The output of this industry has grown from less than a dozen films in the 1990s to seventy-six in 2006.[6] Bhojpuri—a language spoken in the state of Bihar, which until recently was considered one of India's most underdeveloped regions—has always signified "the rural" and "the backward." Bhojpuri cinema—popular among migrant laborers from the state of Bihar—retains the formal elements and populist energies of "old" Bollywood, and its circuits of production and distribution remain routed through the industry in Mumbai. It is not, however, a residual formation since its growing popularity must be viewed in the same context of liberalization that engenders New Bollywood. Mass migration from regions like Bihar and Madhya Pradesh to economic "hot zones" such as Mumbai and Bengaluru, and the easy availability of technologies like video compact discs (VCDs) and the continued existence of single-screen theaters in the B-circuit have fostered this growth.

At the other end of the scale but quite outside of New Bollywood is the global phenomenon known as Rajnikanth Superstar. While some developments in Tamil cinema, including the growth of a vibrant "indie" film movement, show interesting overlaps with New Bollywood, regional cinemas as a whole are a growth industry that need to be analyzed on their own terms. Rajnikanth, though based in the Tamil (and Telegu) film industries, has an audience base spanning the entire globe, including the Tamil- and Telegu-speaking diaspora, long-established immigrant communities in Singapore and Malaysia, fanboys in Germany and Japan, Tamils in Sri Lanka, and so on.[7] It goes without saying that the devotion he enjoys in Southern India crosses classes and the urban/rural divide. The Rajnikanth film is a technologically state-of-the-art, digitally postproduced, capital-intensive extravaganza. It is aggressively marketed in both old and new media and opens wide in both multiplexes and single-screens. His latest release, *Enthiran* (Robot, S. Shankar, 2010, with versions in Telegu and Hindi) had a budget of Rs. 1,600 million and is the most expensive Indian film to date. With fights choreographed by Yuen Woping (*Matrix*), music by the Oscar-winning A. R. Rahman, and special effects by Stan Winston Studios, *Enthiran* is commercial Indian cinema at its biggest. Set to become one of the largest-grossing Indian films of all time, *Enthiran*'s Hindi-language version, *Robot*, had a modest showing in the markets where New Bollywood holds sway.[8] A quick survey of reviews might help us understand why. Anupama Chopra of NDTV warns us that "it takes some time to get used to the film's supremely over-the-top sensibility. *Robot* doesn't have an under-stated moment in its three-hour running time."[9] Nikhat Azmi of the *Times of India* writes, "*Robot* is the perfect getaway film, guaranteed to give you a high with its heady over-the-top Indian flavor. You might just OD (overdose) on the pungent *masala* fare."[10] These comments by two tireless advocates for a reformed cinema reveal the distinctive territory that New Bollywood inhabits today. Chopra's warning that viewers may take some time to get used to a cinematic idiom that is contemporaneous with them and Azmi's fears that they might "OD" on *masala* indicate how strenuously New Bollywood, in search of an aesthetics adequate to the aspirations of the "middle," has abjured "film as magic," which still putatively seduces "a bulk of the people." That *Robot*'s "over-the-top" Indian flavor now appears so exotic speaks to the fact that New Bollywood no longer conjugates with the many worlds of Indian cinema.

# Notes

1.  See David Bordwell, Janet Staiger, and Kristin Thompson, *The Classical Hollywood Cinema: Style and Mode of Production till 1960* (New York: Columbia University Press, 1985) for a definitive account.
2.  Throughout this text I use the terms *Hindi cinema/film* and *Mumbai cinema/film* interchangeably. I use all four permutations to refer to the classic period of Hindi filmmaking—1947–1970.
3.  See Ashish Rajyadaksha, *Indian Cinema in the Time of Celluloid: From Bollywood to the Emergency* (Bloomington: Indiana University Press, 2009), 69–83.
4.  *Chitrahaar*, which first aired in the late 1960s, featured clips from Hindi film song-and-dance sequences and was the most popular television show in the country all through the 1970s. *Phool Khile Hain Gulshan Gulshan* was a talk show that featured the host Tabassum interviewing famous film and TV personalities.
5.  Though *New Bollywood* refers mainly to products of the Mumbai film industry, the term has implications for regional cinema as well. As I argue in chapter 5, some regional cinemas are in the process of reinventing themselves by incorporating the New Bollywood aesthetic.
6.  NRI stands for "nonresident Indians" and denotes the large Indian diaspora settled in various parts of the globe (e.g., Australia, Canada, England, and the United States).
7.  David L. Li, *Globalization on Speed: Economy, Emotion, and Ethics in Contemporary Chinese Cinema* (Stanford, CA: Stanford University Press, forthcoming).

8. Kong Rithdee, "Hope and Fear for the Coming Year: Thai Cinema Looks Set for a Rough Ride in 2008," online at real.time 1/4/2008, http://pages .citebite.com/q1h3q2k1mcrd (accessed 6/25/2009).

9. Chi-Yun Shin and Julian Stringer, eds., *New Korean Cinema* (New York: New York University Press, 2005), 2.

10. Thus All India Radio and Doordarshan (the organization responsible for television) were housed in the Ministry of Information and Broadcasting. They remain there, though India now has numerous private channels in both media.

11. Prabhat Studios, Mumbai Talkies, and New Theatres were the three largest studios in this period.

12. For more on this, see Ashish Rajadhyaksha, "The Curious Case of Bombay's Hindi Cinema: The Career of Indigenous 'Exhibition' Capital," *Journal of the Moving Image* 5 (December 2006): 7–40.

13. By the mid-eighties India had become the world's largest producer of film. In 1985, for example, India produced a staggering 905 feature films, almost double Hollywood's total. See Ashok Banker, *Bollywood* (New Delhi: Penguin Books, 2001), 1.

14. This is how the S. K. Patil Enquiry Report of 1951 described this historical shift:

> During World War II the cinema-going habit spread much further and faster among the population following a greater purchasing power among all classes, particularly the poor and lower middle-classes. . . . Within three months of decontrol [of wartime raw stock rationing] over 100 new producers entered the field, attracted by the prospects held out by the industry. . . . Within three years of the end of the War, the leadership of the industry had changed hands from established producers to a variety of successors. Leading "stars," exacting "financiers" and calculating distributors and exhibitors forged ahead. . . . Film production, a combination of art, industry and showmanship, became in substantial measure the recourse of deluded aspirants to easy riches. . . . Yet such is the glamour of quick and substantial returns which a comparatively small number of producers can secure . . . that the industry has shown no signs of suffering from lack of new entrepreneurs who are prepared to gamble for high stakes, often at the cost of both the taste of the public and the prosperity of the industry.

15. This periodization draws a distinction between colonial and post-independence cinema. Though the two periods share many features—stars, directors, cinematographic styles, and so on—colonial cinema was produced under the studio system and thus bore a greater resemblance to Hollywood cinema. Thus, it categorized its products under separate genres, while—as I show above—the classic period did away with such genres.

16. The term *social* originally usually referred to films that were based on contemporary reality and were entirely fictive, that is, made for cinema as

opposed to genres like "historicals" and "mythologicals" that had extra-cinematic status. See Neepa Majumdar, *Wanted Cultured Ladies Only! Female Stardom and Cinema in India, 1930s–1950s* (Urbana: University of Illinois Press, 2009), 27.

17. Commercial cinema in the 1950s included several movements, including the social realist and bourgeois realist ones. Figures like K. A. Abbas, Bimal Roy, and Zia Sarhadi would represent the former, while Guru Dutt might be viewed as representing the latter. The social film absorbed diverse aesthetic and political emphases.

18. For more on this period, see Bipan Chandra, *India After Independence* (New Delhi: Penguin Books, 2000). For arguments that this period constitutes an early phase of liberalization and commercialization, see David B. H. Denoon, "Cycles in Indian Economic Liberalization: 1966–1996," *Comparative Politics* 31, no. 1 (1998): 43–60; and Vanita Shashtri, "The Politics of Economic Liberalization in India," *Contemporary South Asia* 6, no. 1 (1997): 27–56.

19. A supremely self-conscious example of *masala* might be *Amar Akbar Anthony* (Manmohan Desai, 1977).

20. Filmi-girl, "1970s Nostalgia: A Look at *Tashan* and *Om Shanti Om*," online at http://filmi-girl.livejournal.com/103149.html.

21. The films of Hrishikesh Mukherjee and Basu Bhattacharya, for instance, are exemplary in this regard.

22. This mission statement is taken from the website of the National Film Development Corporation, which replaced the Film Finance Corporation in 1975. See http://www.nfdcindia.com/index.php (accessed 7/1/09).

23. Madhava Prasad, *Ideology of the Hindi Film: A Historical Construction* (New Delhi: Oxford University Press, 1998), 121–22.

24. Nalin Mehta, *India on Television* (New Delhi: HarperCollins, 2008), 154.

25. Vanita Kohli, *The Indian Media Business* (New Delhi: Response Books, 2003), 64.

26. Many parallel film directors moved to television or produced films that resembled the middle cinema of the 1970s. See chapter 4 for more on this point.

27. Action films (many featuring the wrestler-turned-actor Dara Singh) and devotional films were perhaps the only two genres to have any sort of presence during the heyday of the social film and the *masala*. For an excellent study of Hindi action films through the ages, see Valentina Vitali, *Hindi Action Cinema: Industries, Narratives, Bodies* (New Delhi: Oxford University Press, 2008).

28. Singh is India's current prime minister.

29. "India Report," Astaire Research, online at http://www.ukibc.com/ukindia2/files/India60.pdf (accessed 6/30/09).

30. "Ten Ways India Is Changing the World," online at http://across.co.nz/India.html (accessed 6/24/09); and Gurcharan Das, "Freeing India for

Take-off," *Guardian*, June 20, 2006, online at http://www.guardian.co.uk/commentisfree/2006/jun/20/freeingindiafortakeoff.

31. Mckinsey & Company, "The 'Bird of Gold': The Rise of India's Consumer Market," executive summary, May 2007. Online at http://www.mckinsey.com/mgi/publications/india_consumer_market/index.asp.

32. Ibid.

33. Partha Chatterjee, *A Possible India: Essays in Political Criticism* (New Delhi: Oxford University Press, 1997), 146–55.

34. Bevinda Collaco, quoted in Anand, "On the Bollywood Beat," *Hindu*, March 7, 2004. Online at http://www.hindu.com/lr/2004/03/07/stories/2004030700390600.htm.

35. The term *Follywood* (rejected by Collaco) was also used pejoratively to refer to the Hindi film industry. I have found frequent references, the first as early as 1974. See Bunny Reuben, "Sharmila Tagore Discusses Women," *Star and Style*, June 21, 1974, 30.

36. K. A. Abbas, *Mad, Mad, Mad, World of Indian Films* (New Delhi: Hind Pocket Books, 1977), 7.

37. "Round-Up," *Film Blaze*, July 23, 1977, n.p.

38. "Goings On," *Film Blaze*, October 16, 1976, n.p.

39. Monojit Lahiri, "The 'Second Game,'" *Star and Style*, June 7, 1974, n.p.

40. "Rip-Off," *Cine Blitz*, April 1979, 11.

41. I apply here Dipesh Chakrabarty's rich and suggestive concept of "provincialization" as a mode of critical engagement with and localization of "universals"—in this case, the global norms of Hollywood. While journalists would like to define Bollywood as derivative, this project is fruitless, since what emerges is a clear picture of all the senses in which Bollywood is *not* Hollywood but is indeed structured by what Chakrabarty calls "postcolonial difference." To take a rather trivial but telling example, consider the following description of popular 1970s star Dharmendra as "Bollywood's most dedicated disciple of polygamy" (quoted in *Cine Blitz*, February 1981, 43). This phrase appears in a story that refers to the tendency of Bollywood stars to marry their lovers without first divorcing their wives. While the very open manner in which stars take on second wives is viewed as a mark of a Hollywood-inspired loosening of sexual mores, the taboo around divorce and thus the impulse to bigamy are read as a sign of the continued "backwardness" of Bollywood. See Dipesh Chakrabarty, *Provincializing Europe: Postcolonial Thought and Historical Difference* (Princeton, NJ: Princeton University Press, 2000).

42. At the same time, stars who were overly Westernized (e.g., Zeenat Aman) or resolutely vernacular (e.g., Rekha) were seen as less appealing role models.

43. The notable exception is *Filmfare*, which adopts Hinglish relatively late in the decade and then only sporadically. Interestingly, *Filmfare* is also the most nationalist and reformist of the various film publications of this era. It repeatedly promotes "realist" parallel cinema in Hindi and other regional

languages, dedicating columns to the cinemas of Bengal, Kerala, Tamil-Nadu, and Karnataka. Further, it hopes that the government-sponsored parallel cinema will successfully migrate into the popular form and mitigate its commercial excesses. The editor B. K. Karanjia's fortnightly editorials and the work of writers like Monojit Lahiri, Khalid Mohammed, K. A. Abbas, and Sriram Raghavan invest in the project of reorienting film tastes and modernizing institutions.

44. For a fascinating account of Bollywood's impact on the North American diaspora, see Kavita Ramdya, *Bollywood Weddings: Dating, Engagement and Marriage in Hindu America* (Plymouth, U.K.: Lexington Books, 2010).

45. There is considerable agreement among leading Indian film scholars on this chronology. See Madhava Prasad, "The Thing Called Bollywood," *Seminar* 525 (2003), online at http://www.india-seminar.com/2003/525 .htm; Ravi Vasudevan, "The Meanings of 'Bollywood,'" *Journal of the Moving Image* 7 (December 2008), online at http://www.jmionline.org/ jmi7_8.htm; and Ashish Rajyadaksha, *Indian Cinema in the Time of Celluloid* (Bloomington: Indiana University Press, 2009).

46. A London restaurant has recently introduced a hot curry dish named Bollywood Burner! ("Bollywood Burner Vies to Be the World's Hottest Curry," *The Age*, July 11, 2008, online at http://www.theage.com.au/ articles/2008/07/11/1215658075615.html.

47. Thus Ashok Banker's popular book entitled *Bollywood* refers to silent films like *Raja* Harishchandra (1913) and Shakuntala (1920) as Bollywood films, suggesting that the category "Bollywood" stands in for all of Indian cinema.

48. Virginia Wright Wexman, *Creating the Couple* (Princeton, NJ: Princeton University Press, 1993), 3.

49. Ibid., 4.

50. For discussions on the place of romance and marriage in the arts, see David Shumway, *Modern Love: Romance, Intimacy, and the Marriage Crisis* (New York: New York University Press, 2003); and Stanley Cavell, *Pursuits of Happiness: The Hollywood Comedy of Remarriage* (Cambridge, MA: Harvard University Press, 1984).

51. Indrani Chatterjee, introduction to *Unfamiliar Relations: Family and History in South Asia*, ed. Indrani Chatterjee (New Brunswick, NJ: Rutgers University Press, 2004), 5. The marvelous essays in the collection demonstrate that "through the nineteenth century the picture of a complex household with varieties of conjugal relations remains the predominant one. The simple conjugal family of nationalist aspiration can then be understood as a historically contingent 'site of desire' and not everywhere an accomplished fact" (17).

52. For a classic discussion of imperial policy regarding gender and family, see Mrinalini Sinha, *Colonial Masculinity: The "Manly" Englishman and the "Effeminate" Bengali in the Nineteenth Century* (Manchester: Manchester University Press, 1995).

53. See Partha Chatterjee, *The Nation and Its Fragments: Colonial and Postcolonial Histories* (Princeton, NJ: Princeton University Press, 1994); Tanika Sarkar, *Hindu Wife, Hindu Nation: Community, Religion and Cultural Nationalism* (New Delhi: Permanent Black, 2001); and Mytheli Sreenivas, *Wives, Widows and Concubines: The Conjugal Family Ideal in Colonial India* (Bloomington: Indiana University Press, 2008).

54. This is not to say that the family in the West was any more secure from governance. In fact, as Habermas, Foucault, and Donzelot have shown in different ways, the family was anything but immune from mechanisms of the state. However, its imaginative deployment was toward the ends of privacy and interiority. I am suggesting that this was not really the stake in the Indian discourse of the family.

55. See Rochona Majumdar, *Marriage and Modernity: Family Values in Colonial Bengal* (Durham, NC, and London: Duke University Press, 2009), 4.

56. Nancy Cott, *Public Vows: A History of Marriage and the Nation* (Cambridge, MA: Harvard University Press, 2000), 5.

57. Shumway, *Modern Love*, 21.

58. Shumway argues that the inability of romance to accommodate talk about marriage led to the development of a "discourse of intimacy" (ibid.).

59. The nearest Western equivalent for a *mahal* would be a villa.

60. See Sangita Gopal and Biswarup Sen, "Inside and Out: Song and Dance in Bollywood Cinema," in *Bollywood Reader*, ed. Rajinder Dudrah and Jigna Desai (Maidenhead, Berkshire: Open University Press, 2008), 146–57.

61. My view of the relation between aesthetic form and other aspects of social life is influenced by both Giles Deleuze's notion of the assemblage and Bruno Latour's theory of "actants." See Giles Deleuze and Felix Guattari, *A Thousand Plateaus: Capitalism and Schizophrenia* (Minneapolis: University of Minnesota Press, 1987); and Bruno Latour, "Irreductions," in *The Pasteurization of France*, trans. Alan Sheridan and John Law (Cambridge, MA: Harvard University Press, 1988).

CHAPTER ONE

1. A recent collection of essays outlines some of the scholarly approaches to the performance sequence in Indian cinema. See *Global Bollywood: The Transnational Travels of Hindi Film Music*, ed. Sangita Gopal and Sujata Moorti (Minneapolis: University of Minnesota Press, 2008). Other noteworthy book-length studies include Ashok Da Ranade, *Hindi Film Song: Music Beyond Boundaries* (New Delhi and Chicago: Promilla Co. Publishers and Bibliophile South Asia, 2006); Manek Premchand, *Yesterday's Memories, Today's Melodies* (Mumbai: Jharna Books, 2003); and Ashraf Aziz, *Light of the Universe: Essays on Hindustani Film Music* (New Delhi: Three Essays Collective, 2003).

2. See Alison Arnold, *Hindi Filmgit: On the History of Commercial Indian Popular Music* (PhD diss., University of Illinois at Urbana–Champaign, 1991); Peter

Manuel, *Cassette Culture: Popular Music and Technology in North India* (New Delhi: Oxford University Press, 2001); Anna Morcom, *Hindi Film Songs and the Cinema* (London: Ashgate, 2007); and Greg Booth, *Behind the Curtain: Making Music in Mumbai's Film Studios* (New York: Oxford University Press, 2008).

3. Neepa Majumdar, *Wanted Cultured Ladies Only! Female Stardom and Cinema in India, 1930s–50s* (Urbana: University of Illinois Press, 2009), 9.

4. Calcutta was renamed Kolkata on January 1, 2001. I will use the latter name even when I am referring to events before this date.

5. There is much excellent new work on conjugality. See Rochona Majumdar, *Marriage and Modernity* (Durham, NC: Duke University Press, 2009); Mytheli Sreenivas, *Wives, Widows and Concubines: The Colonial Family Ideal in Colonial India* (Bloomington: Indiana University Press, 2008); and Rachel Sturman, "Property and Attachments: Defining Autonomy and the Claims of Family in Nineteenth-Century Western India," *Comparative Studies in Society and History* 47 (July 2005): 611–37.

6. Ashish Rajyadaksha and Paul Willemen, *The Encylopaedia of Indian Cinema* (London: British Film Institute, 1999).

7. Still, genres like the mythological and historical were far from traditionalist in their exploration of conjugal and gender relations; see Priya Jaikumar, *Cinema at the End of Empire: A Politics of Transition in Britain and India* (Durham, NC: Duke University Press, 2006), 195–238.

8. Madhava Prasad, "Cinema and the Desire for Modernity," *Journal of Arts and Ideas* 25–26 (December 1993): 71–86.

9. Another Bombay Talkies production, *Light of Asia* (1925), also included kisses.

10. By the 1930s, a number of film journals were being published from Mumbai, Kolkata, and Madras. Among them were the English-language *Varieties Weekly*, *Talk a Tone*, and *Film India*. These journals located cinema as a part of the nationalist project of modernization and aggressively debated and promoted Indian cinema.

11. "Letters to the Editor," *Film India*, March 1940, 11.

12. Such views of the celluloid kiss have a longer history among the Indian movie-going public. The most concrete evidence can be found in the *Report of the Indian Cinematograph Committee, 1927–28*, vols. 1–5 (Pune: National Film Archives of India, 1928), hereafter cited as *ICC*. See also Jonathan Crary, *Techniques of the Observer: On Vision and Modernity in the Nineteenth Century* (Boston, MA: MIT Press, 1992).

13. "Letters," *Film India*, February 1941, 21.

14. *ICC*, 1:227.

15. "Letters," *Film India*, April 1940, 23.

16. Ibid., 24

17. Baburao Pendharkar, "No More 17,000-Foot Epics: Let Us Cut Down Length of Pictures and Produce Educative and Interesting 'Shorts,'" *Film India*, December 1939, 44–46, 44.

18. Ashish Rajyadaksha, quoted in the entry under "Indian Cinematograph Committee, online at http://en.wikipedia.org/wiki/Indian_Cinematograph_ Committee (my emphasis). See also William Mazzarella, "Making Sense of the Cinema in Late Colonial India," in *Censorship in South Asia: Between Sedition and Seduction*, ed. Raminder Kaur and William Mazzarella (Bloomington: Indiana University Press, 2009), 63–86.

19. Jitendranath Mojumdar, "Cultural Aspects of Indian Films," *Varieties*, July 22, 1933, n.p.

20. Lakshmi Reddy, "Fan Letter," *Film India*, February 1941, n.p.

21. K. A. Abbas, "The Only Three Great Directors of India," *Film India*, June 1930, 52–56, 54.

22. "The Influence of Our Films: Our Stars Don't Even Kiss," *Film India*, May 1942, 65–66.

23. Madhava Prasad, *Ideology of the Hindi Film: A Historical Construction* (New Delhi: Oxford University Press, 1998), 88–113.

24. Adam Phillips identifies the kiss as the "publicly acceptable representation of private sexual life"; see *On Kissing, Tickling and Being Bored* (Cambridge, MA: Harvard University Press, 1993), 97.

25. Sushila Rani, "Give Us a Real Kiss: A Plea for More Realism," *Film India*, October 1942, 31–33, 31. The editor claims that Sushila Rani is his secretary. Though this is most likely a ruse, the use of a female nom de plume for an article advocating kisses is significant.

26. Ibid., 3.

27. Ibid., 33.

28. Gopalan, *Cinema of Interruptions: Action Genres in Contemporary Indian Cinema* (London: British Film Institute, 2002), 37.

29. Rani, "Give Us a Real Kiss," 32.

30. Ibid., 31.

31. Nilanjana Bhattacharjya and Monika Mehta, "From Bombay to Bollywood: Tracking Cinematic and Musical Tours," in Gopal and Moorti, *Global Bollywood* 105–31, 108.

32. Rajyadaksha and Willemen, *Encyclopaedia*, 265.

33. Vijay Mishra, *Bollywood: Temples of Desire* (New York: Routledge, 2001), 18.

34. K. A. Abbas, "These Three: Prabhat, New Theatres and Bombay Talkies," *Film India*, May 1939, 53.

35. Ibid., 53–54.

36. Ibid., 46.

37. The critical reception testifies to this. See K. A. Abbas, "Three Directors," *Film India*, May 1940, 55–56.

38. Jaikumar, *Cinema at the End*, 226–28. *Kammerspiel* was a German film movement of the 1920s influenced by chamber plays and characterized by a focus on character psychology and minimal set design.

39. Mishra, *Bollywood*, 22–23.

40. Neepa Majumdar, "Beyond the Song Sequence: Theorizing Sound in Indian

Cinema," in *Sound and Music in Film and Visual Media*, ed. Graeme Harper, Jochen Eisentraut, and Ruth Doughty (London: Continuum Press, 2009), 303–24.

41. This song was used by Baz Luhrmann in *Moulin Rouge* (2000). The most internationally popular Bollywood numbers in recent years have been item songs. "Chaiyya, Chaiyya" (from *Dil Se*, From the heart, Mani Ratnam, 1998), for example, was used in Spike Lee's *Inside Man*. Most recently, we see the rise of the male item number, usually performed by a star. In *Kraazy 4*, Hrithik Roshan performed an item song during the end credits. Shahrukh Khan's "Dard-de-Disco" from *Om Shanti Om* (Farah Khan, 2007) is another example.

42. Some say that Shilpa Shetty's "Main Aayi Hoon UP Bihar Lootne" (I have come to conquer Bihar and Uttar Pradesh) from *Shool* (E. Nivas, 1999) is the first song to which the term *item number* was applied.

43. A Gupta, "Item Number: Defined," online at http://www.cylive.com/view-Content.do?id=351&vt=pub.

44. See Ashok Da Ranade, *Hindi Film Song*, 304.

45. Ramya Sarma, "Kissa Kiss Ka," *India Times*, June 4, 2004, online at http://movies.indiatimes.com/articleshow/719361.cms.

46. "King Khan Learning French Kissing," online at http://entertainment.oneindia.in/bollywood/gupshup/2008/shahrukh-learning-french-kiss-010208.html.

47. Tyagi, Harish, "Aishwarya Rai's Kiss in *Dhoom 2*: Too Hot for India," online at http://www.monstersandcritics.com/people/news/article_1229091.php/Aishwarya_Rais_kiss_in_Dhoom_2_Too_hot_for_India.

48. Dugal, Jasmeen, "Emraan Hashimi: The Kissing Bandit," *Bollywood Trade News Network*, March 2006, online at http://www.glamsham.com/movies/scoops/06/mar/03emraan.asp.

49. See Biswarup Sen, "Sounds of Modernity: The Evolution of Hindi Film Song," in Gopal and Moorti, *Global Bollywood*, 85–104.

50. See Manuel, *Cassette Culture*, 63.

51. See Anna Morcom, "The Commercial Life of Hindi Film Songs," in Gopal and Moorti, *Global Bollywood*, 63–84.

52. See Neepa Majumdar, "The Embodied Voice: Song Sequences and Stardom in Popular Hindi Cinema," in *Soundtrack Available: Essays on Film and Popular Music*, ed. Pamela Robertson-Wojcik and Arthur Knight (Durham, NC: Duke University Press, 2001), 161–81.

53. As Peter Manuel notes, there is a long tradition of "parody" (borrowing; not pejorative) in Indian music that gets transformed by "cassette-based media democratization." See Manuel, *Cassette Culture*, 131.

54. Ashish Rajyadaksha attributes this weak relation of sound to diegesis to the absence of a perspectival tradition in Indian art. See "An Aesthetic for Film Sound in India," *Journal of the Moving Image* 6 (December 2007): 13–28, 28.

55. PricewaterhouseCoopers LLP, *Federation of Indian Chambers of Commerce and Industry (FICCI) and Pricewaterhouse Coopers' Indian Entertainment and Media Industry: Unraveling the Potential*, March 2006, available online at http://www.pwc.com/en_IN/in/assets/pdfs/ficci-pwc-indian-entertainment-and-media-industry.pdf . These figures are also quoted in Vanita Kohli-Khandekar, *The Indian Media Business*, (New Delhi: Sage, 2006), 143.

56. See Madhava Prasad, "Communication and Signification: Voice in the Cinema," *Journal of the Moving Image* 6 (December 2007): 29–38, 31.

57. See Majumdar, "Embodied Voice," 163–69.

58. Abhilasha Ojha, "What Is Wrong with India's Music Industry?" Posted online, September 5, 2005, at http://www.rediff.com/money/2005/sep/05spec.htm.

59. Ibid.

60. Ananya Kabir notes that a "neo-ethnic" musical has emerged in the Punjabi diaspora. While this bypasses painful aspects of national history, it nonetheless promotes post and transnational modes of belonging; see "Musical Recall: Postmemory and the Punjabi Diaspora," *Alif: Journal of Comparative Poetics* 24 (January 2004): 172–89.

61. Until recently, folk music had a hard time competing with film music and often incorporated its styles; see Manuel, *Cassette Culture*, 56.

62. Nair interview, special feature included on the DVD of *Monsoon Wedding* (Hollywood, CA: Universal Studios, 2002).

63. See Rachel Dwyer, *Yash Chopra* (London: Palgrave, 2002).

64. For an insightful study of religious tolerance in Hindi cinema, see Priya Kumar, *Limiting Secularism: The Ethics of Coexistence in Indian Literature and Film* (Minneapolis: University of Minnesota Press, 2008), 177–229.

65. It is also Vijay Verma's coolie number in Yash Chopra's *Deewar* (The wall, 1975).

66. This was the case with Shantanu Moitra's 1960s-inspired soundtrack for Pradeep Dutta's remake of *Parineeta* (2006).

67. See Ananya Kabir, "Allegories of Alienation and Politics of Bargaining: Minority Subjectivities in Mani Ratnam's *Dil Se*," *South Asian Popular Culture* 1, no. 2 (2003): 141–60; and Anustup Basu, "The Music of Intolerable Love: Political Conjugality in Mani Ratnam's *Dil Se*," in Gopal and Moorti, *Global Bollywood*, 153–76.

68. See Nivedita Menon, *Recovering Subversion: Feminist Politics Beyond the Law* (Urbana: University of Illinois Press, 2004), 27.

69. Chopra regretfully informs us that he wanted to incorporate another song—"Kaha Aah Gayen Hum?" (Where have we arrived?)—but was persuaded otherwise at the editing table (quoted in the special features of the DVD: *Veer Zaara*, Yashraj Films, 2005).

70. See Ronjita Kulkarni, "You Do Not Mess with Cricket in India: An Interview with Nagesh Kukunoor," posted on Rediff.com (August 24, 2005), online at http://in.rediff.com/movies/2005/aug/24nagesh.htm.

71. In the 1970s Mukherjee tried to reform commercial Hindi film form from within, giving it a more realist orientation in films like *Anand* (Happiness, 1971) and *Bawarchi* (Chef, 1972; Kukunoor's favorite film).

CHAPTER TWO

1. Hari Kunzru, *Transmission: A Novel* (New York: Plume, 2005), 103.
2. From the website of the CIA, online at https://www.cia.gov/library/publications/the-world-factbook/index.html. Anthropologists and sociologists point out that these figures do not reflect the many forms of nonlegal marriage dissolution. See Livia Holden, *Hindu Divorce: A Legal Anthropology* (London: Ashgate, 2008), 1–27.
3. See Emily Wax, "In Tradition-Bound India, Female, Divorced and Happy," *Washington Post*, September 19, 2008, online at http://www.washingtonpost.com/wp-dyn/content/article/2008/09/18/AR2008091803911.html?hpid=sec-world; and Purnima Mankekar, "Dangerous Desires: Television and Erotics in Late Twentieth-Century India," *Journal of Asian Studies* 63, no. 2 (2004): 403–31.
4. See Simon Robinson, "Divorce and Remarriage: Indian Style," *Time*, July 5, 2007, online at http://www.time.com/time/world/article/0,8599,1640200,00.html?xid=rss-world; and Meenakshi Ray, "Website Shows Urban India Shedding Divorce Stigma," *Reuters*, August 21, 2007, online at http://www.reuters.com/article/internetNews/idUSDEL28139620070821?feedType=RSS&feedName=internetNews.
5. Cited in Wax, "In Tradition-Bound India." For a history of this phenomenon, see Francis Bloch, Vijayendra Rao, and Sonalde Desai, "Wedding Celebrations as Conspicuous Consumption," *Journal of Human Resources* 33, no. 3 (2004): 675–95.
6. See Sangita Gopal and Sujata Moorti, introduction to *Global Bollywood: Travels of Hindi Film Music*, ed. Sangita Gopal and Sujata Moorti (Minneapolis: University of Minnesota Press, 2008), 1–58; and the essays in Raminder Kaur and Ajay J Sinha, eds., *Bollyworld: Popular Indian Cinema Through a Transnational Lens* (London: Sage, 2005).
7. The excellent body of work on Hindi commercial cinema, the Indian state, and the significance of diasporic audiences includes monographs such as Jigna Desai, *Beyond Bollywood: The Cultural Politics of South Asian Diasporic Film* (London: Routledge, 2003); Rajinder Dudrah, *Bollywood: Sociology Goes to the Movies* (London: Sage, 2006); Rachel Dwyer, *All You Want Is Money, All You Need Is Love* (London: Cassell, 2000); Vijay Mishra, *Bollywood: Temples of Desire* (New York: Routledge, 2001); and Gayatri Gopinath, *Impossible Desires: Queer Diasporas and South Asian Popular Cultures* (Durham, NC: Duke University Press, 2005). See also the following essays: Monika Mehta, "Globalizing Bombay Cinema: Reproducing the Indian State and Family,"

in *Once Upon a Time in Bollywood: The Global Swing in Indian Film*, ed. Gurbir Jolly, Zenia Wadhwani, and Deborah Barretto (Toronto: Tsar, 2007), 20–42; Purnima Mankekar, "Brides Who Travel: Gender, Transnationalism and Nationalism in Indian Film," *Positions* 7, no. 3 (1999): 731–61; Patricia Uberoi, "Imagining the Family: An Ethnography of Viewing *Hum Aapke Hain Koun!*" in *Pleasure and the Nation: The History, Politics and Consumption of Public Culture in India*, ed. Rachel Dwyer and Christopher Pinney (New Delhi: Oxford University Press, 2001), 309–51; and Jenny Sharpe, "Gender, Nation and Globalization in *Monsoon Wedding* and *Dilwale Dulhaniya le Jayenge*," in Jolly, Wadhwani, and Barretto, *Once Upon a Time in Bollywood*, 70–91. Mankekar and Mehta link the content of Hindi cinema to the political economy of liberalization. Desai, Dudrah, and Uberoi look at the sociology of the "family film" and study its appeal through ethnographic research. Uberoi focuses on domestic audiences, while Desai and Dudrah focus on the diaspora. Dwyer studies the films of the Yashraj conglomerate.

8.  Ashish Rajyadaksha, "The 'Bollywoodization' of Indian Cinema: Cultural Nationalism in a Global Arena," in *City Flicks*, ed. Preben Kaarsholm (Kolkata: Seagull, 2004), 113–39.

9.  Johar's most recent film, *My Name Is Khan* (2010), almost completes his transition to the Hollywood mode.

10. This practice might be viewed as part superstition (the letter *K* proved lucky for Karan) and part branding. The Hindi film industry is famously superstitious, but, as Ekta Kapoor's Balaji Telefilms tele-serial franchise showed, a preference for the letter *K* also helped create one of the most recognizable brands on television. Kapoor's success might be attributed to a production model that combined efficiencies of scale with a winning "formula." They resemble the KJo film insofar as they are family sagas that combine displays of ritual and festivities with racy, soap-style subject matter. For more on Ekta Kapoor, see Shohini Ghosh, "Married to the Family: Cultural Apprehensions in the Narratives of Film and TV," *Revue: Indian Horizons* 55 (January–March 2008): 54–62; and Ipsita Chandra, "Kyunki Main Bhi Kabhi Tulsi Thi: Opening and Using the Black Box of Primetime Telereality," *Journal of the Moving Image* 4 (November 2005): 77–100.

11. These statistics are available online at http://www.boxofficeindia.com/cpages.php?pageName=overseas_earners.

12. These statistics are available online at http://www.boxofficeindia.com/cpages.php?pageName=all_time_earners.

13. Vijay Mishra suggests that this is not a totally new phenomenon; see "Bollywood: A Critical Genealogy," Working Paper No. 20, *Asian Studies Institute* (February 2008), 1–31.

14. See Jon Lewis, *Whom God Wishes to Destroy: Francis Coppola and the New Hollywood* (Durham, NC: Duke University Press, 1995); and Timothy Corrigan, *A Cinema without Walls: Movies and Culture After Vietnam* (Philadelphia, PA: Temple University Press, 1991).

15. See James Naremore, "Authorship," in *A Companion to Film Theory*, ed. Robert Stam and Toby Miller (New York: Blackwell, 1999), 10.

16. Sean Cubbitt, *The Cinema Effect* (Cambridge, MA: MIT Press, 2004), 356.

17. Moinak Biswas, "Mourning and Blood Ties: Macbeth in Mumbai," *Journal of the Moving Image* 5 (December 2006): 78–85, 82.

18. Several fine books on this era, including Anupama Chopra, *Sholay: The Making of a Classic* (New Delhi: Penguin Books, 2000) and Connie Haham, *Enchantment of the Mind: The Films of Manmohan Desai* (New Delhi: Roli Books, 2006), provide an overview of the 1970s by focusing on two key directors. See also Ranjani Mazumdar, "From Subjectification to Schizophrenia: The 'Angry Man' and 'Psychotic' Hero of Bombay Cinema," in *Making Meaning in Indian Cinema*, ed. Ravi Vasudevan (New Delhi: Oxford University Press, 2000), 238–64; and Madhava Prasad, "Aesthetic of Mobilization," in his *Ideology of Hindi Film: A Historical Construction* (New Delhi: Oxford University Press, 1998), 138–59.

19. We might view a film like Manmohan Desai's *Amar, Akbar, Anthony* (1977) as a parody of the excesses of Hindi cinema, including well-worn plot-devices like brothers separated at birth, ideologies like nationalist integration, as well as emerging industry practices like the production of "multistar" film, whose producers hope to ensure returns by packing a film with stars.

20. See Madhava Prasad's chapter entitled "The Middle-Class Cinema," in *Ideology*, 160–87, for an excellent reading of the films of this era.

21. See Ajanta Sircar's excellent analysis of this film in "Love in a Time of Liberalization," *Journal of Arts and Ideas* 32–33 (April 1999): 35.

22. For "parafinarrative," see Ravi Vasudevan, "The Melodramatic Mode and the Commercial Hindi Cinema," in *Screening World Cinema: A Screen Reader*, ed. Catherine Grant and Annette Kuhn (London: Routledge, 2006), 104–26.

23. In *Roja* and *Bombay*, the extended versus the nuclear family and tradition versus modernity are spatialized along a rural/urban divide. The couple must leave the village to live out their progressive destiny. While this divide is picturesquely contained in *Roja*, the regressive parents must be left behind to die in *Bombay* so that the couple might enter a brave, new, secular day. In *Dil Se*, Amar puts his family and country at peril for love. Interestingly, though *Dil Se* failed in India, it made the top ten at the U.K. box office. Like the KJo film, it underprivileges the nation. Mani Ratnam's films are the subject of many fine essays, including Madhava Prasad, "Signs of Ideological Re-form in Two Recent Films: Signs of Real Subsumption," in Vasudevan, *Making Meaning*, 145–67; Lalitha Gopalan, *Bombay* (London: British Film Institute, 2006); and Ravi Vasudevan, "Bombay and Its Public," *Journal of Arts and Ideas* 29 (January 1996), 45–63. See also Nicholas Dirks, "The Home and the Nation: Consuming Culture and Politics in *Roja*," in Dwyer and Pinney, *Pleasure and the Nation*, 161–85; Ananya Kabir, "Allegories of Alienation and Politics of Bargaining: Minority Subjectivities in Mani Ratnam's *Dil Se*," *South Asian Popular Culture* 1, no. 2 (2003):

141–60; and Anustup Basu, "The Music of Intolerable Love: Political Conjugality in Mani Ratnam's *Dil Se*," in Gopal and Moorti, *Global Bollywood*, 153–76.

24. See Madhava Prasad, "Realism and Fantasy in Representations of Metropolitan Life in Indian Cinema," in Kaarsholm, *City Flicks*, 82–98.

25. See Ranjani Mazumdar, *Bombay Cinema: An Archive of the City* (Minneapolis: University of Minnesota Press, 2007), 118; Sheena Malhotra and Tavishi Alagh, "Dreaming the Nation: Domestic Dramas in Hindi Films Post-1990s," *South Asian Popular Culture* 2, no. 1 (2004): 19–37; Mankekar, "Brides Who Travel," and Sharpe, "Gender, Nation and Globalization."

26. The exhibitors' cut was tied to revenue, so they were thought to have incentives to market films.

27. Theater owners typically charge 50–60 percent of the revenues for rent. See Valentina Vitali, *Hindi Action Cinema: Industries, Narratives, Bodies* (New Delhi: Oxford University Press, 2008), 134–40.

28. Manjunath Pendakur, *Indian Popular Cinema: Industry, Ideology and Consciousness* (New York: Hampton Press, 2003), 15–34. See also P. Bharadwaj and J. Pillai, "What a Waste of Money!" *Filmfare*, July 1997, 24–30. As Pendakur and the pages of film magazines like *Filmfare*, *Stardust*, and *Cine Blitz* make clear, these decades were characterized by chaos.

29. See Sangita Gopal and Sujata Moorti, introduction to Gopal and Moorti, *Global Bollywood*, 1–58.

30. Vanita Kohli-Khandekar, *The Indian Media Business*, 2nd ed. (New Delhi: Sage, 2006), 117.

31. Anna Morcom, *Hindi Films and Their Songs* (London: Ashgate, 2007), 181–207.

32. Kohli-Khandekar, *Indian Media Business*, 121.

33. Ibid.

34. See Madhu Jain, *The Kapoors: The First Family of Indian Cinema* (New Delhi: Penguin Global, 2006).

35. Rochona Majumdar, *Marriage and Modernity: Family Values in Colonial Bengal* (Durham, NC: Duke University Press, 2009), 210.

36. See Vivek Chibber, *Locked in Place: State Building and Late Industrialization in India* (Princeton, NJ: Princeton University Press, 2003).

37. See Ritu Birla, *Stages of Capital: Law, Culture and Market Governance in Late Colonial India* (Durham, NC: Duke University Press, 2009). See also Vinay Gidwani, *Capital, Interrupted* (Minneapolis: University of Minnesota Press, 2008).

38. Prasad, *Ideology*, 49. The call for reform within the industry regards Hollywood-style efficiencies as a standard. Ram Gopal Varma, for example, wants to streamline the product and the process. Thus he makes genre films—gangster, horror, and so on. His production firm is appropriately called The Factory.

39. See blog entry for 7/3/08, online at http://www.mynameiskaran.com.

40. Mark Lorenzon and Florian Arun Tauebe, "Breakout from Bollywood: Internationalization of Indian Film Industry," DRUID Working Paper No. 07–06 (2007), 22.

41. Ravi Vasudevan, "The Cultural Space of a Film Narrative: Interpreting *Kismet*," *Indian Economic and Social History Review* 27, no. 2 (1991): 171–85, 181, 183–84.

42. Rachel Dwyer, "Shooting Stars: The Indian Film Magazine, *Stardust*," in Dwyer and Pinney, *Pleasure and the Nation*, 247–84; and M. L. Srinivas, "Devotion and Defiance in Fan Activity," in Vasudevan, *Making Meaning*, 297–314.

43. Confederation of Indian Industry and A. T. Kearney, *The New Economics of Indian Film Industry: Creativity and Transformation* (2008); the report can be purchased online at http://cii.in/documents/Publication_List_May2009 .pdf.

44. Lorenzon and Tauebe, "Breakout from Bollywood," 13–14.

45. Gurbir Singh, "The Big Picture," *Business World*, January 9, 2008.

46. Ali Jaafar, "Hollywood Biz without Borders: Film Industry Banking on Foreign Forays," *Variety*, April 17, 2009, online at http://www.variety.com/ article/VR1118002564?refCatId=13; and Arthur J. Pais, "Hollywood Dips into Bollywood," posted on August 31, 2006, online at http://www.rediff .com/movies/2006/aug/31india.htm.

47. See Someswar Bhowmick, *Behind the Glitz: The Enigma of Indian Cinema* (Kolkata: Thema, 2008).

48. The emergence of the "bound script" is essential to the identification of film as property, and also enables copyright enforcement. See Lawrence Liang, "Cinematic Citizenship and the Illegal City," in *Cinema, Law and the State in Asia*, ed. Corey Creekmur and Mark Sidel (London: Palgrave, 2007), 11–27. See also Laikwan Pang, *Cultural Control and Globalization in Asia: Copyright, Piracy and Cinema* (New York: Routledge, 2007), 31–47.

49. Pendakur, *Indian Popular Cinema*, 32–34.

50. Jason Overdorf, "Hooray for Bollywood," *Newsweek*, December 10, 2007, online at http://www.newsweek.com/id/72719/output/print.

51. Jason Overdorf, "Reinventing Bollywood," April 4, 2007, online at http:// money.cnn.com/magazines/business2/business2_archive/2007/03/01/ 8401035/index.htm.

52. Lorenzon and Tauebe, "Breakout from Bollywood," 21.

53. Overdorf, "Hooray for Bollywood."

54. Quoted in ibid.

55. See Wharton's Knowledge@Wharton's Interview with Ronnie Screwvala, June 25, 2008, available online at http://knowledge.wharton.upenn.edu/ india/article.cfm?articleid=4299.

56. Ghai, quoted in Pendakur, *Indian Popular Cinema*, 73. David Dhawan, the maker of successful comedies and an innovator in the genre movie, is also known for his meticulous work ethic. "The solution is simple," says

Dhawan, "planning *honi chahiye* [there must be planning]." See P. Bharadwaj and J Pillai, "What a Waste: Blowing Up the Big Bucks," *Filmfare*, July
1997, 25.

57. Prasad, *Ideology*, 49.

58. For the relation of family ties to globalization, see Jyotsna Kapur and
Manjunath Pendakur, "The Strange Case of the Disappearance of Bombay
from Its Own Cinema: A Case of Imperialism or Globalization," *Democratic
Communiqué* 21, no. 1 (2007): 44–59.

59. Patricia Uberoi, *Freedom and Destiny: Gender, Family and Popular Culture in
India* (New Delhi: Oxford University Press, 2006), 24.

60. See notes 7 and 8 for citations.

61. Mankekar, "Brides Who Travel," 744.

62. Sandhya Iyer, "Interview with Karan Johar," online at http://sandhyai
.blogspot.com/2007/08/interview-with-karan-johar.html.

63. The rich body of work on melodrama includes Peter Brook's classic, *The
Melodramatic Imagination: Balzac, Henry James, Melodrama and the Mode of
Excess* (New Haven, CT: Yale University Press, 1976); Thomas Elsaessar,
"Tales of Sound and Fury," in *Imitations of Life: A Reader on Film and Televi-
sion Melodramas*, ed. Marcia Landy (Detroit, MI: Wayne State University
Press, 1991), 44–79; Christine Gledhill, *Home Is Where the Heart Is: Studies in
Melodrama and the Women's Film* (London: British Film Institute, 1987); Ben
Singer, *Melodrama and Modernity* (New York: Columbia University Press,
2001); and Linda Williams, *Playing the Race Card: Melodramas of Black and
White from Uncle Tom to O. J. Simpson* (Princeton, NJ: Princeton Univer-
sity Press, 2002). For work focused on Indian cinema, see Prasad, *Ideology*;
Sumita Chakravarty, *National Identity in Indian Popular Cinema* (Austin:
University of Texas Press, 1993); Jyotika Virdi, *The Cinematic ImagiNation:
Indian Popular Films as Social History* (New Brunswick, NJ: Rutgers University
Press, 2003). See also, Ashish Rajyadaksha, "The Epic Melodrama: Themes
of Nationality in Indian Cinema," *Journal of Arts and Ideas* 25/26 (December
1993): 55–70; and Vasudevan, "Melodramatic Mode," 104–26, 118.

64. Williams, *Playing the Race Card*, 30, 153.

65. Melodrama is said to thrive on repression; see Elsaessar, "Tales of Sound
and Fury."

66. Rey Chow, *Sentimental Fabulations: Contemporary Chinese Films* (New York:
Columbia University Press, 2007), 18 (her emphasis).

67. Ibid., 23.

68. Vasudevan, "The Politics of Cultural Address in a Transitional Cinema:
A Case Study of Indian Popular Cinema," in *Reinventing Film Studies*, ed.
Christine Gledhill and Linda Williams (London: Arnold; New York: Oxford
University Press, 2000), 131–64, 138.

69. This kind of flashback reverses the logic of what Corey Creekmur calls the
"maturation dissolve"; see "Bombay Boys: Dissolving the Male Child in
Popular Hindi Cinema," in *Where the Boys Are: Cinemas of Masculinity and*

*Youth*, ed. Murray Pomerance and Frances Gateward (Detroit, MI: Wayne State University Press, 2005), 350–76.

70. Critics have argued that frontality—when a character directly addresses the spectator—is a durable representational convention of Indian cinema. For more on frontality in Indian cinema, see Gita Kapur, "Mythic Material in Indian Cinema," *Journal of Arts and Ideas* 14/15 (July–December1987): 79–108; Anuradha Kapur, "The Representation of Gods and Heroes: Parsi Mythological Drama of the Early Twentieth Century," *Journal of Arts and Ideas* 23/24 (January 1993): 85–107; and Ashish Rajyadaksha, "The Phalke Era: Conflict of Traditional Form and Modern Technology," *Journal of Arts and Ideas* 14/15 (July–December 1987): 47–78.

71. Ashish Rajyadaksha, "Viewership and Democracy in the Cinema," in Vasudevan, *Making Meaning*, 267–96.

72. For a succinct summary of these features, see Vasudevan, "Melodramatic Mode."

73. For the concept of cognitive mapping, see Fredric Jameson, *The Geopolitical Aesthetic: Cinema and Space in the World System* (Bloomington: Indiana University Press, 1995).

## CHAPTER THREE

1. See Anupama Chopra, "Can Bollywood Please All of the People All of the Time?" *New York Times*, October 29, 2006, online at http://www.nytimes.com/2006/10/29/movies/29chop.html.

2. See Robin Wood, *Hollywood from Vietnam to Reagan* (New York: Columbia University Press, 1986), 95–134.

3. David J. Russell, "Monster Roundup: Reintegrating the Horror Genre," in *Refiguring American Film Genres: History and Theory*, ed. Nick Browne (Berkeley and Los Angeles: University of California Press, 1998), 233–54, 239–40.

4. The one exception may be action films. In the 1960s a number of films— *King Kong* (1962), *Samson* (1964), and *Hercules* (1964)—all starring wrestler-turned-actor Dara Singh, were substantial hits. See Valentina Vitali, *Hindi Action Cinema: Industries, Narrative, Bodies* (New Delhi: Oxford University Press, 2008), 134–83.

5. See Faiz Ali and Seba Ahmad, "Horror: Bollywood and Lollywood Style," online at http://www.thehotspotonline.com/moviespot/bolly/BollyHorror/bollyhorror.htm (accessed 5/15/09).

6. We can add a few more titles to this list of pre-1970 Indian (and South Asian) horror: *Maut Ka Toofan* (Storm of death, Henry Dargwitch, 1935), *Bhedi Bungla* (House of mystery, Master Bhagwan, 1949), *Aadhi Raat* (Midnight, S. K. Ohja, 1950), *Tower House* (Nisar Ahmad Ansari, 1962), *Kala Jadoo* (Black magic, Mehmood, 1963), *Pataal Nagri* (Underground city, Raj Kumar, 1963), *Kohra* (Biren Nag, 1964), *Gumnaam* (The nameless, Raja

Nawathe, 1965), *Anita* (Raj Khosla, 1967), and *Anmol Moti* (Precious pearls, S. D. Narang, 1969).

7.  Pete Toombs, "The Beast from Bollywood," in *Fear without Frontiers: Horror Cinema Across the Globe*, ed. Steven Jay Schneider (London: Fab Press, 2005). 244.

8.  Kaya Ozcaracalar, "Between Appropriation and Innovation: Turkish Horror Cinema," in Schneider, *Fear without Frontiers*, 205–17, 205.

9.  Viola Shafik, "Egypt: A Cinema without Horror?" in *Horror International*, ed. Steven Jay Schneider and Tony Williams (Detroit, MI: Wayne State University Press, 2005), 273–89, 273.

10. Mauro Ferai Tumbocon, "In a Climate of Terror: The Filipino Monster Movie," in Schneider, *Fear without Frontiers*, 254–62, 255.

11. Stephen Gladwin, "Witches, Spells and Politics: The Horror Films of Indonesia," in Schneider, *Fear without Frontiers*, 219–29, 220.

12. Adam Knee, "Thailand Haunted: The Power of the Past in the Contemporary Thai Horror Film," in Schneider and Williams, *Horror International*, 141–57.

13. Toombs, "Beast from Bollywood," 253.

14. See the introduction and chapter 2. See also Madhava Prasad, *Ideology of the Hindi Film: A Historical Construction* (New Delhi: Oxford University Press, 1998); and Valentina Vitali, *Hindi Action Cinema: Industry, Narrative, Bodies* (New Delhi: Oxford University Press, 2009).

15. See Prasad, *Ideology*, 46–51.

16. Though the first films of this phase were released in the 1970s, the trickle only became a flood in the next decade.

17. Jeff, "Hotel: Ramsay Brothers Horror," online at http://www.cinemastrikes back.com/?p=1221 (accessed 5/15/09).

18. S. V. Srinivas, "Film Culture, Politics and Industry," online at http://www .india-seminar.com/2003/525/525%20s.v.%20srinivas.htm. Srinivas distinguishes the B circuit from other industry classifications that designate markets as A, B, and C, according to size, and rank movie theaters as A, B, and C, according to location and available amenities. The B circuit cuts across these classifications, for it traverses B and C exhibition outlets in A markets.

19. "How to Make a Ramsay Horror Flick," online at http://sify.com/movies/ bollywood/fullstory.php?id=14207829, (accessed 9/16/10).

20. Toombs, "Beast from Bollywood," 245.

21. Other examples of this are *Guddi* (Hrishikesh Mukerjee, 1971) and *Mr. India* (Shekhar Kapur, 1987).

22. For an anthropological account of these supernatural and social beliefs, see Graham Dwyer, *The Divine and the Demonic: Supernatural Affliction and Its Treatment in North India* (London: Routledge Curzon, 2002).

23. Robin Wood, "An Introduction to the American Horror Film," in *Movies and Methods*, vol. 2, ed. Bill Nichols (Berkeley and Los Angeles: University of California Press, 1994), 195–219.

24. A similar point is made with regard to J-Horror (Japanese horror films) in Rajyashree Pandey, "The Pre in the Postmodern: The Horror *Manga* of Hino Hideshi," *Japanese Studies* 21, no. 3 (2001): 262–74.

25. See Linda Williams, "When the Woman Looks," in *Dread of Difference: Gender and the Horror Film*, ed. Barry Keith Grant (Austin: University of Texas Press), 15–33; and Carol J. Clover, "Her Body Himself: Gender in the Slasher Film," in ibid., 66–105.

26. Liberalization entailed a jettisoning of the socialist model that India had adopted at independence in favor of a system that was far more open to the forces of the global market; see the introduction.

27. Lalitha Gopalan provides a history of the Steadicam and its adoption by Hindi cinema. While one school claims that Ram Gopal Varma's 1989 gangster thriller *Shiva* was the first Indian film to make extensive use of the Steadicam, others trace it to an earlier source in 1984. See *Bombay* (London: British Film Institute, 2005), 51–54.

28. See, for example, posts online at http://www.passionforcinema.com; http://www.Indianauteur.com, as well as http://www.imdb.com.

29. Brandt Sponseller, "A Bit Derivative and Meandering but Entertaining," January 25, 2005, online at http://www.imdb.com/title/tt0266875/user-comments.

30. Ram Gopal Varma, "Fearing Fear," September 9, 2008, online at http://rgvarma.spaces.live.com/blog/cns!5187B91811914FB4!3240.entry.

31. Sponseller, "A Bit Derivative."

32. James, "Was This RGV's Rough Draft?" December 7, 2007, online at http://www.imdb.com/title/tt0266875/usercomments.

33. Though Saamri is capable of motion in the film's later section (once his head and body are reunited, he starts to terrorize the surrounding villages), he is never shown in the city.

34. In a list of his favorite films, Varma includes *Candyman* (Bernard Rose, 1992) where, of course, questions of dwelling are central.

35. Sujay Iyer, "Ram Gopal Varma's *Phoonk*: Trademark RGV but Not His Best," online at http://www.daijiworld.com/news/news_disp.asp?n_id=50226&n_tit=Bollywood+This+Week%3A+Phoonk+-+Trademark+RGV+but+Not+at+his+Best.

36. Varma, "Fearing Fear."

37. Mikhail M. Bakhtin, *The Dialogic Imagination: Four Essays*, ed. Michael Holquist and Vadim Liapunov, trans. Vadim Liapunov and Kenneth Brostrum (Austin: University of Texas Press, 1982), 425–26. The term *chronotope* refers to space and time coordinates invoked by a narrator.

38. Gurcharan Das, "The India Model," online at http://www.ccsindia.org/ccsindia/gdas/indiamodel.pdf (accessed 6/25/09).

39. Defined as households whose annual income was above Rs. 70,001, the percentage of middle-class homes increased from 28.10 percent to 47.28 percent; see E. Sridharan, "The Growth and Sectoral Composition of India's

Middle Class: Its Impact on the Politics of Economic Liberalization," *India Review*, 3, no. 4 (2004): 405–28.

40. Das, "India Model."

41. Satish Deshpande, *Contemporary India* (New Delhi: Penguin Books, 2003), 137.

42. See K. C. Sivaramakrishnan, *A Handbook of Urbanization in India* (London: Oxford University Press, 2005); Ranvir Sandhu, *Urbanization in India* (London: Sage, 2003); and Sujata Patel and Kushal Deb, *Urban Sociology* (New York: Oxford University Press, 2003).

43. See Anirudh Paul, Prasad Shetty, and Shekhar Krishnan, "The City as Extra-curricular Space: Re-Instituting Urban Pedagogy in South Asia," *Inter-Asia Cultural Studies* 6, no. 3 (2005): 386–409, 387.

44. See Lawrence Liang, "Porous Legalities and Avenues of Participation"; Solomon Benjamin, "Touts, Pirates and Ghosts"; Anand Vivek Taneja, "Begum Samru and the Security Guard"; and Media Researchers@Sarai, "Complicating the City: Media Itineraries," in *Sarai Reader 05: Bare Acts* (New Delhi: Center for Study of Developing Societies, 2005). See also Awadhendra Sharan, "Claims on Cleanliness: Environment and Justice in Contemporary Delhi," *Sarai Reader 02: The Cities of Everyday Life* (New Delhi: CSDS), 2002; and Awadhendra Sharan " 'New Delhi': Fashioning an Urban Environment Through Science and Law," in *Sarai Reader 04: Bare Acts* (New Delhi: CSDS), 2004.

45. Steve Derne, *Globalization and the Transformation of Culture, Class and Gender in India* (London: Sage, 2008); Leela Fernandes, *India's New Middle Class: Democratic Politics in an Era of Economic Reform* (Minneapolis: University of Minnesota Press, 2006); William Mazzarella, *Shoveling Smoke: Advertising and Globalization in Contemporary India* (Durham, NC: Duke University Press, 2004); Mark Leichty, *Suitably Modern: Making Middle-Class Culture in a New Consumer Society* (Princeton, NJ: Princeton University Press, 2002).

46. Leela Fernandes, "The Politics of Forgetting: Class Politics, State Power and the Restructuring of Urban Space in India," *Urban Studies* 41, no. 12 (2004): 2415–30.

47. Ram Gopal Varma, "The Trailblazer," interview, *Timeasia Magazine*, October 20, 2003.

48. Quoted in Ranjani Mazumdar, *Bombay Cinema: An Archive of the City* (Minneapolis: University of Minnesota Press, 2007), 113.

49. Ibid., 120.

50. Cinema's relationship to consumerism has been documented by Anne Friedberg in *Window Shopping: Cinema and Postmodernism* (Berkeley and Los Angeles: University of California Press, 1994). Ron Inden provides a historical account of the promotion of commercialism in Hindi cinema in "Transnational Class, Erotic Arcadia, and Commercial Utopia in Hindi Films," in *Journeys: Audio-Visual Media and Cultural Change in India*, ed. C. Brosius and M. Butcher (New Delhi: Sage, 1999), 41–68.

51. Vivian Sobchack, " 'Lounge Time': Post-War Crises and the Chronotope of Film Noir," in *Refiguring American Film Genres: History and Theory*, ed. Nick Browne (Berkeley and Los Angeles: University of California Press, 1998), 158.
52. For a sophisticated history of the relationship between sound culture, embodiment, and technology, see Jonathan Sterne, *The Audible Past* (Durham, NC: Duke University Press, 2003). See also Michael Chion's seminal *Audio-Vision* (New York: Columbia University Press, 1994).
53. The zombie movie might be an exception.
54. "Summary: Friday the 13th," online at http://www.fridaythe13thfilms .com/films/friday1.html (accessed 6/27/09).
55. Tina Gray was one of Freddie's victims in *Nightmare on Elm Street*; Steve Christy was the camp counselor in the original *Friday the 13th*.
56. While a few releases (e.g., the *Darna* series) stay with the classic formula, the majority of New Horror films do not.
57. In this it may be closely allied to rock n' roll. One could argue against Woods that these practices do not threaten normality so much as extend it, thus making it compatible with the age of "excessive capitalism" that the prioritizing of consumption over production entails.
58. As such, it is influenced by international art horror, especially Asian horror and its variants. This cinema, as Mitsushiro Yoshimoto notes in an unpublished paper, is preoccupied with the horror of globalization. There are several excellent recent studies of Asian horror cinema, including Jay McRoy, *Contemporary Japanese Horror Cinema* (Amsterdam: Rodopi, 2008); and Patrick Galloway, *Asia Shock: Horror and Dark Cinema from Japan, Korea, Hong Kong and Thailand* (Berkeley, CA: Stonebridge Press, 2006).
59. For the classic formulation of this argument, see Prasad, *Ideology*.
60. Meenakshi Saini, "Horror Strikes Bollywood," *Hindustan Times*, October 2, 2008.
61. Bryan Pearson, "Love, Song, Dance . . . and Suspense," *Variety*, February 13, 2003.
62. David Chute and Anupama Chopra, "Bollywood Beat Takes a Back Seat," *Variety*, March 8–14, 2004.
63. Saini, "Horror Strikes Bollywood."

CHAPTER FOUR

1. Most of these are single-screen theaters, with seating capacities of 600–1,200. Though a prodigious movie-producing nation, India remains seriously underscreened. In 2005, for example, there were 12,000 commercial screens in India, an average of 12 screens per million people. The US average is 117 per million, France's is 77, Italy's is 52, Denmark's 61, Spain's 46, and Germany's 45. The United Kingdom, with the worst screen coverage for a large European economy, has 30 screens per million, almost three times India's ratio. See Anand Kumar, "Quiet Revolution in Film Industry,"

*Dawn*, December 3, 2007, online at http://www.dawn.com/2007/12/03/ ebr9.htm; and Bertrand Moullier, "Whither Bollywood? IP Rights, Innovation and Growth in India's Film Industries," research paper, February, 2007, online at http://www.law.gwu.edu/Academics/research_centers/ciec/ Documents/Notes%200n%20Creativity/WhitherBollywood.pdf, 6.

2. Moullier, "Whither Bollywood?" 20. According to Moullier, this number will grow, as multiplexes are planned for almost all the three hundred malls currently under construction across India. This paper notes that the exhibition revolution underway in India along with the digital delivery of prints are two of the three key factors driving the double-digit growth in India's entertainment sector (17–19). Kishore Lulla, CEO of Eros Entertainment—one of the key global distributors of Bollywood films—also links the growth of multiplex construction to the digital delivery of prints. See Rajesh Unnikrishnan, "Digital Cinema Will Spur Growth: Interview with Kishore Lulla," *Economic Times*, March 17, 2007, online at http://economictimes.indiatimes.com/Opinion/Digital-cinema-will-spur-growth/articleshow/1774181.cms?curpg=2.

3. See Vanita Kohli-Khandekar, *The Indian Media Business*, 2nd ed. (New Delhi: Sage, 2006); and Manjunath Pendakur, *Indian Popular Cinema: Industry, Ideology and Consciousness* (New York: Hampton Press, 2003).

4. *Hat-ke* films are also known as "new age," though they have nothing in common with the New Age culture of the West. Its closest analogue in the United States is the "indie" film, which, however, is not typically screened in multiplexes.

5. Krittivas Mukerjee, "Multiplexes Boost India's Movie Mania," *Reuters News Service*, July 23, 2007, online at http://www.reuters.com/article/technology-media-telco-SP-A/idUSDEL14312420070723.

6. *Page 3* is an edgy exploration of celebrity culture whose plot elements include homosexuality and pedophilia, while *Corporate* examines the evolving workplace in neoliberal India. When the art cinema movement first took off in the United States in the 1950s, there was a similar alliance between "good cinema" and "mature content." In this context, the rise of art cinema is linked to several factors, including the Paramount decision of 1948 that forced studios to divest their ownership of exhibition infrastructure, leading to a sharp fall in the number of films produced, the enforcement of the code that sanitized mainstream cinema through informal censorship, and the spread of television. The rise of the "exploitation" film, which explored topics like youth culture and urban violence, is also noteworthy. The Indian film industry has a completely different relation to exhibition than US art cinema, which was screened in the "arthouse" theaters that mushroomed in the 1950s and showed mainly foreign films, documentaries, and second-runs. See Barbara Wilensky, "Discourse on Art Houses in the 1950s," in *Exhibition: The Film Reader*, ed. Ina Rae Hark (New York: Routledge, 2001), 67–76.

7. Mukherjee,. "Multiplexes Boost India's Movie Mania."
8. Mehra, quoted in Supriya Thanawala, "Despite Successes, Indian Cinema Yet to Be Explored Fully," *Ficci Frames*, March 6, 2007, online at http://www.exchange4media.com/FICCI/2007/sec-film.htm.
9. See Charles Acland, *Screen Traffic: Movies, Multiplexes and Global Culture* (Durham, NC: Duke University Press, 2003); John Clarke, *New Times and Old Enemies: Essays on Cultural Studies and America* (London: Harper, 1991); Douglas Gomery, *Shared Pleasures: A History of Movie Presentation in the United States* (Madison: University of Wisconsin Press, 1992); Miriam Hansen, *Babel and Babylon: Spectatorship in American Silent Film* (Cambridge, MA: Harvard University Press, 1991); Roy Rozensweig, *Eight Hours for What We Will* (Cambridge: Cambridge University Press, 1984); and Gregory Waller, ed., *Moviegoing in America: A Sourcebook in the History of Film Exhibition* (Indianapolis, IN: Wiley-Blackwell, 2001).
10. Notable exceptions include John Belton's masterful study on the widescreen and, more recently, Bruce Isaacs's call for a film aesthetics that articulates form with the conditions of reception. Of course, phenomenologically inclined cultural critics like Siegfried Kracauer and Walter Benjamin had long since connected theater architecture to screen content. To quote Kracauer, "This total artwork of effects assaults all the senses using every possible means. Spotlights shower their beams into the auditorium, . . . [and] the orchestra asserts itself as an independent power, its acoustic production buttressed by the responsory of the lighting. Every emotion is accorded its own acoustic expression and its color value in the spectrum—a visual and acoustic kaleidoscope that provides the setting for the physical activity on stage: pantomime and ballet. Until finally the white surface descends and the events of the three dimensional stage *blend imperceptibly* into two-dimensional illusions" (*The Mass Ornament: Weimar Essays*, ed. and trans. Thomas Y. Levin [Cambridge, MA: Harvard University Press, 1995], 324; my emphasis). See also John Belton, *Widescreen Cinema* (Cambridge, MA: Harvard University Press, 1992); Bruce Isaacs, *Towards a New Film Aesthetic* (London: Continuum, 2008).
11. David Bordwell, *The Way Hollywood Tells It: Story and Style in Modern Movies* (Berkeley and Los Angeles: University of California Press, 2006), 72–103, 74.
12. James Hay, "What Remains of the Cinematic City," in *Cinematic City*, ed. David B. Clarke (London: Routledge, 1997), 210–12.
13. Gomery, *Shared Pleasures*; Hansen, *Babel and Babylon*; and Waller, ed. *Moviegoing in America*.
14. Mark Jancovich, Lucy Faire, and Sarah Stubbings, *The Place of the Audience: Cultural Geographies of Film Consumption* (London: British Film Institute, 2008); Richard Maltby, Melvin Stokes, and Robert Allen, eds., *Going to the Movies: Hollywood and the Social Experience of Cinema* (Exeter: Exeter University Press, 2007); Lary May, *Screening Out the Past: The Birth of Mass Culture and the Motion Picture Industry* (New York: Oxford University Press, 1980).

15. See Judith Thissen, "Next Year at the Moving Pictures: Cinema and Social Change in the Immigrant Jewish Community," in Maltby, Stokes, and Allen, *Going to the Movies*, 113–29, 129.

16. Ravi Vasudevan, introduction to *Making Meaning in Indian Cinema* (New Delhi: Oxford University Press, 2000), 1–36, 25.

17. Stephen Hughes, "Policing Silent Film Exhibition in Colonial South India," in Vasudevan, *Making Meaning*, 39–64, 47–48.

18. William Mazzarella, "Cannibals Enjoy Comedies: Making Sense of the Cinema in Late Colonial India," in *Censorship in South Asia: Between Sedition and Seduction*, ed. Raminder Kaur and William Mazzarella (Bloomington: Indiana University Press, 2009), 71.

19. The most concrete evidence appears in the thousands of pages of interviews with film viewers conducted by the Indian Cinematograph Committee in the late 1920s, which led to the publication of *Report of the Indian Cinematograph Committee1927–28*, vols. 1–5 (Pune: National Film Archives of India, 1928), hereafter cited as *ICC*. This was a high-level commission set up by the imperial government to inquire into film and censorship in India. It goals were to examine the organization and principles of methods of the censorship of Cinematograph films in India; to survey the organization of "Cinematograph films" in the Indian film-producing industry, and to consider whether it was desirable to encourage the exhibition of films produced within the British empire generally and the production and exhibition of Indian films in particular, and to make recommendations. While the express purpose of this research might have been imperial panic about the native's consumption of images of white women on screen, it was also motivated by the need to combat the global dominance of Hollywood and protect British film production at home and in the colonies. While it is difficult to summarize the range of views expressed in this connection, the view that kissing is not appropriate in Indian films dominates many responses. The reasons given vary from middle-class panic at the effect on-screen sex might have on the unwashed masses to the absence of the kiss in Indian culture and society. While some of these objections, particularly with regard to cinema's effects on the masses, reprised arguments made concerning the institution of the Hays Code in Hollywood, others can be explained in terms of Indian cinema's emergence as an instrument of nation-building in a colonial context and the elite's desire to control this technology.

20. As we saw in chapter 1, though the kiss is prohibited, the romantic duet—a type of song-and-dance sequence essential to couple-formation—is entrusted with delivering the intensities proper to a sensuous medium like the cinema. Predictably, the continued presence of performance sequences has also been viewed as jeopardizing the development of cinematic realism. These critiques typically proceed from the vantage of an elite, urban middle class. See Ravi Vasudevan, introduction to *Making Meaning*, 6–7, for an elaboration of these positions.

21. Manishita Dass, "The Dreamlife of Modernity: Debating Cinema's Impact in 1920s India," paper presented at the annual meeting of the Society for Cinema and Media Studies Conference, Chicago, 2007 (a version of this paper is now available as "The Crowd Outside the Cultured City: Imagining the Mass Audience in 1920s India," *Cinema Journal* 48 (Summer 2009); and Amit Rai, *Untimely Bollywood: Globalization and India's New Media Assemblage* (Durham, NC: Duke University Press, 2009).

22. Ashis Nandy, "Indian Popular Cinema as a Slum's Eye View of Politics," in *Secret Politics of Our Desires: Innocence, Culpability and Indian Popular Cinema*, ed. Ashis Nandy (New Delhi: Oxford University Press, 1998), 1–19; and Madhava Prasad, *Ideology of the Hindi Film: A Historical Construction* (New Delhi: Oxford University Press, 1998), 46.

23. Nandy, "Indian Popular Cinema," 3.

24. The stabilization of the middle-class viewer as the norm in Hollywood meant that the cinematic apparatus did not have to account for these different vantages. Historians have documented that this bourgeois spectator was more an aspirational ideal than an accomplished fact, yet exhibitors, regardless of the phenomenology of the single-screen theater, continued to assume a unified, narrative-driven spectator. Thus, as Herbert Blumer and Philip Hauser show in *Movies, Delinquency and Crime*, censors often attributed the corrupting effects of cinema to the narrative and attempted to impose a moral order on it, when in fact cinematic spectacle held a far greater interest for youthful spectators. The realist assumption led to this marginalization of spectacle. See Maltby, Stokes, and Allen, *Going to the Movies*, 13.

25. Prasad, *Ideology*, 42.

26. Ashish Rajyadaksha, "Viewership and Democracy in the Cinema," in Vasudevan, *Making Meaning*, 267–96.

27. Partha Chatterjee, *Politics of the Governed: Reflections on Popular Politics in Most of the World* (New York: Columbia University Press, 2006), 27–52.

28. For frontality, see chapter 2, note 71.

29. Ravi Vasudevan, in a series of carefully argued essays, has documented the coexistence of realist and frontal codes as a mark of a transitional cinema, but one could also connect his analysis of film form to the dominant form of exhibition. See "The Melodramatic Mode and the Commercial Hindi Cinema," in *Screening World Cinema: A Screen Reader*, ed. Catherine Grant and Annette Kuhn (London: *Routledge*, 2006), 104–26; and "The Politics of Cultural Address," in *Reinventing Film Studies*, ed. Christine Gledhill and Linda Williams (London: Arnold; and New York: Oxford University Press, 2000), 131–64.

30. I owe this point to one of the anonymous reviewers of this manuscript.

31. Statistics available online at http://www.researchandmarkets.com/research/26bcb5/multiplex_india. Further, a recent article in the *New York Times* notes that the health of the movie industry globally relies on the flow of capital into the growth of exhibition, not only in India but also in other

booming economies like that of Russia. See Laura Holson, "Hollywood's Road Trip," *New York Times,* April 3, 2006.

32. A recent study proposed that exhibitors have always enjoyed a competitive advantage in the film industry because of this chronic shortage of venues. The author meticulously documents the continuous complaints of producers against the extortionist practices of exhibitors. See Valentina Vitali, *Hindi Action Cinema: Industries, Narratives, Bodies* (New Delhi: Oxford University Press, 2009), 134–40.

33. Pendakur, *Indian Popular Cinema,* 16–18.

34. A government-owned multiscreen art theater complex, Nandan, was built in Kolkata in the 1980s, and there had been double screens in the South of India since the 1970s, but the multiplex chain can probably be dated to the late 1990s.

35. Anupama Chopra, "Hindi Films Get the Indie Spirit," *New York Times,* November 13, 2005; and Aparna Sharma, "India's Experience with the Multiplex," online at http://www.india-seminar.com/2003/525/525%20aparna%20sharma.htm.

36. See Patrick Frater and Tatiana Segal, "Bombay Dreams," *Daily Variety,* July 29, 2008.

37. Kaveree Bamzai, "How India Watches Movies," *India Today,* December 6, 2007.

38. Kohli-Khandekar, *Indian Media Business,* 47–48.

39. Ibid., 49.

40. William Paul, "The K-Mart Audience at the Mall Movies," in Hark, *Exhibition: The Film Reader,* 77–88, 81–82.

41. Ina Rae Hark, "General Introduction," in ibid., 1–19, 4.

42. Ibid., 6–7.

43. Ibid., 5.

44. Ibid., 2.

45. Paul, "K-Mart Audience," 84.

46. Ibid., 84; see also Acland, *Screen Traffic,* 107–29.

47. Acland, *Screen Traffic,* 112–13.

48. Adrian Athique and D. P. Hill, "Multiplex Cinemas and Urban Redevelopment in India," *Media International Australia* 124 (August 2007): 108–18.

49. About 25 percent of Hollywood revenue comes from the box office. See Confederation of Indian Industry-A. T. Kearney, *The New Economics of Indian Film Industry: Creativity and Transformation* (2008); the report can be purchased online at http://cii.in/documents/Publication_List_May2009 .pdf. (Hereafter cited as CII-Kearney, *New Economics.*)

50. Rem Koolhaas, "Generic City," in *S, M, X, XL,* by. Rem Koolhaas, Bruce Mau, and Hans Werlemann (New York: Monacelli Press, 1997), 248–64.

51. Gyan Prakash, introduction to *The Spaces of the Modern City: Imaginaries, Politics and Everyday Life,* ed. Gyan Prakash and Kevin Kruse (Princeton, NJ: Princeton University Press, 2008), 1–18.

52. While 25 percent of the population is still living under the poverty line, es-

timates of the size of India's middle-income classes, both rural and urban, are between 220 to 300 million people, and 61.2 percent of the population is under the age of thirty. The 15–34 age group—the demographic driver of filmed entertainment consumption all over the world—is set to increase by 30 percent between 2001 and 2011, reaching 134 million. See the introduction and Moullier, "Whither Bollywood?" 16.

53. See Leela Fernandes, *India's New Middle Class: Democratic Politics in an Age of Reform* (Minneapolis: University of Minnesota Press, 2006); and Rupal Oza, *The Making of Neoliberal India: Nationalism, Gender and Paradoxes of Globalization* (New York: Routledge, 2006).

54. Sahri, quoted in "India 360: Ten Years of Multiplexes," online at http://www.ibnlive.com/printpage.php?id=42441&section_id=.

55. As Manishita Dass suggested to me, we might go even further back and consider films like *Footpath* (Zia Sarhadi, 1953) and *Naya Daur* (The new age, B. R. Chopra, 1957) as engaged in a rethinking of the commercial form. Indeed, the 1950s represent some of the same diversity of commercial formats that the current decade is witnessing. Perhaps that is why it is called the "golden age" of Hindi cinema.

56. Prasad, *Ideology*, 160–87.

57. Among Ratnam's most significant Hindi-language output are *Bombay* (1995) and *Roja* (1992), while Ram Gopal Varma's oeuvre includes *Rangeela* (Full of color, 1995), *Satya* (Truth, 1998), and *Company* (2002). Also noteworthy in this regard is director Vidhu Vinod Chopra, whose *Parinda* (The pigeon, 1989) and, to a lesser extent, *1942: A Love Story* (1994) anticipate the figurations of the contemporary witnessed in the *hat-ke*/multiplex films. For excellent analyses of these filmmakers, see Moinak Biswas, "Mourning and Blood Ties: Macbeth in Mumbai," *Journal of the Moving Image* 5 (December 2006): 78–85; Anustup Basu, *Bollywood in the Age of New Media: The Geotelevisual Aesthetic* (Edinburgh: University of Edinburgh Press, 2010); Corey Creekmur, "Bombay *Bhai*: The Gangster in and behind Popular Hindi Cinema," in *Cinema, Law and the State in Asia*, ed. Corey Creekmur and Mark Sidel (London: Palgrave Macmillan, 2007), 29–44; Lalitha Gopalan, *Cinema of Interruptions: Action Genres in Contemporary Indian Cinema* (London: British Film Institute, 2002); and Madhava Prasad, "Realism and Fantasy in Representations of Metropolitan Life in Indian Cinema," in *City Flicks*, ed. Preben Kaarsholm (Kolkata: Seagull Books, 2004), 82–98.

58. Madhava Prasad, "Contemporary Indian Cinema and the Figure of the Culturally Backward Spectator," working paper, n.p.

59. Shubham Roy Choudhury, "Sounds of Horror: Sound and Dread in Hindi Cinema," *Journal of the Moving Image* 6 (December 2007), online at http://www.jmionline.org/jmi6_8.html.

60. CII-Kearney, *New Economics*.

61. In the last three years that figure has declined to an average of between 65 percent and 78 percent.

62. Moullier, "Whither Bollywood?" 6–7.

63. Tandon, quoted in "Inox Leisure Launches Third Multiplex in Jaipur," *India PR Wire*, October 13, 2007, online at http://www.indiaprwire.com/print/?type=news&id=24947.

64. Sonia Kolesnikov-Jessop, "India Plans Multiplex Blitz," *International Index*, January 30, 2008.

65. Moullier, "Whither Bollywood?" 7, 9–10.

66. Bordwell, *The Way Hollywood Tells It*, 72–73.

67. For a classic account, see Manuel Castells, *The Rise of Network Society* (London: Wiley-Blackwell, 2009).

68. David Bordwell, *Poetics of Cinema* (New York: Routledge, 2007), 198.

69. Gopalan, *Cinema of Interruptions*, 63–105.

70. The narrative premise of Inaaritu's multiplot global hit *Amores Perros* (Love's a bitch, 2004) was adapted by Mani Ratnam in his *Yuva* (Youth, 2004). I have not included this film in my discussion since an auteuristic homage to Inaaritu's template of three colliding stories does not belong to the genre of the multiplex film.

71. Benedict Anderson, *Imagined Communities: Reflections on the Origin and Spread of Nationalism* (London: Verso, 1983), 24–25.

72. Fredric Jameson, "The Experiments of Time: Providence and Realism," in *The Novel: Forms and Themes*, ed. Franco Moretti (Princeton, NJ: Princeton University Press, 2006), 95–127.

73. See Prasad, *Ideology*, 88–113.

74. Patricia Uberoi, *Freedom and Destiny: Gender, Family and Popular Culture in India* (New Delhi: Oxford University Press, 2006), 24.

75. Vivian Sobchack, "Phenomenology and the Film Experience," in *Viewing Positions: Ways of Seeing Film*, ed. Linda Williams (New Brunswick, NJ: Rutgers University Press, 1994), 36–58.

76. The conception of the social emerging in these network narratives seems to exemplify the current theoretical work on the subject by philosophers like Bruno Latour. Latour draws on actor-network-theory (ANT) to suggest that to conceive of the social as a higher, more complex organization that acts upon the individual is fundamentally to mischaracterize it. For him, the social emerges in the connections and associations that various actors form with each other. Nor does the social occupy a separate sphere, as opposed, for instance, to the economic or the political. See Bruno Latour, *Reassembling the Social: An Introduction to Actor-Network-Theory* (New York: Oxford University Press, 2007).

77. Neepa Majumdar, "The Embodied Voice: Song Sequences and Stardom in Popular Hindi Cinema," in *Soundtrack Available: Essays in Film and Popular Music*, ed. Pamela Wojcik and Arthur Knight (Durham, NC: Duke University Press, 2002), 163–65.

78. Mitry, quoted in Sobchack, "Phenomenology and the Film Experience," 58.

CHAPTER FIVE

1. *Bhadralok* can be literally translated as "respectable folk."
2. My translation.
3. This phrase was used by practitioners of the French New Wave, especially Truffaut, to distinguish their own work from the genteel cinema of the previous generation that supposedly exemplified "Frenchness." A similar tradition, I suggest, existed in Bengali cinema. For more on the French "Tradition de Qualité," see Alan Williams, *Republic of Images: A History of French Filmmaking* (Cambridge, MA: Harvard University Press, 1992), 278.
4. Saratchandra Chatterjee's novella has been the source of multiple film adaptations in different Indian languages. Bhansali's *Devdas* had a much-publicized opening in Cannes and is said to have marked Bollywood's formal arrival on the world stage. See Bhaskar Sarkar, "Melodramas of Globalization," *Cultural Dynamics* 20, no. 1 (2008): 31–51.
5. I use the word *vernacular* in its linguistic sense to refer to Bengali. Regional cinema connotes movies made and viewed in a particular region—here, the state of West Bengal. In India, the national language, Hindi, is distinguished from various "vernaculars" like Tamil, Telegu, Bengali, and so forth. In idiomatic usage, the word connotes provinciality. Hindi's status as a national language and Hindi cinema's bid to national dominance remain contested claims.
6. See Martin Heidegger, "The Question Concerning Technology," in *The Question Concerning Technology and Other Essays*, trans. William Lovitt (New York: Harper & Row, 1977), 3–35; Jacques Ellul, *The Technological Society*, trans. John Wilkinson (New York: Vintage Books, 1967); and Harold Innis, *The Bias of Communication*, 2nd ed. (Toronto, Canada: University of Toronto Press, 2008).
7. Jim Gerries, "Was Foucault a Philosopher of Technology?" *Techne* 7, no. 2 (2003): 14–24, 14.
8. While the diffusion of cinema through culture is no new phenomenon, the current capitalization of cinema's effects is certainly remarkable. The name *Bollywood*—with its nod to that cinema-industrial complex par excellence—captures this change. See Ashish Rajadhyaksha, "Rethinking the State After Bollywood," in *Journal of the Moving Image* 3 (June 2004): 47–89. Contemporary East Asian cinemas have similarly been theorized as paradigmatic of globalization processes. For recent work, see Gina Marchetti and Tan See Kam, eds., *Hong Kong Film, Hollywood and the New Global Cinema: No Film Is an Island* (New York: Routledge, 2007); and Rey Chow, *Sentimental Fabulations: Contemporary Chinese Films* (New York: Columbia University Press, 2007).
9. Ghosh, quoted in Mahua Das and Kushali Nag, "Facelift: Tollywood's Changing Look," *Telegraph*, August 7, 2009, 8.

10. Bengali groups playing a modern sound are commonly referred to as "Bangla bands." Bhoomi, Parash Pathar, and Chandrobindu are notable examples.

11. Many lead actors in the classic period—Soumitra Chatterjee for example—were almost professorial in their attire and demeanor.

12. In Kolkata, the Bengali film industry is often designated as *Tollywood*. The *T* comes from the neighborhood (Tollygunge) where the film studios were located. This can lead to confusion because the same name is used for the Telegu-language film industry as well. For a sample of responses to the *Japanese Wife*, see "Treat or Torment," *Telegraph*, May 1, 2010, 7–8.

13. See, for example, Ashish Rajadhyaksha, *Indian Cinema in the Time of Celluloid: From Bollywood to the Emergency* (Bloomington: Indiana University Press, 2009).

14. One popular overview lists only six films made before 1950 as must-see Bollywood (as opposed to ten films made between 1995 and 2001); see Ashok Banker, *Bollywood* (New Delhi: Penguin, 2001).

15. We might view *Moulin Rouge!* (Baz Luhrmann, 2000) and *Slumdog Millionaire* (Danny Boyle, 2008) as films that have borrowed Bollywood technologies. See Sangita Gopal and Sujata Moorti, "Bollywood in Drag: *Moulin Rouge!* and the Aesthetics of Global Cinema," *Camera Obscura* 25, no. 3 (2011): 29–65.

16. For an economic history of Kolkata, see Sukanta Chaudhuri, *Calcutta: The Living City* (New Delhi: Oxford University Press, 1995).

17. To use Gerard Genette's categories, Tagore's novel is a hypotext, whereas Ray's adaptations of Tagore are intertexts; see *Palimpsest: Literature in the Second Degree* (Lincoln: University of Nebraska Press, 1997). More recently Linda Hutcheon uses *intertext* more broadly to designate different modes of adaptation; see *A Theory of Adaptation* (New York: Routledge, 2006), 15–22. For adaptation as a mode of translation, see Robert Stam, "Beyond Fidelity: Dialogics of Adaptation," in *Film Adaptation*, ed. James Naremore (New Brunswick, NJ: Rutgers University Press, 2000), 54–76. Susan Bassnett describes Ghosh's turn to Bollywood as "intercultural and intertemporal communication," since he uses the cultural resources of Bollywood to represent nineteenth-century Bengal; see *Translation Studies* (London: Routledge, 2002), 9.

18. For a more in-depth discussion of some of the issues I raise in this and the next paragraph, see Tithi Bhattacharya, *Sentinels of Culture: Class, Education and the Colonial Intellectual in Bengal* (New Delhi: Oxford University Press, 2005); John McGuire, *Making of a Colonial Mind* (Canberra: Australia National University Press, 1983); S. N. Mukherjee, *Calcutta: Essays in Urban History* (Kolkata: Subarnarekha, 1993); and Swati Chattopadhyay, *Representing Calcutta: Modernity, Nationalism and the Colonial Uncanny* (New York: Routledge, 2005).

19. See Moinak Biswas, "Bengali Cinema and the Literary Liaison," *Journal of the Moving Image* 1 (Autumn 2000): 1–22; and Abhijit Roy, "The New Popular and the *Bhadralok*," unpublished paper, 14. Some arguments found here appear in Abhijit Roy, "Bringing Up TV: Popular Culture and the Development of the Modern in India," *South Asian Popular Culture* 6 (April 2008): 29–43.

20. Sharmishtha Gooptu, "The Glory That Was: An Exploration of the Iconicity of New Theatres," *Comparative Studies of South Asia, Africa and the Middle East* 23, nos. 1–2 (2003): 286–300. See also Goophi's excellent history of Bengali Cinema, *Bengali Cinema: An Other Nation* (London: Routledge, 2010).

21. Madhuja Mukherjee, "New Theaters: New Perspectives," *Deep Focus: A Film Quarterly* (January–May, 2005): 94–104.

22. Ibid., 101, 107.

23. Shoma Chaudhury, "Interview with Amit Chaudhuri," *Tehelka*, October 1, 2005, online at http://www.tehelka.com/story_main14.asp?filename=1001 05Bengalis_stand.asp (my emphasis).

24. See Bhaskar Sarkar, *Mourning the Nation: Indian Cinema in the Wake of Partition* (Durham, NC: Duke University Press, 2009), 157–65. See also Kironmay Raha, *Bengali Cinema* (Nandan: West Bengal Film Center, 1991), 66–69; and Moinak Biswas, "The Couple and Their Spaces: *Harano Sur* as Melodrama Now," in *Making Meaning in Indian Cinema*, ed. Ravi S. Vasudevan (New Delhi: Oxford University Press, 2000), 122–42.

25. Swapan Mullick, "Bengal Has Lost Its Only Real Star," *Filmfare*, August 16–31, 1980, 31–33, 30.

26. Rajiv Gandhi, quoted in "People Shall Give a Fitting Reply," *People's Democracy*, 33, no. 17 (2009), online at http://pd.cpim.org/2009/0503.pd/ 05032009_1.htm (accessed March 3, 2011).

27. Shakti Samanta, who worked in both Mumbai and Kolkata, was a pioneer in this regard.

28. Satyajit Ray, *Speaking of Films*, trans. Gopa Majumdar (New Delhi: Penguin Books, 2006), 94–95.

29. Yves Thoraval, *Cinemas of India* (New Delhi: Macmillan, 2001), 230.

30. Raha, *Bengali Cinema*, 80–83.

31. Sanjoy Chakravarty, "From Colonial City to Global City: The Far from Complete Spatial Transformation of Kolkata," online at http://astro.temple .edu/~sanjoy/calpap.html.

32. Fredric Jameson, *Postmodernism; or, the Cultural Logic of Late Capitalism* (Durham, NC: Duke University Press, 1991).

33. A 2002 survey shows that about 80 percent of single-screen theaters in Kolkata now show Bengali films—double the figure from the 1990s. Arijit Dutta, president of the East India Motion Pictures Association, says, "Bengali Cinema is big and safe business today" (quoted in Krittivas Mukherjee, "Bengali Film Industry Buoyant on Spate of Big Hits," *Indo Asian New Service*, March 5, 2004).

34. While Rs. 25 million was a huge sum for a Bengali film, this budget was puny compared to those for Bollywood films. *Devdas*, for example cost Rs. 500 million! (One US dollar = forty-six rupees.)

35. Shreekant Mohata, interview with author, July 14, 2006.

36. Representative reviews of *Chokher Bali* are available online at http://www .rottentomatoes.com/m/chokher_bali/articles/1345761/.

37. Khemka, quoted in Sambit Saha, "Bengali Cinema Zoom In on Profits," *Business Standard*, January 10, 2004.
38. Prosenjit, quoted in Aparna Harish, "Tollywood Looks West," *Telegraph*, December 11, 2005.
39. Dasgupta, quoted in ibid.
40. Gowri Ramnarayan, "In Favour of the Parallel Line," *Hindu*, August 31, 2001.
41. Sangeeta Dutta, "Bengali Audiences in UK-Tolly Travelogue: Our Films, Their Sensibilities," online at http://www.nriinternet.com/ENTERTAINMENT/Bengali/1_Bengali_UK.htm.
42. For theoretical writings on this global/vernacular relation, see Arjun Appadurai's classic *Modernity at Large: Cultural Dimensions of Globalization* (Minneapolis: Minnesota University Press, 1996); and Rob Wilson and Wimal Dissaynayake, eds., *Global/Local: Cultural Production and the Transnational Imaginary* (Durham, NC: Duke University Press, 1996).
43. Amit Chaudhuri, "Madmen, Lovers, Artists," *Telegraph*, December 14, 2003.
44. Srabonti Narmeen Ali, "Bangaliness Bollywood Style," *Daily Star*, January 2, 2004, 3.
45. See Mandakranta Bose, "The Political Aesthetic of Nation and Gender in Rituparna Ghosh's *Chokher Bali*," in *Indian Literature and Popular Cinema: Recasting Classics*, ed. Heidi R. M. Pauwels (New York: Routledge, 2007), 191–202.
46. See Moinak Biswas, introduction to *Apu and After: Re-Visiting Ray's Cinema*, ed. Moinak Biswas (Chicago: University of Chicago Press, 2005), 2. See also Keya Ganguly, *Cinema, Emergence and the Films of Satyajit Ray* (Los Angeles: University of California Press, 2010).
47. As scholars have noted, this celluloid refashioning of the past characterizes the cinema of other globalizing economies like China and Brazil. See Rey Chow, *Primitive Passions: Visuality, Sexuality, Ethnography and Contemporary Chinese Cinema* (New York: Columbia University Press, 1995); Christopher Berry and Mary Ann Farquhar, *China on Screen: Cinema and Nation* (New York: Columbia University Press, 2006); Lucia Nagib, *Brazil on Screen: Cinema Nuovo, New Cinema, Utopia* (London: I. B. Tauris, 2007); and Tom Zaniello, *Cinema of Globalization: A Guide to Films about the New Economic Order* (Ithaca, NY: ILR Press, 2007).
48. Rituparna Ghosh, "Even at 50 Crores, Unsatisfying," *Anandabazar Patrika*, July 20, 2002, 1–3.
49. The attention to "authentic" detailing in Bollywood films might be contrasted to earlier period films like *Mughal-E-Azam* (The great mughal, K. Asif, 1960), whose mise-en-scène, though lavish, does not stand up to historical scrutiny. This marks a shift from a symbolic to a cognitive relationship to commodities. See Moinak Biswas, "Early Films: The Novel and Other Horizons," in Biswas, *Apu and After*, 75, n. 24; see also Vivian Sobchack, " 'Surge and Splendor': A Phenomenology of the Hollywood Epics,"

in *Film Genre Reader 11*, ed. Barry Keith Grant (Austin: University of Texas Press, 1995), 280–307.

50. No mainstream Hindi film since Mehboob Khan's *Mother India* has garnered this level of international attention. *Devdas* became paradigmatic not only of Bollywood product but also of Indian culture. Representative reviews are available online at http://www.rottentomatoes.com/m/devdas/.

51. Ackbar Abbas, "Play It Again Shanghai: Urban Preservation in the Global Era," in *Shanghai Reflections*, ed. Mario Gandelsonas (Princeton, NJ: Princeton Architectural Press, 2002), 37–55.

52. Intertextuality is a key aesthetic principle of all "new waves" including, of course, the French New Wave. See Jeff Menne, "A Mexican *Nouvelle Vague*: The Logic of New Waves under Globalization," *Cinema Journal* 47, no. 1 (2007): 70–92; and David Wills, "The French Remark: *Breathless* and Cinematic Citationality," in *Play It Again Sam*: *Retakes on Remakes*, eds. Andrew Horton and Stuart Y. McDougal (Berkeley and Los Angeles: University of California Press), 147–61.

53. Ghosh makes this same point in his review of *Devdas*, "Even at 50 Crores," 2.

54. Corey Creekmur's essay "Remembering, Repeating and Working Through *Devdas*," in Pauwels, *Indian Literature and Popular Cinema*, 173–190, is essential reading for a theory and history of the remake in Indian cinema.

55. The opening recalls the aesthetics of what Andrew Higson has termed *heritage cinema*. See *Waving the Flag: Constructing a National Cinema in Britain* (Oxford: Clarendon Press, 1995), 112–14.

56. This phrase is Bhaskar Sarkar's; see "Melodramas of Globalization," 45.

57. See the reviews by Ekanshu Khera, online at http://www.planetbollywood .com/Film/ChokherBali/, and Jake Wilson, online at http://www .urbancinefile.com.au/home/view.asp?a=10474&s=Reviews. Also see reader's reviews online at http://www.mouthshut.com/readreview/55372–1 .html.

58. Shoma Chatterji, "Chokher Bali Will Widen My Horizon: An Interview with Rituparna Ghosh," online at http://timesofindia.indiatimesonline.com.

59. The film's art director, Bibi Ray, outlined Ghosh's relentless quest for period authenticity. He even aged costumes, a relatively unknown practice in Bengali cinema (interview with author, July 16, 2006).

60. See Partha Chatterjee, *The Nation and Its Fragments* (Princeton, NJ: Princeton University Press, 1993); Dipesh Chakrabarty, *Provincializing Europe*, 2nd ed. (Princeton, NJ: Princeton University Press, 2007); Tanika Sarkar, *Hindu Wife, Hindu Nation* (Bloomington: Indiana University Press, 2002); Meredith Borthwick, *Changing Roles of Women in India* (Princeton, NJ: Princeton University Press, 1994).

61. For the relation of cinema to history and historiography, see Pierre Sorlin, *The Film in History: Restaging the Past* (Totowa, NJ: Barnes and Noble, 1980); Marcia Landy, ed., *The Historical Film*: *History and Memory in Media* (New

Brunswick, NJ: Rutgers University Press, 2000); and Philip Rosen, *Change Mummified: Cinema, Historicity, Theory* (Minneapolis: University of Minnesota Press, 2001).

62. Ravi Vasudevan, "Nationhood, Authenticity and Realism in Indian Cinema: The Double Take of Modernism in Ray," in Biswas, *Apu and After*, 80–115; and Keya Ganguly, "Carnal Knowledge: Visuality and the Modern in *Charulata*," *Camera Obscura* 37 (January 1996): 155–86.

63. Creekmur, "Remembering, Repeating and Working Through *Devdas*," 183–86.

64. Ranjani Mazumdar, *Bombay Cinema: Archive of the City* (Minneapolis: University of Minnesota Press, 2007), 121.

65. Menne makes a similar argument with regard to *Amores Perros*; see "Mexican *Nouvelle Vague*," 76.

66. Rabindranath Tagore, *Binodini: A Novel*, trans. Krishna Kripalani (Kolkata: Sahitya Academy, 2001), 74.

67. See Shohini Ghosh, "Passionate Involvement: Love and Politics in Satyajit Ray's *The Home and the World*," in *Rabindranath Tagore's The Home and the World: A Critical Companion*, ed. P. K. Datta (New Delhi: Permanent Black, 2001), 82–107, 88.

68. Ray had this to say about the use of background sound: "A director seeks refuge in background music only when he feels the need to highlight or heighten the emotional content in a scene by adding music to what has already been conveyed through the visual images, words and sounds" (*Speaking of Films*, 112).

69. Michael Sprinkler, "Homeboys: Nationalism, Colonialism and Gender in the Home and the World," in Datta, *Critical Companion*, 107–26.

70. Ghosh, quoted in Shahla Raza, "No More a Man's World," *Hindu*, January 5, 2004, online at http://www.thehindubusinessline.in/life/2004/01/05/stories/2004010500130100.htm.

71. Tagore, quoted in Chakrabarty, *Provincializing Europe*, 134.

72. Ibid., 279, n. 36.

73. Madhumita Bhattacharyya, "Designs on Paro and Binodini: Ash's Adornments Travel Far and Wide, Set Jewelry Trends," online at http://www.telegraphindia.com/1030917/asp/calcutta/story_2372327.asp.

74. See Sangita Gopal and Biswarup Sen, "Engines of Desire: Hindi Film Song-Dance," in *The Bollywood Reader*, ed. Rajinder Dudrah and Jigna Desai (Maidenhead, Berkshire: Open University Press, 2009), 146–58.

75. Tagore, *Binodini*, 180

76. Ibid., 200.

77. Ibid., 215.

78. In our July 29, 2007, interview, Ghosh drew attention the homoeroticism in Tagore's novel.

79. Himani Banerjee, *Inventing Subjects: Studies in Hegemony, Patriarchy and Colonialism* (New Delhi: Tulika, 2001), 101.

80. This scene, not in the novel, recalls a similar sequence in Satyajit Ray's *Ghare Baire*, in which the modern husband, Nikhilesh, encouraged his wife, Bimala, to wear blouses so she could venture outside.

81. Purnima Mankekar, "Brides Who Travel: Gender, Transnationalism and Nationalism in Indian Film," *Positions* 7, no. 3 (1999): 731–61; and Patricia Uberoi, "Imagining the Family: An Ethnography of Viewing *Hum Aapke Hain Kaun*," in *Pleasure and the Nation: The History, Politics and Consumption of Popular Culture in India*, eds. Rachel Dwyer and Christopher Pinney (New Delhi: Oxford University Press, 2001), 309–51.

82. For a study of the heteronormative drives of postcolonial Bengali cinema, see Sangita Gopal, "Sex Outside: Postcoloniality and the Erasure of Ethnosexual Queerness," *Journal of Postcolonial and Commonwealth Studies* 10, no. 1 (2003): 11–33.

83. This phrase is from Gayatri Gopinath, *Impossible Desires: Queer Diasporas and South Asian Popular Cultures* (Durham, NC: Duke University Press, 2005).

CONCLUSION

1. The phenomenon of male family members killing a female relative to protect the honor of the family is on the rise in India. It is most common among middle- to upper-middle class, semi-urban families. Sociologists note that honor killings often occur in the context of marriage choices by women. For an overview, see Anjali Puri, Chander Suta Dogra, Arpita Basu, and Neha Bhatt, "Dreams Girl," July 12, 2010, online at http://www.outlookindia.com/article.aspx?266071.

2. MMS is an acronym for Multimedia Messaging Service. "MMS scandals" refer to secretly made "sex tapes" that go viral.

3. Chidananda Dasgupta, "Report on National Film Policy: Is Big Cinema Bad Cinema?" *Filmfare*, December 1–15, 1980, 37–39, 39.

4. Bharat Rungachary, "Mani Kaul Is More Expensive Than Manmohan Desai," *Filmfare*, November 16–30, 1980, 35–37, 37.

5. Amit Rai, *Untimely Bollywood: Globalization and India's New Media Assemblages* (Durham, NC: Duke University Press, 2009).

6. For an excellent analysis, see Ratnakar Tripathy, "Bhojpuri Cinemas: Regional Resonances in Hindi Heartland," online at http://juxtcinema.blogspot.com/.

7. See Selvaraj Velayutham, "The Diaspora and the Global Circulation of Tamil Cinema," in *Tamil Cinema: The Cultural Politics of India's Other Film Industry*, ed. Selvaraj Velayutham (New York: Routledge, 2009), 172–88.

8. See Taran Adarsh, "*Robot* Stumbles in Bollywood," October 22, 2010, online at http://www.bollywoodhungama.com/trade/top5/index.html; and "Box Office Update," October 6, 2010, online at http://www.ibosnetwork.com/newsmanager/templates/template1.aspx?a=22203&z=.

9. Anupama Chopra, *"Robot* Review," NDTV, October 1, 2010, online at http://movies.ndtv.com/movie_Review.aspx?id=551&cp.

10. Nikhat Azmi, *"Robot* Review," *Times of India,* September 30, 2010, online at http://timesofindia.indiatimes.com/entertainment/movie-reviews/hindi/Robot/moviereview/6658514.cms.

# Index